To Simon, Lyra and Sophie,
My family mountain.

Psychology
for Creative Artists

Rediscover Creativity with
Tools from the Therapy Room

Dr Anna Haigh

Psychology for Creative Artists:
Rediscover Creativity with Tools from the Therapy Room

Published by:

Pavilion Publishing and Media Ltd
Blue Sky Offices
25 Cecil Pashley Way
Shoreham by Sea
West Sussex
BN43 5FF

Tel: 01273 434 943
Email: info@pavpub.com
Web: www.pavpub.com

Published 2023

A catalogue record for this book is available from the British Library.

ISBN: 978-1-803882-83-3

Pavilion Publishing and Media is a leading publisher of books, training materials and digital content in mental health, social care and allied fields. Pavilion and its imprints offer must-have knowledge and innovative learning solutions underpinned by sound research and professional values.

Author: Dr Anna Haigh
Editor: Mike Benge
Cover design: Emma Dawe, Pavilion Publishing and Media Ltd
Page layout and typesetting: Tony Pitt, Pavilion Publishing and Media Ltd
Printing: Independent Publishers Group (IPG)

Contents

Acknowledgements

Lots of people have been instrumental in the writing of this book and I owe a great debt of thanks to each of them. The people in my life have offered inspiration and advice, have kept the plates of my life spinning so I could attend to writing, and have offered endless words of encouragement and support.

I would like to thank Simon, my partner in this life and in music. Thank you for the long days spent parenting, and the long nights spent listening. Your perspective helps me see through the trees, and your support means that I can have a life full of love and still be a person of my own. I am endlessly grateful that we chose, and keep choosing, each other. I love you.

To my two daughters, Lyra and Sophie. You have shown me what it is to love something so deeply that it becomes part of the fabric of who you are. We are constantly humbled to have your souls entrusted to us as you make your way through childhood. I hope that we can honour your spirits and your creativity in the way that you deserve and fill you with the love you need for your journey through life. Being your mummy is like being given a well of joy that never runs dry.

To my mum, David, Peter and Chris, my family of origin. Mum, thank you for the words, thank you for showing us how to write, for reading to us and for honouring all our creativity in the way you did. You opened doors to worlds so much bigger than we knew and allowed us to walk through them. We can never be grateful enough. Thank you for holding the fort and making space for me to write. To David, thank you for the love and gentleness you brought to our family. You showed us what kindness and grace are and we carry that with us. To Peter, thank you for your wisdom and logic, for being my constant companion through our childhood and for tolerating my weaknesses when I am not the person I want to be. To Chris, you are an inspiration and have taught me what it looks like to dedicate your life to your art and the hard graft of being true to yourself. The light that came on in my life when you were born has never gone out; thank you for the laughter. And to Natalie, your energy is like caramel that soothes and sweetens life and our family. I love you all.

To the Family; Matt, Emma, Paul, Nick, Cristina, Christo, Caroline, Karl, Jess, Ed and Hannah. The family that we chose. My words falter when I try and convey your importance. You are the constellation in which I have found real belonging and I am thankful every day that we found each other. You are my village and my tribe. I love you all.

To Mel, Hannah and Kyle, my friends and soulmates. Thank you for your wisdom, your love, and your belief in me. Thank you for challenging me when I need it. I would not be the person I am without you.

To Evan, the energy and inspiration generated by our conversations was the 'big bang' of this book. Your mind is a magical place, and I am so grateful that you shared it with me. Your art is powerful and called to my own in a way that I will not forget. The telegraph wire of thoughts and inspiration that ran between us sustained me throughout this process and I cannot thank you enough.

To all the artists that have shared their experiences and work with me over the years, thank you. Your words and thoughts are reflected throughout this book and in the way I see the world. Thank you to Lucy for reminding me of the power of yes and of freefalling into the arms of the universe. May the rivers of inspiration and creativity flow always through your life.

To Darren, thank you for taking a risk on this book and on me. I have loved every minute.

Preface

This book has been many years in the making and constitutes a bringing together of two fields which have been slowly approaching each other in my life, much like tectonic plates. When I began the study and practice of psychology, creative arts were something I practised around the edges; at times a form of self-care that maintained my sanity and at other times a guilty secret that would have me sneaking into lectures still wearing make-up from a gig the night before. I viewed creative arts as a necessary part of me, a way of being in the world that was as integral to my sense of self as other parts of my personality. I viewed psychology as what I *did*; the legitimate thing that I studied and developed over many years, which luckily led to a professional career I genuinely love. It did not occur to me then that these elements may have relevance to each other, and even when the idea began to dawn, the significance of the connection took a long time to emerge. For many years I held my creative and professional selves as discrete and often competing parts; the professional self becoming increasingly demanding of time and resources as I became more senior, and the creative self holding less and less validity as I also sought to integrate parenthood into the balance of my life. At one point, I stopped creating almost entirely as the flood of demands had me up till late and without any energy or motivation to make or write.

Around this time, I was lucky enough to attend some training at an arts university with Steve Potter, a writer, Cognitive Analytic Psychotherapist (CAT) and friend. He presented the CAT concept of 'mapping' relational patterns to a group of artists and writers and suggested that this may be a concept that they wished to continue to explore in a supervision group, which I subsequently offered to facilitate. Over the next few years, we met regularly, a group of textile designers, journalists, creative writers and painters, and me. I found myself using techniques that I would normally only employ in a therapy room with patients in my 'day job' as a psychologist in a busy mental health team. What we discovered is that the very same methods used to explore early life experiences and present-day difficulties in therapy also opened avenues of enquiry and understanding about both the artistic process and the work.

Over time, what emerged between us resulted in a deepening of creative practice, a move towards greater self-understanding and understanding of the work, an increase in authenticity and output and, ultimately, a rising conviction that there was something in the interface between their world as artists and mine as a psychologist that needed to be explored. Many of the group members were students on one of the degree courses, and these discoveries began to make their way into coursework, degree shows and ultimately manifested in their practice once they graduated. When I left Cornwall, the group disbanded, and the members went on to do a myriad of amazing creative projects including opening a gallery, authoring a journal, and illustrating any number of creative works. I, however, reverted to type, working as a psychologist during the day and then writing and performing music, or working as a ceramicist in the evenings.

The ideas didn't leave me though, and whenever I encountered another artist, conversations about the cross-over between art and psychology would flow (as would the wine, usually) and I would be reminded of all I had learned. I found that, again, many of the techniques and methods that I would use in therapy seemed applicable to the experience of the practicing artists I surrounded myself with. Managing critical voices, dealing with imagined, hostile audiences, coping with shame and exposure – all themes that I regularly encountered in both my professional and creative lives. Finally, I took the hint and began to jot things down and intentionally started to sound out the idea to those around me; could the practice of clinical psychology have something to say to creative artists? The answer appeared to be an overwhelming 'yes', and so this book was born.

As I began to map out the concepts, I started to take steps to redress the balance in my life, asking myself the same challenging questions that I will present to you as we move through this book. The answers came thick and fast; provocative, urgent and requiring action. I changed my work hours, set up a studio at the bottom of my garden, began to write and play music again, and finally got round to penning this book. I drove to the Highlands of Scotland to collect a second-hand pottery wheel, and after ten years of borrowing other people's equipment, I installed 'Colin', a shiny turquoise kiln, in my cellar so I could fire my own work. It is not an easy process, and it can mean taking a long, hard look at many of the things that have become a given in life, but it is a journey that has the power to lead you closer to whatever that quiet voice in your gut is urging you towards. If you have no sense of that instinct but are aware of a subtle dissatisfaction with the 'what is', then this book will help you to pay closer attention and tune in to what the next steps should be.

It is worth mentioning that it is not an easy process for those around you either; rediscovering, reprioritising, or deepening your creative life might require a renegotiation of assumptions and roles that have been at play for many years. It may come as a shock, perhaps even to the closest people in your life who might be unaware of the creative part of you that has been hidden or concealed behind a mound of obligations and commitments. For those already with an established artistic practice, you might discover renewed vigour that keeps you in your studio longer, demanding your attention until late in the night. You may have to find ways to articulate, negotiate and make space for the new 'dance' that is emerging with the important people in your life. This might sound daunting, but I would ask the question, 'what is the alternative?' If there is one thing that being a clinical psychologist has taught me, it is that we can all be guilty of carrying the illusion that life is endless, or at the very least long enough to accomplish all the things that we set our minds to. Every day, I hear stories that shake this belief, and it is one of the things I am most grateful for in my work. Life is not endless; it is unpredictable and uncertain, and at times it can throw you a curve ball that no one could have seen coming. The only defence against this is to ensure that the life you lead is as close to the life you want for as much of the time as possible. The greatest cause of regret that I encounter in my work is people having not lived bravely and authentically under the guise that they would get round to it when the kids were older, the job less demanding, the mortgage paid… I would argue, then, that the risks of making change must be weighed up against the (not insignificant) risks of not making change.

This book is not just for people who consider themselves 'proper' artists (whatever that means); it is designed for anyone that wants to develop and sustain their creativity and address anything that might act as a 'block'. Many jobs require innovation and originality without being considered typically 'artistic'. Entrepreneurs, therapists, software developers, architects, designers, investors and researchers; all require access to the same creative 'well' as those with a career in the arts. This book takes methods, techniques and models from contemporary clinical psychology and applies them to the process of creating. It doesn't matter if you are an established artist with a long-term practice, or a creative person that has not yet found a way to implement their artistic leanings, this book will provide questions and exercises to support you to take another step towards the sort of creative person you want to be. The concepts can be applied regardless of your medium and discipline, pulling from the experiences of photographers, painters, musicians, ceramicists, writers and performance artists.

Psychology is a lot like art in the way that people are drawn to different approaches and ways of making sense of the world; what works for one person leaves another cold. This book therefore draws from a wide range of psychological disciplines and models, and you will likely find that some really suit you and some do not. That is fine. I would urge you to try each exercise, particularly the ones that you are initially cynical of, and just be interested about why something does or does not work. If you take nothing from the exercise apart from the knowledge that a particular way of thinking does not 'fit' you, then that is enough. I have included a reference section with recommendations for further reading if any of the exercises particularly resonate, however it is not necessary to have a full grasp of the theoretical underpinning for them to be useful. It is enough to work through this book with an open mind and see what arises.

The most important thing to know is that this is not an 'expert' guide, but a set of field notes from someone who is still working through their own relationship with their creativity and art. I am not setting myself up as someone with all the answers, but as someone whose experiences have generated some helpful questions. I am offering the tools that I use in my work, the reflections from my own creative life, and the lessons that I have learned from working with other artists, in the hope that they will be of use to you as you explore what it means to live your creative life. As with therapy, leave anything behind that is not useful or does not fit, but be open to experiment and curiosity wherever possible.

Chapter One: Setting the scene

If you have picked up this book, it is likely that you are wanting to explore your creativity further, and may be struggling with blocks or hurdles when trying to make work that satisfies the part of you trying to express itself. Most creative artists will encounter 'dry spells' during their career, or will find that they are missing a certain ingredient in their art that is hard to define, sitting just outside of language but niggling and irritating them. Some people have always felt that they have a project waiting to be realised; a painting that crops up in daydreams, a book that they return to regularly in their mind, but something stops them from acting. Whatever your reason for choosing this book, I hope that you will be able to use the concepts and exercises to make sense of these experiences and move past them. That is not to say that all human experiences can or should be brought into our awareness to be fully processed; it is merely asserting that, where there exists a block, there exists an opportunity for enquiry and exploration.

I am not a fan of didactic learning and I try to move away from this style of delivering information wherever possible. Not only does assuming the role of 'teacher' set me up to disappoint you, but it also sets you up to receive a whole host of information that may or may not be relevant. Instead, this book is intended to be *interactive*. I have included many of the techniques and exercises that I regularly use in therapy to guide self-exploration and enquiry. I will ask the same questions that I ask my patients and hope that this will allow you to generate answers that are specific and meaningful to you, that will speak to your unique experiences. Of course, this demands a level of effort and commitment from you that a manual or self-help guide might not, but the resulting insights and discoveries are likely to be far more relevant to your personal situation and will therefore better support you to build the sort of vital creative life that you are looking for.

This book uses a psychological lens to look in detail at every point in the creative process; how you develop as a creative being, how context shapes the way you and others respond to your work, how psychological blocks can prevent action and how you can ensure your version of creative success. We will consider the powerful role of emotions and inspiration and develop ways to harness both to deepen and sustain your creative life over the longer term, not just for the time you are engaging with this book. My hope is that you will reach the end of this experience with a far greater insight into your specific needs as an artist and a clearer idea of how to move forward to make work that is as radical, inspiring and authentic as you want it to be.

It is my advice that setting aside some time each week to read and complete the activities will give you the greatest chance of getting the most out of this book, however the chapters are not designed to be completed in a set amount of time. Some people process thoughts and feelings quickly, and some people require more 'mulling' time to reflect on and integrate what they encounter. The important thing is that you invest sufficient time and resources so that the process gathers momentum and pulls you along, reducing the risk that you will give up part way through without having made meaningful, enduring changes.

It is important to note that many of the exercises in this book will concern you, the reader, and your individual thoughts, feelings and behaviours. Choosing to focus on you as an individual does not mean that the central and important role of social context and power is overlooked; quite the contrary. We will explore some of the contextual factors that can impact the process of making and disseminating creative work in Chapter Two, and will give some thought as to how these can be worked with or, when necessary, resisted. The book is structured in such a way as to present you with an opportunity to think about how these factors impact you personally, and to empower you to decide whether you want to make changes in your relationship with them. There remains the job of tackling, challenging and ultimately changing the structures that are designed to exclude, however this book focuses on how that work can be done inside of each of us as individuals, in the hope that it will contribute to the wider process of change.

The most important thing

When you are looking to make a change, there are several places that you can focus your attention, which includes the way you think or feel about an issue. When it comes to art and creativity, the best place to start is with behaviour – with *doing*. It is entirely possible for you to work your way through this book focusing on how you think and feel, but to reach the end with nothing material having changed. All thinking and no action can give us the convenient impression that we are doing the work, while we continue to remain stuck. As such, we are going to start with action. We are going to make the change and then make sense of it.

From the moment you start this book, until the time you finish, you are going to commit to spending *30 minutes per day* creating, using any medium you like. It is totally up to you what form this takes, but you must dedicate 30 full minutes to using your creativity. You do not have to stick to your usual medium but can use this opportunity to explore unchartered territories that you may have felt drawn to but have never given yourself the chance to experiment with. If you do not regularly create, then this is a wonderful chance to try your hand at different things without any risk. It doesn't matter what time of day you allocate for your creative time, and it doesn't even need to be the same time each day, but it does need to happen, even if that means making some temporary sacrifices or changes to your timetable.

Your creative time does not have to be 'productive' in the usual sense, in fact it is likely to be more effective if you purposefully push any thoughts about 'usefulness' and 'output' right out of your mind. Instead, view this time as a kind of island from the usual way of doing something. If you are a musician and you are used to practising or writing for several hours each day, then use your daily creative time to play the sort of music you don't usually allow yourself. Experiment with jazz, or play folk songs from your childhood, learn pieces from television shows you love. If you are a painter who works to commission, use your daily creative time to play with the paint in a way that you would usually deem frivolous. Try using a different brush, painting onto a different surface, even using parts of your body to create different effects. What happens if you paint with your hands, or your hair, or your whole arms? If you are a writer, then ask yourself if you could write anything, what would it be? And then just write the answer. It might be that inside of you is a horror novel when you are known for romance, or a light comedy when you have made your name as a writer of dark thrillers. This is a golden opportunity to play and have fun. To court your creativity and show it some appreciation, to set it free and allow it to expand.

The most important tenet is that you *do not show your work to anybody*. Not one soul. We are going to work through how you unhook yourself from unhelpful relational patterns that impact creativity, but for now we will remove all external input and distractions by making the commitment to keep any work private. The time between starting and finishing this book is for you to experiment with your creativity without censorship or fear about what others might think or say. It is a chance to work out what you like, what you dislike, what you are good at, what needs work, what inspires and flows easily and what feels effortful. If you have days where your creativity feels dry and forced, then allow yourself to just make pretty patterns on a piece of paper with felt tip pens, or simply arrange flowers in a beautiful vase. Your daily creative time does not need to be highbrow, productive, or useful. It just needs to *be*.

I have found it best to have a sketchbook in which I keep anything I have drawn, painted, or written, but it might be that your given medium would benefit more from a locked box or drawer. Either way, you need to be absolutely sure that no one will stumble on it by mistake so you can make art unencumbered and without any self-consciousness. Take some time to create a space that is conducive to creativity and that allows you to work in private without distraction for the duration of your creative time.

It is important that you do not get so caught up in the process of preparing that you delay starting, however. If you are anything like me, then you may be very skilled at deferring making changes by busying yourself with the process of preparation. "I can't start today because I don't have a dedicated notebook", or a new set of pens, or the right paints. I enjoy accumulating such items immensely, and have a whole shelf dedicated to blank notebooks. Though enjoyable, the need to acquire and prepare can serve as a defence against what actually needs to be done: the work. If you have a pen and some paper, then you can start today. If you don't have that, then you can make salt dough using just flour and water. If you don't have flour, then you can take out your old camera or even the camera on your phone and go for a walk. If the battery is flat, then you can find a space in your yard and use chalk. Do not allow yourself to listen to and get caught up in the internal 'chatter'; move straight into action and just make. Anything, something, for 30 whole minutes. Every single day.

I am a great believer in not reinventing the wheel, particularly when the wheel has had such a great impact on your own life. To this end, for the duration of your time working through this book, I invite you to also complete the 'morning pages' suggested by Julia Cameron in her wonderful book '*The Artist's Way*' (1992). The 'morning pages' create a very helpful foundation for artistic recovery and growth and can form a lifelong habit that many artists find essential. The idea is deceptively simple, you commit to writing three pages of longhand writing each morning, allowing whatever comes up in the moment to be transferred to the page. The morning pages are the first thing you do when you wake up, before you begin the tasks of the day. It is so instinctive to me now, that I roll over and feel for my pen before I even open my eyes. Of course, there are days when the demands of work, children, or sometimes even pets, derail my best intentions, and they are more like the 'midday pages', however I strive to write them every single day. Once again, the importance of not sharing these with anyone is fundamental to ensure there is no selective editing or censorship. Writing in this way offers a unique opportunity to meet with the 'self' in all its banality, complexity, beauty and ugliness. It allows you to hear what you think, and that in turn empties your mind in preparation for creativity. Once you have got the daily gripes and worries out of the way, what flows onto the page is often the very thing you need for your creative work. It is how this book was born.

Making space for your morning pages and your daily creative time may mean getting up an hour earlier than usual to get space alone before the family wake, or finally clearing out the garden shed so you can hide away with drawing pencils and a sketch pad. It might require you to find a quiet space in your lunch break, or to work while eating so you can finish earlier and rush home to have some creative time. Whatever it takes, this is an essential part of this process that requires unequivocal commitment from the outset. If there are times when you didn't do your morning pages or have been unable to find the 30 minutes for your creative time, then be curious about it, and then be clear about your reasons why. Identifying and exploring barriers to creativity as we go along will give you helpful information about the sort of internal and external blocks that need addressing to ensure lasting change.

A warning

Like all journeys into the human mind, this one comes with a warning. When we foray into our early experiences and begin to enquire about how we have come to be, we cannot always predict or control what we encounter. As such, I would advise you to be mindful of your support networks and ensure that you are clear where you will take difficult emotions if they arise. That's not to say that everyone will require the input of a therapist (though I personally believe that therapy is an excellent space to do this sort of work); a partner, a friend who knows you well, or even liked-minded colleagues can be invaluable sounding boards and offer scaffolding as you go through the process. At the back of the book, I have listed resources and agencies that you can approach if you feel like you do require some professional support, and I would urge you to contact these if necessary. This warning is not meant to sound dramatic, is it merely to acknowledge the unintended consequences of any process of exploration and change, and to ensure you are equipped to deal with them.

One of the most challenging aspects of a book like this is to stick with the process to the end. We are experts at creating defences against things that are too painful to know, or too difficult to feel, and it is likely that you will encounter these defences as you move through the chapters. It might be that thinking about a teacher that dashed your hopes to be an actor is too difficult to sit with, as it raises questions about how different your life might have been, or brings up feelings of rage or sadness that are frightening. It is tempting in these moments to put the book down, promising ourselves that we will pick it up again in due course and then consigning it to the far reaches of our bookshelves. Or you might find yourself rubbishing the book and wondering what on Earth the publisher was doing when they printed it. Instead of throwing the book in the bin, I would urge you to see these thoughts and feelings as red flags – indicators that you have hit on something that requires your focus and enquiry so you can process and move past it. In order to do this, you may have to increase your self-care and support. If you still feel the same once you have spent some time considering your relationship with the material, then feel free to use this book to prop up your sofa or keep your local charity shop in business.

It is important to note that this process is likely to bring about change, and while there is a part of you that welcomes this, there may be other parts that are less comfortable or committed, to the extent that they may sabotage the process. It is often the case in therapy that when we are nearing a breakthrough, or an important discovery, or are standing right on the periphery of change, the person will begin to experience fear, dread, anxiety or ambivalence that can result in them stepping back, missing sessions, or becoming caught up in a life circumstance that suddenly demands their attention. As a general rule, humans prefer things to stay the same, even if the current setup is not working well. We prefer the familiar, we like our risks to be clear and predictable, and the payoffs to be well-tested. Moving into an unknown space where there may be unforeseen dangers or at the very least discomforts, can be daunting.

One analogy that I find useful comes from the world of eye movement desensitisation and reprocessing (EMDR) therapy; the process of change is like entering a tunnel in a car. If you go as fast as you can tolerate and is safe, and keep moving, you will reach the end with the least suffering possible. If you keep stopping to check tyres, maybe have a snack, make a phone call, read a magazine, you are prolonging your time in the tunnel and making the process more challenging than perhaps it might have been. The key is to balance self-care and support, with the challenge of change so that you remain moving in a way that feels manageable and gets you where you need to go.

Self-care

Self-care is something that I talk about endlessly with my patients, and it is only in the last few years that I have begun to realise that many of the people around me do not have the faintest idea what I am talking about when I use this term. It is a concept that is central in mental health, and yet it is not taught in schools, is rarely considered in the workplace, and is frequently overlooked when people are trying to make sense of why they are experiencing mental health difficulties outside of formal therapy. Self-care is a broad term that means something different for each individual; it is essentially the answer to the question about what things restore, sustain and resource you.

The most useful way to conceive of what constitutes self-care is to imagine your energy and resilience like water in a jug. Some things take energy, even positive things such as socialising with friends, or exercise. Other things replenish and fill the jug, allowing you to sustain yourself and function. What gives and takes energy will differ for each person and the key is to take an honest look at what demands energy from you, and what gives it back. For example, a night in a pub with a trusted friend fills my jug and invariably I wake the next day with renewed energy and motivation. For others, a night in a pub would be enjoyable, but ultimately draining. For them, it might be that time alone reading or playing computer games is the ultimate rejuvenator.

The key is not to get into value judgements about the relative merit of each activity. I am often told by people that they feel guilty for playing computer games in a way that they wouldn't if they were going out for a run, even if the outcome is the same with regard to self-care. We tend to label some activities as productive and valuable, and others as wasteful or pointless, value judgements that often stem from childhood. If you were told that you would get 'square eyes' because you enjoyed television or were constantly admonished for gaming on a console rather than playing outside, then it stands to reason that it will be more difficult to view these as valid uses of your time as an adult. I personally love to watch gentle television shows that focus on people being creative, during which nothing terribly bad happens. I find they give my mind and body a rest and allow me some downtime that I might not have afforded myself otherwise. It is easy at times of stress to see this time as 'wasted' and to replace it with a 'productive' activity: however, if you can come to view self-care as an activity in and of itself, then you are setting yourself up for a life that is both productive and sustainable. I would urge you to notice any judgements you make about the activities you find restorative, and then place them to one side in order to complete the exercise below. Whatever your self-care preference, the outcome is not the activity itself, but the impact on your emotional wellbeing and ability to respond to adversity.

Exercise 1: A menu of self-care

Take a pen and list all the things that you enjoy doing. Don't think about it too much, just write whatever comes into your mind. Include anything that you find pleasurable, regardless of how big or small. Try not to censor or second-guess yourself. You might include things such as taking a walk, speaking with a friend, drinking freshly made coffee, painting a picture, riding your bike, gardening, taking a bath, riding a horse, writing a letter, visiting a gallery, meeting friends for lunch or dancing.

Take a look at the list you have compiled. Which of these activities take energy and which replenish you? Which activities leave you feeling depleted and in need of a rest, and which leave you feeling energised? Write down the ones that fill your energy 'jug' on a separate list, this will constitute your 'menu' of self-care activities.

Once you have your list, look at what you have written and notice if you experience any value judgements about what you have identified. Are any of the activities considered more virtuous, or less? Give yourself permission to indulge in any activity that provokes a negative judgement for the length of time that it takes you to complete this book. If you love to build Lego, or watch old re-runs of 1990s sitcoms, then these constitute valid self-care activities for the duration of this process. Give yourself permission to enjoy them.

It is important to have both time-intensive and 'quick-fix' options on your self-care menu, as you will not always have the time and resources available for both. There are some days when finding just ten minutes for yourself is the difference between making it through the day and becoming completely overwhelmed. I find throwing pots extremely restorative, but up until recently I didn't have a wheel or kiln at home, so would have to rent studio space, travel the distance to get there, throw the pots, clean up fully and then travel back home again. It was important for me to build this into my weekly time planning, but it did not serve as a quick response to times when I encountered challenging emotions or needed to top up my 'jug' quickly. In contrast, I find gardening extremely restful, and notice that even short amounts of time with my hands in the earth can have a remarkable impact on my mood and energy levels. I am lucky enough to have a garden right outside my back door, so I keep this high on my list of self-care activities. Take a look at your 'self-care menu' and ensure that you have some options that can be accessed quickly and without too much 'faff'.

It is not enough to plan your self-care; you must also identify the cues that you actually need to use the things you have identified. These signs are likely to be different for everyone; we all have prompts that tell us that we are mentally or physically reaching the end of our tether. For example, you might find yourself becoming irritable at the people around you in a way that is more pronounced than usual or is uncharacteristic. You might find that you become disorganised, and stop being in the right place at the right time when you are reaching overwhelm. You may find that your sex drive decreases, or the attention you pay to your physical health – all of these are potential indicators that you need to increase the time you devote to self-care. When adversity arises, there can be a temptation to work harder and meet the challenge head on. Being aware of the subtle signs that you are pushing yourself past your tolerance level can remind you to pause and attend to filling your 'jug'. Though counterintuitive, this stacks the odds that you will be able to endure whatever challenge you are facing and remain resilient.

If you start to notice these cues while working through this book or realise that you have a strong desire to stop doing the exercises, or to put the book down entirely, then take this as an indicator that you need to increase your self-care. It is not always practical or possible to take large chunks of time, but perhaps it is possible to take a bath instead of a shower or set aside an extra 30 minutes to prepare food from scratch in an evening. Find ways to build in breaks during your day, for example go for a walk at lunchtime with your camera rather than eating at your desk, or finish a meeting ten minutes early and allocate the time to listening to a piece of uplifting music. The process of change is tiring and demanding but even small acts of self-compassion can be the difference between staying the course and abandoning ship.

There are also times when our minds and bodies clearly give us the cue that they need to stop. Entirely. For a period of time. These times can sometimes be accompanied by physical illness that forces us to respond and pay attention to whatever is demanding so much of our mental energy. I regularly encourage the people I work with to take annual leave, or arrange childcare, or allocate one full day where their tasks remain untouched, way before this point. If we keep pushing, our body finds a way of pushing back that takes far longer to recover from than a one-off duvet day or a weekend without the children. Most of us encounter some stress in our day-to-day lives, but, if left unchecked, then the demands placed on us can leave little space to do the work of enquiry and self-development that books such as this encourage. If this is you, then try to find ways to make space for yourself as you work through this process. This is likely to have a significant impact on your ability to complete the book and, ultimately, to become the sort of creative artist you are hoping to be.

Sources of support and sources of attack

There are very few absolutes in psychology, but one of the 'near absolutes' is the positive impact of social support on the process of discovery and change. The need for social support does not end with this book however, but is likely to be an essential component of how you move forward and sustain yourself as an artist. A supportive network helps to buffer you against criticism, maintain inspiration, remain resilient in the face of failure, and continue creating well into old age. What we are talking about is the sort of support that allows you to openly share who you are in all your complexity, mess, uncertainty, strength and vulnerability, with a person or people, and feel bolstered, seen and encouraged by the response. This is not to say that the response must be entirely positive and without constructive criticism, but that any feedback is helpful in moving you towards your goal and does not leave you doubting yourself to the point that you are paralysed.

When it comes to creativity, it is essential to differentiate between those people in our lives that are likely to offer helpful, healthy support, and those who may intentionally or unintentionally sabotage the process. The process of realising your creativity and starting to unblock can bring up envy in the people around you – an emotion that is distinct from jealousy in that it is accompanied by the urge to destroy or scupper the thing that we crave when we encounter it in others. Being aware of this means we can think carefully about who we share a project with and at what stage. If a person has long harboured the wish to write a book, and then you tell them of your strides to finish a writing project, you might find that the response is critical in a way that is difficult to recover from. If you share your dilemmas about performing your music with a person who is also a frustrated musician, then you might find that their response does not offer the encouragement you are looking for but reinforces your concerns. This is not to say that envy cannot be managed, or that the person is even aware of the emotion underpinning their actions, but it is to say that envy is something to be mindful of and guard against.

Envy is also an extremely helpful signpost in your own creative life. If you notice you have a reaction to something someone else is doing, if you recognise the 'stab' of jealousy or find yourself being uncharacteristically harsh in your criticisms, then that might just be a clue regarding what your next project should be. If you hear yourself running down someone else's film, book, or painting, this strongly suggests a part of you wants what they have – the opportunity to express yourself in that way. The fastest way to move past those feelings is to make a move towards whatever it is you want. Write the book, pitch the film, learn the instrument. Being aware of our own envy where possible stops us from acting unconsciously to sabotage others and allows us to concentrate on our own creative lives.

Exercise 2: Identifying sources of support

Take a pen and paper. Make a list of the people that you most often consult about developments in your life, including creative work. This might include fellow artists, friends, family members or teachers.

Imagine you have an idea for an artistic project and picture discussing this with each of the people on your list. Pay attention to what happens in your body as you imagine the conversation – does any part of you tighten and brace for what you predict will be a negative or unhelpful response? Does any part of you relax in anticipation of the support and thoughtful response you are likely to receive? Make a mark next to the people who you intuitively know will be balanced and helpful, and be mindful of your 'gut instinct' response to those who might not be.

While you are building your creative muscles, it makes sense to be thoughtful about who you surround yourself with, and who you involve in the process. If you know in your gut that there is a risk of envy attack, or that the person is likely to sabotage you for another, sometimes well-meaning reason, then it is perfectly fine to protect yourself by being selective in what you share. That may even include family: for example, a parent might have concerns that your hopes to be a filmmaker will be dashed, and so prefaces any related conversation with a warning of how difficult the industry is to penetrate (in fact, there are many successful film makers, both commercial and independent). This may be a misguided attempt to protect you but serves the function of demoralising you and reintroducing doubt. These are not the people to show pieces of new work or fledgling bits of writing, save that for those people who you know will take great care with what you are producing and whose opinion you can trust. An old lecturer of mine used to use the phrase 'hold your council', and I have to say I was initially terrible at doing that. Over the years I learned that being thoughtful about what you share and with whom can be as much an act of self-care as booking a massage or taking a walk.

It is just as important to intentionally spend time with people who restore and uphold you as it is to put distance between yourself and those who demoralise, and I would strongly suggest getting dates in the diary to make this happen. Reflecting on your own processes and experiences can be tiring work, and even if you don't necessarily want to talk about it, just having an evening spent with good company on the horizon can be restorative. If you are not normally someone who looks to others for support, then see this as part of the process of building a life that can sustain your creative work over the longer term. If, when you have completed the exercise above, you realised that there are few or no people in your life that you can rely upon for support, then this might be a really good place to begin investing your energies. It may be time to join a local writing club, or art critique group, or even explore something unrelated to your field such as a community choir. What you are looking for is a place to fill your jug when your own resources or perspective do not carry you alone.

There is often a concern that asking for support will be experienced as a burden, or will be met with judgement, or may even risk a friendship. The only way to counter this is to ensure that we ask cleanly and honestly in a way that gives the other person space and permission to say no. It is also important to remember that, by asking for support, we also give permission to the other person to bring their own vulnerabilities, concerns and experiences to the table, perhaps in a more authentic way.

When I was in my early 20s, I met a wonderful woman called Hannah, who I considered to be clever, savvy and ethical, and whose company I enjoyed immensely. We struck up a friendship and would spend long evenings in the pub discussing politics or sharing interesting things we had read or comedies we had seen. I unconsciously considered Hannah a 'friend for best', a person who I held in high esteem and quietly considered above the messy and confusing situations that I was regularly encountering in my own life as an early-twenty-something. One evening, after a particularly upsetting fight with my then partner, I was too tired, fed up and sad to bring my 'best' self, and when she asked how I was I told her; about the fight, my confusion about the relationship, the messy feelings I was experiencing – the lot. Hannah's shoulders visibly dropped by two inches, and she responded by sharing her similar anxieties about the state of her relationship, her uncertainty about the future and her conflicting feelings that stubbornly refused to be pinned down. By dropping the mask, I had offered an invitation for her to do the same. Hannah and I continue to share the mess and beauty of life 24 years later, and both joke about the years we spent being 'friends for best'. Perhaps there are relationships in your life that could bear a bit of testing, a risk or two, or a complete drop of the mask. This is likely to pave the way for a more authentic encounter with yourself and with others, and I would strongly suspect that this will translate into your creative work.

Exercise 3: Identifying barriers to support

Imagine that you have had a setback and you experience a negative emotional reaction- perhaps a manuscript has been rejected and you are disappointed, a painting is not developing in the way you intended, and you are frustrated, or something in your personal life is vying for your attention in a way that is making it more challenging to make work and you are anxious. Imagine you have uninterrupted time with one of the people you identified as helpful and supportive in the last exercise and are sharing this difficulty or challenge. What thoughts and feelings do you experience as you imagine this scene? Do you feel confident that the person listening is interested and motivated to lend their support, or do you worry that they are judging you, are disinterested or may resent the time spent focusing on your experiences? Do you feel able to tolerate your vulnerabilities or do you feel a flush of shame that you aren't doing better and don't have it 'sorted' yet? Note down any thoughts and feelings that make you feel like pulling away and putting distance between you and the other person. Set the list to one →

side and leave it for a while; long enough that the feelings subside but not so long that you forget it entirely.

Next time you are spending some time alone, reconsider the list with the 'wise', logical part of yourself. How true or likely are the things you have written? What would the other person say if they saw the list and the things that stop you from sharing with them? What would you say to another person who experienced these thoughts and feelings when sharing their challenges or difficulties with you?

The importance of time alone

This might seem like an obvious point, and in contradiction to the above argument about the need for support, but I believe that it is also worth considering the important role of time spent alone before we embark on this journey, and to identify the internal and external barriers to this. Time alone, doing nothing but pottering and listening to our internal 'voice', is an essential component of deepening or discovering creativity and of sensitising us to inspiration and insight; however, it is perhaps one of the hardest practices to establish and maintain.

Unfortunately, it is not as simple as suggesting 'spend some time by yourself' as we have many inbuilt mechanisms that, without our awareness, will sabotage these attempts by bumping it down the list of priorities. Our brains are extremely well-developed machines, whose purpose is to help us to survive and to thrive in a world that presents an overwhelming amount of information and numerous dangers, both overt and subtle. We have myriad ways of responding to this, almost all directly impacting our capacity to be alone with our thoughts and feelings.

In many ways, the society that we now find ourselves in is a direct result of these survival mechanisms: however, many of us now find ourselves caught in a loop, snared by the systems we have set up in a way that is difficult to free ourselves from. In his work on compassion focussed therapy (CFT), Paul Gilbert (2014) presents a helpful model for understanding this, and suggests a solution. By dividing our cognitive processes into three 'systems', we are able to think about what parts of our brain are dominant at any one time and consider the implications for creativity.

At the core of our brains is the 'threat system' that is responsible for orchestrating our response to danger. This system is instinctive, fast-acting and often unconscious, and impacts our physiology as much as our psychology. When we encounter a perceived threat – and it's helpful to note that our brains are not able to distinguish between an imagined or hypothetical threat and a 'real' one, on a neurological level – we release adrenaline and prepare our body to respond. Our response depends on the threat, but can include fight, flight, freeze, play dead and 'fawn' (acting in a manner that is most likely to neutralise the threat). These have a significant impact on our physiological state, and can result in an increased heart rate, restlessness, dilated pupils, numbness, a sense of dread and a tight jaw, to name a few.

The other important system to note is the 'drive' system, which plays an important role in motivating us to seek out resources; to pursue, achieve and acquire. When the drive system is rewarded with a 'win', we release dopamine, a profoundly rewarding neurotransmitter. This 'win' can be a material gain but can also be social rewards or reinforcement such as a 'like' on social media.

Both the threat and drive systems can be activated by our environment, and advertisers and businesses are fully aware of the potential of this to impact our behaviour. Social media gives us almost constant access to material that taps directly into our innate wish to scan for and predict danger, and our wish to pursue, acquire and gain positive feedback from one another. As devices have become more and more portable, to the extent that I can now easily check my emails from my watch, the compulsion to access social media can be satiated pretty much anywhere at any time.

There has been a lot of research undertaken to explore the impact of this 'hyperdistraction' on our mood and our attention. A recent study showed that the amount of social media that a person consumed during the COVID-19 pandemic directly impacted how much of a threat the person felt the virus posed to them and how anxious they were (Alrasheed *et al*, 2022). Interestingly, this compulsion to read about the pandemic didn't actually impact the behaviour of participants, who, despite feeling at greater risk, didn't take any more precautions than their peers, who read less and therefore were less anxious.

This finding has huge implications for our understanding of how social media and our brains interact. It suggests that it is entirely possible to spend large amounts of time reading material and becoming increasingly anxious about a subject, but not moving into action that allows us to reduce the risk. This constant barrage of threat-related information and social reward in the form of feedback can be addictive to the extent that time spent in quiet contemplation can begin to feel risky, resulting in an uncomfortable niggling as the brain seeks to habitually activate and satiate either the threat or drive system. This has a profound effect on our ability to create, as the quiet voice of inspiration and creativity must fight through the competing environmental 'noise' which we are biologically programmed to attend to. This means that to overcome this, we have to understand the pull to 'scroll' and must intentionally cultivate and turn on the 'contentment and soothing system'.

To be creative, we must be able to turn and sustain our attention towards our internal creative urge or inspiration for long enough to create work. We need to be able to give enough space for ideas to emerge gently and be translated into creative work using whatever medium we have chosen. This usually means taking time to exist in an undistracted state of 'mulling'; a mental state where ideas, thoughts and emotions can be encountered as they arise, rather than being summoned or directed. This is not a state that is particularly valued or cultivated in a capitalist society where the focus is often on productivity and outcome. It also sits at odds with the urges of our brain which can constantly feel pulled towards the threat and drive system. However, without this space, it is impossible to truly encounter the sparks of imagination and inspiration that are often at the heart of creative work. What this space looks like might be totally different for each person, for example some people find that ideas emerge best when they are walking, or cycling, or gardening. For others, it is time in their studio or work area without distraction. The common factor is the importance of moving out of the 'threat' and 'drive' systems and into the 'contentment and soothing system'.

This self-soothing system is governed by the endorphin oxytocin – if you don't know what that is then imagine the feeling as you sink into a warm bath, or gaze at a sleeping baby, or sing along to a favourite band with the people around you at a gig. Oxytocin is the bonding, soothing, 'everything is just fine' chemical that allows us to stop acquiring or scanning for danger for a time. The difficulty with our physiology is that these systems are not given equal credence – we prioritise those that are most likely to secure our survival, meaning that 'threat' and 'drive' are likely to win out whenever there is competition. The way to manage this is to understand the discomfort that arises when you stop and find ways to remind your brain that it is safe and can relax. How this looks will be different for everyone, but there are tried and tested methods that can be a good place to start.

Some people can be more tolerant of unstructured time alone with their thoughts if they are also engaging in repetitive tasks that do not require conscious effort. Knitting, crocheting, doing a jigsaw puzzle, all prevent you from anxiously scrolling or texting a friend, but do not interrupt the process of mulling over thoughts and listening for the 'voice' of inspiration. Many of the insights that have made it into the pages of this book occurred when I was driving or cycling. Other people find taking a walk is an essential way of turning off their threat and drive systems long enough to have time to think and process. For some, it is important to create a sensory environment that cultivates a sense of comfort and safety; you may find the smell of incense creates the environment for pottering and thinking as it reminds you of your yoga class, or you might prefer wrapping yourself in a large, soft blanket and sitting at a sunny window. The state you are trying to induce is one of alertness but not hypervigilance, thoughtfulness but not rumination, a kind of relaxed, introspective space that allows ideas to flow freely. Experiment with what things induce this state for you as you work through this book and try to find time to allocate to just 'mulling' at least once a week.

Why are you here?

Before beginning any journey, it is helpful to be somewhat clear about why you are embarking on it and where you might be heading. That is not to say that the entire path should be laid out before you; it is reasonable to expect some twists and turns, but a general sense of your motivation and hopes will provide a guide when you feel lost or off-course.

Perhaps you are clear in your reasons for selecting this book: however, it is also entirely possible that a part of you, not quite in your awareness, picked this book off the shelf while other parts were busy trying to catch a train or buying a bottle of water. Either way, one of the best ways to bring about change is to articulate and commit to a particular goal and the course of action most likely to realise it. Putting it in writing, and, even better, creating a vivid mental picture of what achieving your goal is likely to look and feel like, is a fantastic way to stack the odds that you will get exactly where you want to go.

When trying to identify a goal or outcome, I find that this exercise from Solution Focused Therapy is extremely helpful:

Exercise 4: The miracle question

Begin by asking yourself the question, 'If a miracle happened, and this book was totally successful in bringing about the change I am looking for, what would be different?' Imagine that the problem, aim or goal that brought you here has been totally realised or solved – what has changed? What is the first thing you notice when you wake up in the morning? What do other people notice is different about you? What do you feel in your body? Try and be as specific as possible, imagine waking in the morning and vividly picture the first thing you would feel, the first thing that would go through your head. What does your day look like now a miracle has happened? Write down everything that comes to mind and keep it to refer back to as you move through the book. If you are more of a visual thinker, then you can draw or paint the scene in as much detail as possible or use cuttings from magazines and newspapers to collate a visual representation of your felt-sense.

Identifying potential barriers

Another task when embarking on any successful journey is to identify and plan for any barriers that you might encounter that might prevent you from reaching your goals. Like many things in this book, this is likely to be entirely personal to you, but a clue is often found in what hurdles you have encountered when you have tried to make changes previously. If you have had resolutions to get fit, for example, but have never quite become the athlete that you envisioned, what happened? If you had plans to learn an instrument, but it never quite got off the ground, why? Identifying what has gotten in the way in the past will support you to plan and navigate differently in the future.

Some things that people describe as barriers include the demands of work and the number of hours left in a day or week, family and parenting or caring commitments, a lack of confidence or belief that change can happen, ambivalence and uncertainty about whether change would be positive, and financial constraints. It might be that you struggle to estimate how long something will take, and therefore find yourself getting further and further behind your original plan until you give up. Or you may start well, but then prioritise the needs of others until your original project is left neglected to the extent that all motivation is lost. Sometimes, we simply think that we want something because we believe that we 'should', but repeatedly find that this is not enough to sustain us through the course.

Often, we begin a journey of change because we believe something to be a problem. 'I leave things to the last minute', 'I'm always busy and I need to slow down', 'I always put others before myself'. These things may indeed pose a problem, however they may also come with 'payoffs' that, unless recognised, can create ambivalence when it comes to making changes. Perhaps leaving things to the last minute helps you overcome anxiety about failure? Perhaps being busy all the time protects you from difficult feelings, or means that you can pack a lot into your life in a way that is quite enjoyable? Maybe putting others before yourself gives you a sense of self-worth and makes you feel good? If you are going to begin a process of making change in your relationship with creativity, then it might help you to really understand how things are now and to see if there is any space for recognising what is working as well as what is not.

Exercise 5: Exploring the 'what if...?'

Bring to mind a change you would like to make in your creative life, perhaps something you have identified as a goal in the earlier exercise. It might be that you want to devote more time to creative pursuits, or to spend more time with other creative people or start a new creative project that has been on your mind for a long time.

Now ask yourself, what is the payoff against how things are currently? What would be the downside of making a change? Would anything have to be sacrificed or risked? Is there a counterargument to making this change?

Take time to argue from both sides and try to hear each perspective fully, without interruption. It can be very powerful to alter your →

physical position between the two perspectives, perhaps moving into a different chair as you 'voice' each part of you. What are the real benefits of things staying the same? What are the real benefits of change?

It is absolutely fine if you do not reach a firm conclusion as you move between the two roles, we are not trying to find resolution, but to add depth and colour to both sides of the argument. To create some space that allows us to view the issue in all its complexity. If we miss a vital part of the puzzle, we are likely to sabotage ourselves in a way that is out of our awareness.

Completing this exercise will hopefully have given you a deeper insight into what some of the subtle barriers might be to completing this process, and may have given you a greater sense of your relationship to those barriers. It will be interesting to keep an eye on this as you move through the book, what shifts and what doesn't shift, and to continue to ask yourself deeper questions about what you do and do not want to change.

Conclusion

Beginning any process of exploration and change can come with a range of emotions, from trepidation to cynicism to hope. Identifying what is motivating you, creating a vivid picture of what change looks like, and being clear about any ambivalence you feel will make it easier to commit to the process and see it through to the end. Ensuring that you have the support mechanisms in place to catch any emotional fallout will ensure that you can tolerate what you encounter and can reach the end of the tunnel without crashing your car. Committing to action in the form of the daily creative practice and the 'morning pages' is the quickest and most effective way to start the process of change – we will spend the next few chapters ensuring your thoughts and feelings can catch up.

References

Alrasheed M, Alrasheed S & Algahtani AS (2022) Impact of Social Media Exposure on Risk Perceptions, Mental Health Outcomes, and Preventative Behaviours during the COVID-19 Pandemic in Saudi Arabia. *Saudi Journal of Health Systems Research* **2** (3) 107-113.

Cameron J (1992) *The Artist's Way*. Atlantic Books.

Gilbert P (2009) *The Compassionate Mind*. Hachette, UK.

Chapter Two: The creative self in context

Of all the chapters in this book, this one has been the trickiest to write, and I have noticed myself stopping, reading, correcting, re-writing, and then stopping again in a way that is different to my usual process. There is something about identity politics that can feel uniquely silencing, even though it is one of the most important aspects of working as an artist within a society, and arguably the area of human experience in greatest need of meaningful dialogue. I have a suspicion that this sense of being unable to speak is related to the powerful feelings that the subject elicits: fear, shame, rage, sadness, longing. This is an area covered with landmines that, if detonated, are armed with emotions that can feel uncontained and raw. We risk retaliation, exposure and getting it wrong, a process that is increasingly public, and social humiliation. It is my experience that if we shy away from these topics, however, we miss a vital part in understanding our experience of being human and can mistakenly begin to locate things in the individual person that belong out in the social world.

This chapter is written from my perspective as a working-class, white, queer, cis woman who was born in the UK. Within my culture, I experience privilege in the form of race and gender conformity, but also exclusion and rejection of parts of my sexuality and socioeconomic class. There are many lives and worlds that I do not inhabit and cannot hope to convey accurately, therefore I have tried to speak as authentically as I can about my experiences in the hope that this will invite you to think critically and openly about your own. Most importantly for this book, we are going to consider the impact that these experiences have had, and continue to have, on your creative life.

The social context

Human beings are hardwired to relate to each other, both in groups and as individuals, right from birth. We are socialised into existence by our families, our communities, and our culture, and it is within this context that our creativity develops and ultimately might get blocked. There has been a real trend in Western psychology to look for the root causes of distress and pathology in a person's family of origin, and much psychological enquiry currently focuses on 'who did what to you?' or 'who failed to do what?' Though our 'origin stories' might hold some clues to our development, they risk overlooking the important role of context, politics, power and culture, and of attributing 'cause' to something that is best thought of as 'effect'.

It is for this reason that I have taken the somewhat radical decision to put this chapter before the one that explores your personal experience of growing up and developing as a creative individual. In the original chapter plan, I followed the agreed psychological hierarchy of attending to the 'origin story' and then giving a nod to social context. However, it seems important to focus our lens on the bigger picture first, as our culture and society is the stage on which our origin stories are performed.

The novelist, David Foster Wallace (2009), opened his address to the 2005 graduating class of Kenyon College, Ohio, with the following story:

> 'There are these two young fish swimming along and they happen to meet an older fish swimming the other way, who nods at them and says, "Morning, boys. How's the water?" And the two young fish swim on for a bit, and then eventually one of them looks over at the other and goes, "What the hell is water?"'

He went on to observe that 'the most obvious, important realities are often the ones that are hardest to see and talk about', even though these realities have a formative impact on the people whose lives they govern. The society you are born into dictates the images, messages, narratives and norms that you are exposed to on an immersive level right from the outset. They shape your view of the world in both conscious and unconscious ways, and become an integral part of how your identity forms and ultimately how your creativity develops.

If you are a fish, how do you come to understand and negotiate the water if that is all you have ever known? How do you step back from something you are immersed in and consider its impact? In this chapter, we are going to shine a light on aspects of our cultural experiences that form an inescapable part of how we see the world and constitute the 'water' in which we swim. We will consider how these experiences have the power to block our ability to make authentic, meaningful, radical art, and can be transformed into powerful creative tools.

When talking about issues of diversity and difference, it can be easy to fall into polarising narratives – for example, concentrating either on 'risk and vulnerabilities' or 'resilience and bravery' narratives (Asakura *et al*, 2020). However, human experience is nuanced and complex, and exploring it requires us to resist shortcuts and move past how things appear at 'face value'. This is not about finding *a* truth, but rather illuminating *your* truth, so that you can use it to serve you as an artist and to make sense of your experience of being in the world. As you move through this chapter, notice what themes resonate with you and which don't, and be curious about why. Pay attention to times that things co-exist together in a way that creates tension and complexity; for example, times when an element of your identity has been both an asset and a liability, or times when your experiences have been both helpful and painful. I hope that by the end of this chapter, you will be able to define your own water and that of the people around you. To see yourself in context and make some sense of how that context has shaped the trajectory of you as a person and as an artist. We might not be able to get out of the water completely, but we can at least hold it as a factor in the way we make sense of ourselves and our art.

Societies differ in terms of their attitudes towards gender, socioeconomic status, sexuality, race, age, disability, and other individual characteristics such as body shape and neurotype. These attitudes are often linked to the religious and political ideologies that have exerted an influence as the culture developed. They can manifest overtly, such as being enshrined in law, and covertly, through culturally agreed norms and unwritten 'rules' of behaviour. Sadly, there are themes that seem to resonate across cultures which result in the same groups being repeatedly marginalised, for example people with disabilities, women and people who have a different ethnicity to the dominant group. In every society, some groups have more power than others and are afforded greater opportunity, greater resources, and greater right to speak.

Exercise 6: The words that define us

Before we start to explore social context, take a pen and paper and write down all the nouns that are relevant to you; the naming words that others might use to describe you and where you are located in society. These may include words that describe the colour of your skin, your gender – both sex and gender identity, your age, the amount of money and resources you have, your professional role, your role within your family, the area or country you reside in or originate from, your sexuality and your relationship status. They can be formal words or colloquial slang, they can be 'hot' words, laden with emotion, or merely factual descriptions.

Now, take a look at the list you have written. Which words would be considered part of the 'dominant' group in your society, and which are further to the margins? You might want to visually represent this using a map, with the more culturally confluent words in the middle and the more marginalised words towards the edges. What feelings emerge as you consider your map?

Be curious about these identity words as you read through the following chapter, noticing any emotions that arise or moments of resonance or disconnect

Your individual characteristics, and the subsequent way that your society relates to you, can impact your creative practice in many ways, both psychologically and practically. It can open or close doors, both in your own mind and in the physical world around you. Some forms of expression may be deemed acceptable within your social group, and some considered off limits; some will be commonplace throughout your childhood and others will be alien and unfamiliar. Some subject matters are fair game, and some are taboo. Some groups will find it easier to distribute their work and be taken seriously, and some will meet with open resistance or silent rejection. If we are going to accept the premise that, to make art that has resonance, we need to be able to speak from an authentic place about our own experiences, then we need to understand the context of speaking and identify the covert and overt limits that our social system places on our creativity. We must ask the question, what does speaking your reality, your experience, your 'truth', mean in your context, and what support mechanisms might you need to push past these limits?

Diversity in the arts

Depending on what circles you move in, it may be easy to conclude that we have moved into a fairer and more equal era as a human collective, and to some extent that is true. We are beginning to consider the importance of diversity and representation in the arts and to call out discrimination where we encounter it. However, if you dive beneath the narratives of inclusion, the data suggests that whether your art is seen still depends to some extent on what social group you belong to. Work by women, by artists of colour, by queer people, by people with disabilities, is still vastly under-represented in galleries and in the media. One of my favourite activist groups, the Guerrilla Girls, have spent decades shining a light on this and the quiet shaping of what is considered art by those in power (www.guerrillagirls.com). It is still the powerful groups that make choices about what art is published, displayed, applauded and, inevitably, what art is remembered.

As the Guerrilla Girls so clearly point out, the history of Western art could more accurately be thought of as the history of power: who held it and what they did with it. Identity politics has resulted in the erasing of entire groups from archives and collections: for example, of the more than 2,300 works in the National Gallery in London, only *21* of these works are by female artists (www.nationalgallery.org.uk/paintings/women-in-our-collection). The invisibility of marginalised groups from the history of art has a contemporary impact on the way in which people from those groups can connect with their heritage and legacy. It removes the ability to build on the works of others and requires a kind of reclamation and renewal that prevents the establishment of tradition. All of this is not to say that if you dwell on the periphery of power you cannot make art; quite the contrary, it means that in order to do so you may have to look harder, think more critically, support yourself more and search for the subverted and silenced narratives to find your tribe. It means creating a platform in the water from which you can survey what is around you and find a way to speak.

As we discussed in the previous chapter, humans use stories to shape their reality, therefore if the story does not exist, then the concept itself does not exist. We cannot underestimate the power of representation when becoming a creative artist; if you can't see it, it is much harder to be it. This means that the lack of representation for marginalised groups doesn't just impact the generation of creative artists that are practising now, but also those that are coming up behind them and looking around for role models of what is possible. Education has an enormous part to play in this, and I would argue that institutions such as schools and colleges have a moral responsibility to curate curriculums that present artistic works which represent the communities in which they operate. Again, this is an area in which things are changing, but even a casual glance at the course content of many school-based art courses will show you that there is still a long way to go.

What does this mean for you and your creativity? What was the impact of growing up in your community on your emerging, creative self?

Exercise 7: Representation

Take your notebook and jot down whatever comes to you as you complete this exercise. Remember, you do not have to be fair or unbiased in your responses, you are looking for your subjective experience and reality, not an objective 'truth'. Tuning into your 'gut' response will tell you far more than searching for an objective answer.

Think back to your childhood, both at home and at school. What were the images that surrounded you and who created them? What books did you read and what films were watched in your home? What artists did you study or become aware of in your childhood? What images and artistic representations did you see of people who looked or lived like you and what story did those images tell? Who created these stories and images?

Now look back at what you have written and compare this with the list of words you completed earlier to describe yourself. How do these two lists compare? Did you see work made by artists whose 'naming words' would be considered similar to yours? With the same colour skin as you, the same gender identity or background, or the same sexuality as you? How were those people spoken about by your teachers or by →

family members? If you did see yourself represented in the characteristics of the artists, how well did that translate into your connection with their work; did it resonate or was there a disconnect? Why?

Now for the big question: how did these experiences shape your emerging creativity? How did what you saw around you impact your choice of creative medium? Were there disciplines that weren't available to you, or that it never occurred to you to try? Were there subjects or feelings that you innately felt you were not allowed to convey? If you are unsure, pause here and return to this question at the end of the chapter.

Structures and subversion

As humans, we have a whole host of emotional responses to ensure that we do not stray too far from the agreed social contract, the most notable and powerful of which is shame. The role of shame is to get you to conform to your group, and to keep you conforming. If you experience shame, your natural instinct is to hide the thing that has elicited the feeling; to become smaller and less visible. It stands to reason, then, that this process can powerfully inhibit the ability to make and share authentic, non-conforming work; it can quite literally block you.

Shame can arise whenever we do not find support in our environment for a need, for example to be understood as an artist, to be taken seriously, or for our work to be received. If we can understand that society is not a benign force, but a structure that attempts to maintain itself, then we can begin to see how support might be given or withheld according to the context of you as an artist and your work. Shame therefore becomes more about a relationship with the environment and less about personal failing. Art that pushes boundaries and pushes buttons is often heavily criticised and shamed in order to maintain the system, not because the art has no merit but because it may provoke and destabilise. Of course, as the structure changes, so does its relationship with the work, and we all know of artists whose work has not been applauded until some time later, perhaps even after they have died.

Think back to times when you have experienced shame in relation to your creativity, and you will probably be able to see an underlying need that went unmet. Perhaps you showed a picture to a teacher in need of validation but received critique. Or perhaps, in need of encouragement, you disclosed an ambition to a parent but were shut down and dismissed. Even thinking of these experiences has the power to set in motion the psychological and physiological responses to shame, a phenomenon I often see in the therapy room as patients turn red or begin to squirm as they recall a shameful memory. This has a powerful inhibitory effect that curbs our behaviour and makes us less likely to reveal those parts of ourselves again.

So, how do we push past this and get back to the business of creating? The antidote to shame is *support*, both internal and from others. If we are going to speak from or subvert the space that we have been allocated and create meaningful art, we must learn how to harness self-compassion and consciously seek social support. This may be particularly pertinent if you make a transition between social groups, for example moving to a country where there are different established norms or moving between socioeconomic groups.

Cultivating internal and external support

There are two ways of inoculating ourselves against the paralysing impact of shame: support from others, and internal support in the form of self-compassion. The concept of compassion is central to compassion focused therapy and is differentiated from kindness or self-care in its focus on action. Gilbert (2014) defines compassion as *'sensitivity to suffering or distress in self and others, with a commitment to try to alleviate and prevent it'*. It is a radical commitment to treat even the parts of ourselves that we don't like, or we feel ashamed of, with compassion, and to do what is necessary to alleviate distress. Sometimes the compassionate thing to do is not gentle but is challenging and requires great bravery. It is not the 'easy option' and does not constitute taking the way out of difficulties, it is a commitment that sometimes requires us to be accountable to ourselves for the sake of our work.

This is easier said than done, however, as we are often far better at levelling harsh criticism than we are harnessing radical compassion. In therapy, many people find it useful to use Gilbert's technique of identifying a compassionate person (either in their lives, a figure from popular culture, or even an imagined figure) and considering how they might respond to a given situation as a guide. It is a case of 'fake it till you make it', or 'borrow it' until you develop the skill for yourself. For example, if you experience a negative review and usually respond by berating yourself and spiralling into self-doubt, you will stop and ask yourself how your compassionate guide might respond? Would they suggest you call a friend, or take a walk? Would they empathise with your understandably hurt or angry reaction, but also remind you that this is one review and does not constitute the totality of the responses to your work? Would they advise you do something that you know you find restorative, or suggest you stop and rest and let yourself recover? This 'fake it till you make it' approach can be very effective in starting the journey towards tolerating shame.

Exercise 8: Creating a compassionate figure

This exercise draws from Paul Gibert's work on compassion focused therapy. Further reading can be found in the resources section of this book.

Bring to mind someone or something that you have experienced as compassionate. If no one from your life comes to mind, then recall someone you have seen on television or read about that you feel embodies wisdom, kindness and compassion. You may also prefer to choose an animal or to create a totally imagined figure.

How would you like your compassionate figure to look and behave? What is the tone of their voice like, their body language? What sounds, colours and sensations do you associate with them? How would they demonstrate their compassion towards you? How would you like to respond? What feelings arise as you imagine your compassionate figure, does it feel comfortable to be related to like this, or does it bring up uncomfortable feelings? If you are a visual thinker, then you may prefer to paint, draw or photograph your compassionate figure. Try to create an image that is full and evokes the characteristics of compassion that you feel are important.

Practice bringing your compassionate figure to mind at neutral times when you are not experiencing a powerful emotion, or at times when you feel calm and secure. Bring them to mind when you are driving, or walking, or just before you go to sleep. Becoming familiar with your figure during neutral times will make it far easier for you to envision them at times of challenge or distress.

One important note here is that people are often concerned that, if they allow themselves to be compassionate, they will somehow become lazy, self-indulgent, or will lose what they perceive to be the power of their internal critic to spur them on to better things. In therapy, patients are often deeply wedded to their internal critic and convinced that they somehow protect them or inoculate them against the criticism of others. In my experience, an internal critic is often vastly skewed and has more of a paralysing impact than a facilitative one. It is unlikely that you will achieve anything through self-criticism that you could not achieve through self-encouragement and care. I would go so far as to argue that using self-compassion will get the results that you want faster, as it will free you up from the paralysing impact of shame.

The other way to respond to shame is to take support from other people. The role of social support can be easily underestimated, though the research is unequivocal about the role it can play in protecting us from the worst of human experience, including trauma (Hérbert et al, 2014) and even natural disasters (Xi et al, 2020). It appears as a mediating factor when predicting whether someone will develop PTSD, or whether they will experience mental health issues of any kind at every stage in our lives.

Representation is also important when considering your social group and the support it is able to provide. Research shows that it is a basic human need to see ourselves and our experiences reflected in the people around us, and the lack of this can result in the development of mental health issues (Anglin et al, 2020). If your life circumstances have meant that you are not held in a community that is representative of your lived experience and identity, then it is important to address this as a vital way to increase your resilience to shame.

Exercise 9: Evaluating your support network

Go back to the list of supportive people that you formulated in Chapter One and make a note of who occupies a similar place in society to you or who can connect with parts of your identity that are not considered dominant. If there is no one that fulfils that role on your list, then deliberately set out to forge those connections; join a queer writing group, a women's screenwriting development programme, or an autistic animation group. If these don't exist locally then either set them up or look online.

Case example

Within the UK, there is a heavily ingrained class system that carries with it implicit expectations and behaviours. A person's class background can shape their ethics, beliefs, taste, the way they communicate emotions, the language they use, their accent, aspirations and even physical health and mortality. It also dictates the likelihood of whether you will work as an artist or not; startlingly, working-class people make up only 7.9% of practising artists in the UK (Tapper, 2022), despite making up 48% of the population (Social Mobility Commission, 2021).

Like many issues of diversity, social class plays a significant role in dictating a person's relationship with the arts right from early childhood. Schools with less funding tend to have less access to costly equipment such as cameras and kilns, which can exclude students from whole creative disciplines. Children from households with less disposable income are less likely to have opportunities for extracurricular activities that develop creativity such as music lessons, drama groups or dance lessons. It might be harder for working-class children to access exhibitions, events and performances that carry a ticket fee, or even to transport themselves to free events that might be happening in other locations.

All of this adds up to less 'cultural capital' that the person takes with them into adulthood. Cultural capital is the social knowledge and advantages that make it easier to operate in the world; it is the likelihood that, if you were invited to a swanky party, you would speak 'properly', behave in the 'correct' way and have a clue what people were talking about when they start critiquing a new play or citing classic literature. If working-class people do find a way to enter the creative arts, they do so with less cultural capital than their peers, and therefore encounter a host of barriers which they have to overcome to claim and defend a space at the table.

Mark is a talented musician who came to see me in his early 20s for support with anxiety and panic. Mark was working class by background and had grown up making music with friends in his neighbour's garage. He lived on an estate that was predominantly owned by the local council and attended a large comprehensive school that 'required improvement', but which luckily had a thriving music department. He grew up regularly seeing other working-class musicians in his city in the north of England; his dad had played in a locally well-known folk band, and he often accompanied him to gigs from a young age.

Mark loved writing and performing, and played in local pubs throughout school and college. Mark was gifted and emerged just at the time when artists began relying less on major labels to promote them and began self-publishing online. His band quickly gained momentum and his audience grew. He got a manager and started being invited to parties and social events by promoters. Having predominantly played pubs and bars in his local area, he suddenly started being offered gigs in larger and more upmarket venues and was asked to appear at a few prestigious industry events.

When I met Mark, he was well on his way to a successful career as a musician. He had been invited to play large festivals and was regularly travelling to London for events. As he became more successful however, he became more paralysed by anxiety, to the extent that he was regularly experiencing panic attacks and was increasingly drinking alcohol to cope. We began meeting regularly and he shared how he still loved playing and writing music but found the demand to 'network' with other musicians and people in the industry overwhelming and alienating. He described vividly his experience of being subtly excluded from conversations when people referenced art, music, locations and restaurants he had no experience of. He would find himself losing his words halfway through a sentence as he was engulfed in a wave of anxiety and self-consciousness and was often unable to respond at all. He was taken for dinner by a record label executive and a publisher, and was given chopsticks to eat with which he had never used before; cue an awkward hour of trying to hold up his end of a conversation while attempting to work out the mechanics of eating. People made well-meaning jokes about his broad, northern accent and clothing choices, which made him increasingly conscious of his differences. Even the architecture and acoustics of the buildings he played in had changed and become an alien environment that subtly conveyed 'you don't belong here'. Many of the other working-class musicians he had regularly been in contact with had fallen away as he progressed in his career, and he increasingly found himself unable to relate to the people around him. This left him with an uncomfortable dilemma: either try and conform to this new normal but feel fake and anxious, or hold on to his identity but feel excluded and ashamed.

In some ways, Mark's background was immensely positive and provided him with a coherent, artistic identity and a great deal of support in his early career. However, as soon as he moved out of his context and began 'stepping out', he developed a sense of unease and an awareness of his differences. The space that he was 'allowed' to occupy as a working-class person did not always extend as far as his music took him. By the time he came into treatment, he was drinking heavily and was turning up late to events to avoid the pressure to network. He felt increasingly like a fraud as he started to change his accent and clothing to fit in, and ultimately stopped writing. Mark had no words or explanation for this, so he did what most people do in this situation: internalise the power imbalance, assume that it reflected a deficit or flaw in him, and become terrified that it might be exposed or found out.

As we worked together, we began to disentangle his experiences and make sense of them within the context of social class. We were able to identify how his transition from a working-class to a predominantly middle-class space initiated an imposter syndrome that was less to do with him, and more to do with the structure of the society around him. We explored the importance of 'cultural distance' (how close or far away you are from what is considered the 'majority group' in society) as a risk factor for mental health (Jongsma *et al*, 2021) and think about how this distance grew as he moved from a culture in which he was a majority, into one in which he was suddenly a minority.

Mark began to make some major changes, which included reconnecting with old friends and spending more time with family, but most importantly he began to understand what was happening and gain some distance from his experience of shame and unease. He was able to prepare himself in a different way for events at which he knew there was a good chance he would feel out of his depth, and learn strategies to manage the anxiety, which began to reduce along with his drinking. He began writing again, drawing on the experiences of the past few years as excellent writing material.

The sense of shame and unease described by Mark is not limited to social class but is also familiar to the other groups whose identities sit outside the dominant norms of their society. People from minority ethnic groups, queer people, people whose gender identity does not conform to binary social constructs, people from neurominorities – all describe encountering overt and covert barriers as they move into different professional or personal arenas. When you are a minority in an environment, there can be a quiet assumption that you are in the wrong and an implicit pressure to change that starts early in childhood. Without an awareness of identity politics and the power dynamics at play, this can quickly manifest as shame, imposter syndrome or a nagging sense of not getting it right.

I would argue that these experiences are particularly challenging in the arts, both early in one's career and as a person's practice develops. I hear many accounts of young people who expressed their identity in their art and were heavily criticised by teachers for not conforming to expectations or were made to feel 'other', as the people around them simply could not relate to what they were trying to convey. Some of these adolescents continued to create regardless, mercifully finding a group of like-minded peers either in their community or online, which offered the support they needed to keep going. Others either changed their style or stopped creating altogether, only recovering their creativity in adulthood.

The role of education

One of the most powerful mechanisms that conveys and initiates young artists into the social structures they are to occupy is education. It does this in a myriad of ways; through the content of what is studied, the process of how that is delivered, and within the relationship between teacher and student. The syllabus dictates what work is selected for study and the parameters for assessment, the institution determines how subjects are prioritised for resources and credibility, and the politics and perspectives of the teacher inform how they deliver the material. Some schools employ creative artists to teach creative subjects, and some employ teachers who have an academic knowledge of the subject but do not have a practice of their own. All these things will have a direct impact on how a young person encounters creativity and begins to develop their work.

When children are very small, they create without self-consciousness and want to show you everything they have made. I have a four-year-old and our walls are covered in paintings, drawings, cards, masks and even a 'stained-glass window' made from tissue paper that she brought home from school. She is so proud to show off her creations and to share the experience of making in a way that is playful and open. Research suggests that this willingness to experiment and playfully create does not last; we experience a 'slump' in our creativity around age nine or ten, during which we stop taking risks and the originality of our ideas and our work starts to deteriorate (Lin & Shih, 2016). This is the age where the brain develops quickly and we become increasingly aware of our place in society and more concerned about what other people, especially peers, think of us. We develop an intense awareness of ourselves and the importance of wearing the right clothes, and liking or disliking the same things as the people around us increases dramatically. Children who sit outside of the agreed social norms begin to be rejected and ostracised in a way that is noticeably different to their younger counterparts.

At the same time, the education system is also increasingly dictating what can be considered 'right' and 'wrong', with increasing numbers of tests and assessments and a focus on achievement and comparison with peers. Children are made very aware of their academic ranking and the playfulness that was part of the early school experience has all but disappeared. Writing becomes increasingly about sentence structure, grammar and 'correctness', and many young people have their work handed back to them covered in red pen. Instead of a totally natural form of self-expression that is an extension of communication through spoken word, writing takes on a formal quality that can be done 'right' or 'wrong' with some people being able to do it, and others considered less able. Painting and drawing also starts to be a structured activity that is demonstrably right or wrong, with the focus almost entirely on output rather than process.

Sir Ken Robinson gave one of the most-viewed TED talks of all time about the impact of formal education on the development of a child's creativity and the disastrous impact that it can have (2006). He made the stark observation that public schooling did not exist before industrialisation; therefore, the purpose of education must be viewed as cultivating skills that will deliver young adults who are ready to be part of the workforce. I am not being sceptical when I say that education systems are less focused on bringing forth a well-rounded, critically thinking, creatively expressive, knowledgeable, physically aware and socially functioning human, but instead is geared towards fulfilling the needs of the industrialised society for a continual procession of workers. The reason that is important is that it leaves us with the task of unpicking some of what we have learned and been socialised into in order to reclaim and recover aspects of our creativity.

This focus on adult productivity helps us to understand why there is a sort of universal 'pecking order' of school subjects that is topped by maths and science, followed by the humanities, with the arts bringing up the rear. Even within the arts, Robinson argues that there is a hierarchy, with art and music being considered more respectable and prioritised over dance and drama. No wonder most people grow into lives where the majority of the time is dedicated to work-related tasks, and creativity is either side-lined entirely or pushed to the periphery and practised in snatched bits of time here or there. No wonder we struggle to connect with our bodies and recognise our own and other people's feelings, when dance and drama come at the bottom of the pile.

Thinking critically about the role of education is essential for creative people, as it is likely that you will have been exposed to a system that encouraged you towards 'convergent thinking' (ie there is one right answer and you need to know it) rather than the sort of 'divergent thinking' (there are many possible answers that come from many different sources) that is essential for creativity. Formal education sets up the idea that there is one way of doing something, and only rewards a child for getting the 'right' answer, rather than reinforcing the thought processes that are involved in arriving at an answer. When a child creates something, they are told whether they have done it right or wrong and are often critiqued on their technique, rather than supported to critically evaluate what has worked well and what could be developed. There is little room for experiment, playfulness, error or mistakes. Couple this with the pre-adolescent self-consciousness and desire to be accepted and you have a perfect storm for the destruction of creativity. It is possible that you were told that you weren't good at something as a child because you couldn't do it in the way that mainstream education and rigid assessment procedures deemed 'right'. This approach is misguided and does not take into consideration the role of creative thinking as an essential component to problem solving and innovation. Advances in technology and science depend on the capacity of a person to have the sort of knowledge gained in education, coupled with the cognitive flexibility and creativity to link these together and conceive of the 'next step'. Teaching children how to think critically, to tolerate failure and to problem solve, is essential if they are to succeed in the working world into which they are now being delivered.

Educational institutions are also not benign figures with regard to identity politics and are susceptible to the same cultural biases and norms as the rest of society. Some are better than others at acknowledging this and striving for balance, others are less so and end up operating from the very same power structures that exist in the wider community. The inclusion or exclusion of work by groups other than the dominant ones will have a measurable impact on how a young person conceives of themselves and the options available to them as they move into adulthood, as will the unconscious messages about how the arts are valued and who is and isn't allowed to engage with them.

When I look back at my experiences of art education at school, I don't recall writing one single essay about an artistic work that was created by a woman, let alone a working-class woman. I do not recall studying a film that was written and directed by a woman, or by someone that came from a remotely working-class background. Now, as a white, cis-gendered person, I didn't face the additional exclusion that artists of colour, trans artists, or gender non-conforming artists experience, but I did feel a complete disconnect from the visual arts, which seemed to represent both a gender and socioeconomic reality that differed entirely from mine.

I count myself extremely lucky that my mother is a writer, and a great lover of both literature and music. I watched her write prolifically throughout my childhood and knew many other women that regularly wrote and performed their work. I was intentionally introduced to female authors such as Alice Walker, Maya Angelou, Susie Orbach and Jeanette Winterson, and listened at home to female songwriters such as Melanie, Joni Mitchell, Tracey Chapman and Carol King. As such, I had a strong sense of a world in which women could express themselves with words and through music, even if this was not always the reality I experienced at school. You could argue that it is pure chance that I grew up to be both a writer and a musician and not a painter or a film director, but I would argue that this is absolutely by design and not by accident. I was merely enacting what I had seen, repeating what I knew to be 'true'.

When I began researching for this book, I was fascinated to learn that my experience is by no means unique; Jennifer Higgie (2019) wrote:

> 'I studied painting at art school in Canberra and Melbourne in
> the 1980s and 1990s. Apart from a few feminist artists of the late

twentieth century, I can only recall, at best, a couple of pre-twentieth-century women artists being mentioned.'

She also interviewed the Director of Tate Modern, Frances Morris, in 2018. Morris studied art history at Cambridge University and at the Courtauld Institute, and reported:

'…not one female artist was mentioned in the entirety of her studies apart from, curiously, the Bauhaus weaver Anni Albers, possibly because she was the first female textile artist to be granted the honour of a solo exhibition at New York's Museum of Modern Art in 1949.'

Higgie summarised her paper in the most striking of ways:

'History is a story told in words as well as deeds: if the accomplishments of creative women aren't acknowledged, they may as well have never existed.'

I would argue that if the accomplishments of all marginalised groups aren't acknowledged, then the chances are drastically reduced that they will ever exist. If you cannot see it, you cannot be it. When you think back to your experiences of school, it is highly likely that you will be able to map some of the choices you have made with regard to your creativity to your experiences and the way in which you were made to feel you fit within the world of creativity.

Exercise 10: Art and education

Take a pen and paper and allow your mind to drift back to your experience of school, starting in early years education and moving up into adolescence and early adulthood. What things were said about your creativity and the things that you were 'good' and 'bad' at? What were you told that you 'could' and 'could not' do right? What impact did this have on you and your creativity? Were there any things that you stopped doing as a result of the feedback, or any things that you began to only do in secret? How have these experiences translated into adulthood and your beliefs about what you 'can' and 'cannot' do?

The role of social structures and power in education does not stop once a person leaves school but follows them into further education. The dominant narratives about what sort of art is acceptable, and what is not, continues to directly impact how a student's work is received and marked, even as the focus seemingly becomes more about self-expression and developing an artistic 'voice' in preparation for setting up in practice. If a person chooses to study art in higher education, the curriculum becomes heavily reliant on 'crit' sessions during which a student's work is interrogated and critiqued with a view to developing their integrity and identity as an artist. These sessions are usually curated by older, more established artists and lecturers who wield a level of power within the institution but will also be imbued with whatever power their social group affords them. The problem with this model is that it assumes that everyone comes to the arts with a sense of self that is robust and supported enough to tolerate such a transformative but often bruising experience. If you arrive at that place from a minority background with a pre-existing belief that you are different and/or not good enough, then it is almost impossible to withstand the process and many students drop out or develop mental health issues as a result.

This inequity amplifies as an artist moves into practice and is expected to be able to tolerate public critique and exposure while also developing and making daring choices that risk failure. Of course, some people are going to feel more robust and can withstand this better than others. Research strongly suggests that the willingness to take risks is positively associated with 'radical creativity' and innovation (Madjar *et al*, 2011), however, the amount of risk one is taking will vary depending on the personal stakes at hand. If you are financially comfortable and can rely on pre-existing funds to sustain you, you may be less concerned with commercial success. If you have the backing of your family who have contacts within the art world, then you might be more at liberty to take risks about what you produce, knowing that you have support and do not need to rely on the patronage of strangers. Whether an artist is commercially successful or not does not always reflect the quality of their art, but the ego strength and self-confidence of the artist to push through barriers and put themselves forward. How resilient you are and how many barriers you encounter will depend on your formative experiences and the privilege (or lack thereof) that your social identity affords you.

Again, we are looking for nuance and complexity here; even if you are making art from right at the centre of the enclaves of power within your society, there will still be an invitation to conform, a pressure to succeed and a dominant narrative that it is difficult to deviate from. The question is what impact your experiences had on you, your identity, and your ability to occupy different spaces and be heard as an artist.

The good news

Coming from a marginalised group may present some challenges in terms of becoming an artist, but it also offers some advantages that it is important to know about. There is a whole body of research focusing on the role of 'diversifying experiences' in the development of creativity. These experiences are 'events and circumstances in childhood and adolescence that set a young person on an unconventional and divergent developmental trajectory' (Simonton, 2020) and include things like having a physical disability, having a parent who is different from the 'dominant culture' in terms of their ethnicity, religion or socioeconomic background, and experiencing 'disruptive experiences' such as economic instability (Damian & Simonton, 2015). Such experiences seem to loosen the association between the person and the conventions of their culture in a way that appears to increase their creativity and ability to make novel work. If you have childhood experiences that differed from the people around you, then this may actually serve to improve your creative practice, rather than hinder it.

One of the processes behind this appears to be an increase in the tendency towards 'divergent thinking', ie your ability to explore all the available answers and possibilities when considering how to solve a problem. If you are able to use your experiences to consider many perspectives and options, then you are more able to think expansively and creatively. In contrast, people who take a 'convergent thinking' approach tend to quickly appraise which option is likely to be the best and will narrow their options early in the process in a way that limits the possibilities and creative opportunity (Zhu *et al*, 2019). If you can allow yourself to experiment, play, risk failure and consider all possible insights and inspirations as worthy of pursuing, then you increase the chances of making original work.

A note on neurodiversity

One of the great and I would argue unchallenged structures that exist in society is a bias towards that which is considered 'neurotypical'. By that, I mean the way in which we would 'typically' expect humans to communicate, to navigate their relationships, to think and to respond to the world around them. We base our policies and practices on assumptions that work for a large percentage of people, but not for everyone. This includes people that belong to what is sometimes termed 'neurominorities' such as autistic people, dyspraxic people, ADHD people (attention deficit hyperactivity disorder) and people with specific learning difficulties such as dyslexia.

When it comes to creativity, developing in ways that might be considered as different to the norm can actually be a real benefit. Many neurodivergent people are profoundly creative and their work is sometimes able to shine a light on things that may be taken for granted or unnoticed by neurotypical people. For some, being in a neurominority greatly enhances their sensitivities to the sensory world, meaning they are able to observe colour or symmetry in a striking way, or can notice tiny details that others would not. Hypersensitivity to sound can result in the ability to differentiate between the make and model of an amplifier, for example, or the slightest hint of music being off-key. Differences in social communication can result in canny observations of human behaviour, and the ability to see patterns can give rise to complex and beautiful art. Having ADHD appears to promote the sort of flexible, 'divergent' thinking style that promotes novelty and creativity. Having the sort of focused, intense interests associated with autism can lend itself to the kind of perseverance that builds technical skill.

However, the bias towards the 'neurotypical' can create real barriers for neurominority artists when it comes to studying and practising, and requires that we reconsider some of the commonly held practices and do better. I have met and worked with many, many autistic students in a range of disciplines whose work is acknowledged to be full of promise, but who stumble when they are required to articulate their design process in neurotypical ways or explain the constructs behind their work in abstractions that make no sense to the autistic brain. ADHD people are often full of creative thoughts and ideas, but without adequate support may struggle to meet coursework deadlines or are told early on that they are unlikely to have what it takes based on little evidence other than academic assignments. Art departments can be noisy and full of equipment, making them intolerable for people with sensory processing difficulties, particularly in the absence of a quiet place to de-escalate.

This is another area where things are improving, and we are beginning to understand the sort of reasonable adjustments that might increase the likelihood that someone can learn and practise their creativity unscathed. If you are neurodivergent and have found the barriers overwhelming, then there are a host of resources for you in the section at the end of this book. The important thing is to work to keep locating the problem in the space between you and the world around you, not inside yourself, regardless of how often you are invited to become 'the problem'.

Writing for the gallery

The social forces that exert pressure on individuals interact with the innate, human mechanisms that are designed to improve social cohesion (such as the shame response) and can ultimately result in you producing work that is derivative in an attempt to conform; work which does not convey your unique perspective in a way that feels frustrating and limiting. We can end up 'writing for the gallery', as David Bowie so eloquently put it, creating things in answer to the imagined (or real) audience in your mind. This is a mistake that usually results in work that lacks the 'truth' of your self-expression and therefore is less likely to connect with and resonate with others. It is easy to see how a vicious cycle can develop where the harder an artist tries to fit in and conform, the less positive feedback they receive and the more they double up their efforts to conform. Does this resonate with you and your approach to creativity?

One place to begin to tackle this is to explore who is in the gallery. Who are the internalised audience that appear when you begin to make creative work? How do you relate to that audience and what impact does this have on your work?

Exercise 11: Relating to the gallery

Imagine you have an idea for a creative work. It might be a screenplay, a book, a painting or a photograph. Now imagine you set about creating it. You are in your flow and the work is coming effortlessly. Suddenly, you imagine a person or people seeing this piece of work and you pause. You begin thinking about how they might perceive what you are doing, and the moment of flow is broken. →

Who is it that you tend to 'see' in your mind's eye at that moment? Is it someone from your current life, perhaps colleagues, other artists, your partner, or friends? Or is it someone from your past, maybe a teacher or a parent? Whose opinion has the power to move you to reconsider your work? What is their 'voice' in your head? Is it encouraging, critical, doubtful, or full of praise? Is there a particular mental image that comes to mind, perhaps a moment in the past or a snapshot of a feared future scenario?

How do you respond to this experience? Do you continue with your plan, or do you begin to make changes to avoid perceived criticism or to gain approval? What is your emotional experience? What do you do in response? Do you strive to please or abandon yourself and your art in order to avoid a painful dynamic? Do you make changes to make your work less threatening or less likely to provoke attack? Do you continue to make work for yourself, or begin to make work for the gallery?

Take a pen and paper and write a letter addressing this internal audience. As with all of these exercises, try not to filter or censor yourself to be 'fair' or even accurate, just write as it comes. How does the presence of this audience make you feel? What would you say to them if there were no consequences? How would you like to move forward as an artist and resolve whatever pattern of relating to them you have in your head?

Now sign it off and date the letter with a declaration of resolve about what will be different from now on. Keep this to hand so that you can refer back to it if you notice that you have reverted back to writing for whoever is in your mental gallery.

Money and worth

This leads us to a point about money and our relationship with it. One of the great stereotypes about artists is they are broke and struggling. Whether you are an actor, writer, or painter, there will be a narrative about what poverty looks like for you. This can create a sort of anxiety that can leave you bound to work that you are certain has a market value and will sustain you. In a capitalist society, it is very difficult to disentangle money and worth – if something doesn't sell then it can be challenging indeed to consider it a 'success'.

This can result in a dilemma that feels polarised; either you make what you know will sell but feel frustrated and limited, or you create what you really want but risk losing your income. This is another area where it is important to consciously create a balance. It is perfectly fine to create things that you know will generate a stable income, but guard against the creeping invasion of the time and energy, and protect space to also produce new and experimental work that is less assured but might be more personally rewarding. It is this work that will sustain you and feed your creativity. If you have found a practice that both pays and sustains you, then enjoy the work fully, but heed Bowie's final bit of advice and keep an eye out for times when you perhaps feel too safe or too settled and find ways to push yourself to the edge of your comfort zone again. Maybe swap out the medium for something else, for example using porcelain instead of stoneware if you are a ceramicist, try a screenplay rather than a novel if you are a writer. Shake your work up to the point that you perceive a thrill of uncertainty and encounter the unknown.

Rage against the machine

So, what happens if you want to step outside of the accepted norms that your society has tacitly agreed to and begin to make art that is 'out of place'? To do this, you must consciously develop tools to help you to tune in to your personal experience and to withstand the pressure to conform. We will be looking at how to manage difficult emotions as they arise in Chapter Four. However, besides managing the difficult feelings that creating non-conforming art can elicit, one of the best ways to avoid being totally derailed by the society we live in is to identify and define our values and then to use these as a compass to guide our actions.

In his book, *The Happiness Trap*, Russ Harris (2008) outlines how we can differentiate our values from goals or beliefs and use them as a tool to navigate any situation that arises in life. A value is a guiding principle that you live your life by but which you can never 'complete' or finish. In contrast, a goal is a defined objective that can be 'ticked off' a list. A value is something that develops over time in response to our experiences and the relationships we encounter. A goal is something we select, which may be indicative of our values, but does not require the same ongoing commitment. For example, 'I want to use my creativity to the best of my ability' is a value; 'I want to publish my first novel this year' is a goal. The two are related, but the value is the broader, overarching principle that gives rise to the goal.

It is very easy to become goal-orientated and to lose sight of what values are underpinning your life. As we described in Chapter One, we have a nifty 'drive' system that keeps us working to achieve and accumulate the things we need to survive. This system can be so successful and rewarding that, before you know it, your goals and actions are at odds with your values. For example, a writer may have the value 'I want to make art that is authentic and real', and to that end they set about writing a short story that connects deeply to their personal experience. A publisher is initially positive about the project, but once the story is complete begins to critique it heavily and suggest edits that feel contrived or at odds with the writer's initial intentions. The writer may have a goal to 'get three pieces published this year', or 'to make writing my sole source of income', which would dictate that they make the changes and get the piece published. This may sit at odds with their value, though, which is not just about numbers and success but is about the integrity and meaning of what they produce. If the writer makes the decision about how to proceed based on their personal values, they will insist that the integrity of the piece is maintained and find another publisher who better understands the vision.

There is no right or wrong when it comes to values, the things that we prioritise are personal to us and need no excusing. However, we need to define and consciously commit to them, otherwise they are quickly derailed by other processes.

Exercise 12: Defining your values

The values we are going to explore apply directly to your art, but you may wish to do this exercise with a wider lens that incorporates other areas of your life. If you work better with some suggestions, then Russ Harris has compiled a helpful list of possible values here www.actmindfully.com.au/wp-content/uploads/2019/07/Values_Checklist_-_Russ_Harris.pdf

Imagine you can fast-forward into the future and are listening to a lecture about your creative work and career. What sort of creative life would you like to have had? What words would you like to be used about your art and the impact it has had? What sort of meaning ➔

would you like people to take from your work? How would you like your approach to your art to be described? What role would you like your creative practice to have played in your life? How would you like your creative works to be remembered?

What values did you uncover in relation to your art when doing this exercise? What things have you identified that matter to you in the way you approach creativity? Can you formulate them into some clear sentences that can be easily remembered and referred to when making decisions about your work? What commitments could you make based on the values you have identified?

It can be helpful to remind yourself regularly of your core values, as there will be many opportunities to act in a way that is inconsistent with them. Some people find it useful to have them written down or represented visually and placed somewhere obvious in their workspace as a prompt.

Conclusion

The cultural tides are changing when it comes to diversity in art, and there is now a far greater focus on representation and inclusion. However, there is still a way to go before we can consider these issues resolved. It is important to be able to notice, name and understand the power imbalances in whatever social group you exist. Otherwise, there is a risk they will be internalised and manifest in ways which include shame, imposter syndrome and a longstanding sense of not being able to get it quite right. Over the longer term, this can extinguish even the most passionate of artistic practices.

Considering your relationship to society can help you to gain some distance from the pressure to conform, and the difficult feelings that can arise if you don't. If you are able to stay with your unique experience and perspective, you are more likely to make art that conveys something of these in an authentic way that therefore connects with the lived experience of others. Deliberately finding ways to bolster and sustain yourself makes it more likely that you will be able to continue to create such work and to withstand whatever response you encounter. It also makes the process much more enjoyable.

Thinking about the power of representation also affords us the wonderful opportunity of experimenting with mediums and areas that might not have occurred to us before, or might be considered off limits. Not only does this broaden our horizons but constitutes a radial act that paves the way for others to follow. If you need any incentive to do so, then the following tiny snapshot might inspire you:

- A survey completed in 2020 indicated that only 4% of film directors in the USA are female (Guerilla Girls, 2020).

- Out of 1,000 films surveyed in 2017, only 34 had an Asian director, and only three of these were female (Smith *et al*, 2018). This number had not changed in the past decade.

- In the 65 years that the Grammy Awards have been presented, only 11 black artists have won album of the year.

- In 2019 in the UK, 74% of students studying Art & Design A-level courses were female. In that same year, only 35% of artists represented by commercial galleries in London were female.

Whatever your social group, and whatever the impact of your past experiences, it is perfectly possible to use your values as a guide to your next steps. Whether that is invading spaces that were previously considered 'off-limits', or changing your relationship with the space you already occupy, a conscious eye on your own context will offer perspective and awareness and will help you to locate issues of identity politics in the world around you, rather than inside of yourself.

Exercise 13: Review

Before we launch into the next chapter, it is useful to pause and review how your daily creative practice is going. Hopefully, by now you are in the swing of creating something each day. How is that working out for you? Have you found this easy, hard, frustrating, enlightening? Do you feel looser and more able to play, or are you having to force yourself to do your creative time each day? Are there days when you haven't done your creative time? What was happening on those days and what does that tell you about the things that enable and block you as a creative artist? →

Take a pen and paper and write, uninterrupted for 15 minutes about the experience of your daily creating time. Do not censor, don't think too much about what you are writing, and do not read it back until you have finished. Allow yourself to pour out onto paper the big thoughts, the niggling thoughts, the trivial and banal thoughts. Just write and hear yourself think for 15 minutes. What do you notice? Did anything come out onto the page that was unexpected or interesting?

By now it might be becoming tempting to lose momentum and stop the daily practice. Don't. The only way to reliably overcome blocks, limits and creative doubt is to keep making. Every single day. The word 'practice' is chosen intentionally in this context as both a verb and a noun; the daily creative practice is both an opportunity to practise your art, and a practice in the sense of a religious or spiritual pursuit. It is an intentional commitment to showing up, every day and creating something regardless of what else is happening in your life and what other things are competing for your time and resources. This commitment will be tested and will certainly be challenging at times, but if you persevere you will find that it brings about the change that you are looking for and that brought you to this book.

References

Anglin DA, Lui F, Schneider M & Ellman LM (2020) Changes in perceived neighbourhood ethnic density among racial and ethnic minorities over time and psychotic-like experiences. *Schizophrenia Research* **216** 330-338.

Asakura K, Lundy J, Black D & Tierney C (2020) Art as a Transformative Practice: A participatory Action Research Project with Trans* Youth. School for Social Work: Faculty Publications, Smith College, Northampton, MA.

Damian R I & Simonton D K (2014). Diversifying Experiences in the Development of Genius and Their Impact on Creative Cognition. In D. K. Simonton (Ed.) *The Wiley Handbook of Genius*. Wiley-Blackwell, New York.

Foster-Wallace D (2009) *This is Water: Some Thoughts, Delivered on a Significant Occasion, about Living a Compassionate Life*. Little, Brown. USA

Gilbert P (2014) The origins and nature of compassion focused therapy. *British Journal of Clinical Psychology* **53** (1) 6-41.

Guerrilla Girls (2020) *The Art of Behaving Badly*. Chronicle Books.

Harris R (2008) *The Happiness Trap: Stop struggling, start living*. Robinson Publishing.

Hébert M, Lavoie F & Blais M (2014) Post-Traumatic Stress Disorder/PTSD in adolescent victims of sexual abuse: resilience and social support as protection factors. Ciênc. *saúde coletiva* **19** (3).

Higgie J (2019) *Plain Facts: The importance of Acknowledging Women Artists. In, 'Representation of Female Artists in Britain During 2019'*. Report, The Freelands Foundation.

Jongsma HE, Karlsen S, Kirkbride JB et al (2021) Understanding the excess psychosis risk in ethnic minorities: the impact of structure and identity. *Soc Psychiatry Psychiatr Epidemiol* **56** 1913–1921.

Lin W & Shih Y (2016) The developmental trends of different creative potentials in relation to children's reasoning abilities: From a cognitive theoretical perspective. *Thinking Skills & Creativity* **22** 36-47.

Madjar N, Greenberg E & Chen Z (2011) Factors for Radical Creativity, Incremental Creativity, and Routine, Noncreative Performance. *Journal of Applied Psychology* **96** (4).

Simonton D K (2000). Creative Development as Acquired Expertise: Theoretical Issues and an Empirical Test. *Developmental Review*. **20** 283-318

Smith S L, Choueiti M, Pieper K. (2018). Inclusion in the Director's Chair? Gender, Race & Age of Directors across 1,100 Films from 2007-2017 *Annenberg Inclusion Initiative*. https://assets. uscannenberg.org/docs/inclusion-in-the-directors-chair-2007-2017.pdf

Social Mobility Commission (2021). *State of the nation 2021: Social mobility and the pandemic.* www.gov.uk

Tapper J (2022) Huge decline of working class people in the arts reflects fall in wider society. *The Observer, 10th December 2022.*

Xi Y, Yu H, Yao Y, Peng K, Wang Y & Chen R (2020) Post-traumatic stress disorder and the role of resilience, social support, anxiety and depression after the Jiuzhaigou earthquake: A structural equation model. *Asian Journal of Psychiatry* **49**.

Zhu W, Shang S, Jiang, W, Pei M & Su, Y (2019) Convergent Thinking Moderates the Relationship between Divergent Thinking and Scientific Creativity, *Creativity Research Journal*, **31** (3)

Chapter Three: The development of creativity

In this chapter, we will bring the focus of our lens right in and start to think about how you and your creativity developed within the context of your family and the community that directly surrounded you. We are going to explore how creativity was talked about, valued and facilitated in your childhood home, and recall your early forays into creative expression, considering what (if any) implications that has for your creativity now.

Whenever we explore the origins of how we have come to be, we run the risk of unearthing experiences that have been long-buried, and emotions that we were unaware of until we turned over the rock and discovered them. Even if we stay in seemingly shallow water, we can still unintentionally hit a 'drop off'. If this happens to you as you work through this chapter, then I urge you to refer to your menu of self-care and prioritise activities that offer comfort and return you to a state of balance. Take support from the people you identified as trustworthy at times of distress, keep writing your morning pages, and keep doing your daily creative time as this will give you space to process what you encounter. As ever, if you feel like you unearth something that is best explored with a therapist, then there are resources at the end of this book.

Why do we create? The role of art in human society

Before we begin exploring how and why your creativity has developed, it is worth taking some time to think about the role of creativity in human societies, and the question of why we create. This is a huge question that speaks to our ancestry, our biology, the way we have evolved to live together in groups, our consciousness and sentience, our reliance on language, and our need to make sense of and share the things we experience. Creativity is evident in children from infancy and develops along with all the other essential faculties they need to function as adults. Despite its universality, there is a noticeable lack of a coherent 'model' of creativity, neatly outlining why and how we create, which is surprising as we have models for pretty much everything else. How we remember, how we relate, how we behave. This alludes to the complex nature of creativity and the way in which it straddles the practical, psychological, spiritual and social elements of our lives. It does not package itself neatly or cleanly, but wriggles and shimmers, and eludes being pinned down, much like the things that many of us use creativity to convey. We use creative means to express ourselves as individuals and as societies, to pass on information to subsequent generations, to express the mysterious elements of human experience, to emulate or connect with spirituality, to develop new ideas and innovations, to transform and to change. What is clear is that the human tendency to create is tenacious and enduring; we appear to have always made art, and we continue to do so, even in the most unlikely or adversarial of circumstances. Many of the artists I spoke to when formulating this book talked about creative expression as a fundamental need, as keen and urgent as basic biological needs.

When I first started researching creativity, I spent much of my time looking backwards, exploring art and music history, the evolution of story and song, of visual image and the photograph, and thinking about how this shapes our current creative expression. This is not uncommon, as much of the writing regarding creativity dwells either in the past or makes reflections and observations about where we are currently. Creative expression has shaped the development of humanity and has given rise to the incredible leaps we have made in innovation, technology, and science. We have used our creative minds to build complex societies, to prolong our lives, to colonise previously uninhabited spaces, and even to venture past our own earth and out into the cosmos. Looking back paints a clear picture of how creativity and the arts have shaped civilisation, however I confess that it was not until recently that I began to fully consider the essential role of the creative arts in pointing the way forward and shaping the future.

Human beings use story and language to construct reality, if we do not have a word or a story for something, then we struggle to imagine it, much less to communicate it to others. The human world is a world shaped by stories, it is how we understand the order of things, the patterns and 'rules' of existence. Stories are prophetic, they predict and shape our behaviour by telling us what to expect and making clear what is expected of us. We use them as a sort of shorthand, to deliver warnings and learning to the next generation and even as ways of making sense of ourselves and our identity. When something traumatic or unexpected happens, we quickly begin to construct a story, telling and retelling it until it makes sense and can be understood within the accepted order of things.

Our reliance on story and language means that we struggle as a collective to formulate and make 'real' anything that sits outside the narratives already available to us, anything that falls outside of our direct experience. This makes creating large changes at a group or societal level particularly challenging; we cannot find a shared way to think about the future if it doesn't refer to something we already know. If what we already know is not enough, or is rendered obsolete by changing circumstances, then we are in trouble. Facing global pandemics, economic and political shifts and the huge changes that are happening within our environment, we are now required to generate novel solutions that radically adapt the way in which we function, not just as individuals but as a group. We are poorly evolved to think as a collective, as many of our psychological survival mechanisms are based on our survival, or the survival of those very close to us. We struggle to reach consensus when we are dealing with the unknown, and we look for clear leadership. However, the systems we have developed to provide this leadership within democratic systems make those in power dependent on public opinion to stay in power; a system that makes it very challenging to make unpopular or anxiety-provoking decisions.

If we are going to rise to the challenges that face us, we need artists to light the way so we can find a path to follow. We need new stories, songs, images and narratives that fill the void of uncertainty. We need people to use their creativity to conceive of new ideas, propose new solutions, innovate and generate suggestions so that we can reduce the uncertainty and begin to debate how we move forward in whatever group we are in. As in the past, humans need to use their creative minds to illuminate the future so that we can collectively see a way forward. This makes the work of developing and supporting creativity within individuals and societies urgent and essential.

The reason I mention this is that the work of developing creativity within individuals happens on both a macro, societal scale, and on a micro, individual scale. Children develop within small systems, most often families, within which they learn to navigate the world, to express themselves, manage feelings and operate socially. We have considered some of the factors that impact creativity on a societal level, now let us turn our attention to your personal experience of growing up to be a creative being.

How do we develop as creative beings?

The answer to the question of how we develop is different depending on which area of psychology you consult, and which model is used as an explanation. Some models focus on the physical, neurological changes that occur in our brains, some focus more on the environmental factors that we encounter, and more recently the field of epigenetics has begun to account for how the physical and environmental interface with each other. There are common themes and areas of divergence, but the consensus is that there are important factors that shape the way we develop in both the 'nature' and 'nurture' camps.

A full overview of developmental psychology would fill this book and is not necessary for the purpose of understanding how you came to relate to yourself, and your creativity, in the way that you do. We could choose to focus on our biological dispositions, or even our epigenetics, however I tend to find it helpful to think about how we become a person through the relationships we encountered and the people we were close to in our childhood. We are social beings and are essentially socialised into existence. We develop our ability to be creative in the same way as we develop anything else, in relationship with each other. The way creativity is spoken about, valued, expressed and recognised by the people around you as a child will usually form the template for how you eventually learn to relate to it yourself. If your parents speak about creativity as if it is a waste of time, then you may grow up to also view art as wasteful or frivolous. If creativity was valued above all else by the people around you, then you might prioritise it highly in your adult life. Like most things in therapy, the foundations of our relationship to ourselves and creativity can be understood and changed; it is not a life sentence but a template that is open to reworking if it no longer works for you.

One way of understanding the transmission of ideas and patterns within relationships is using cognitive analytic therapy, or CAT; a model developed by Dr Tony Ryle (Ryle *et al*, 2002). He is responsible for one of the quotes that I use most when training health professionals, despite the fact that I had to read it several times before the meaning became entirely clear to me: 'human beings are biologically predisposed, to be socially formed'. What he meant by that, is that we are equipped right from birth with the inbuilt mechanisms necessary to get people to relate to us, and us to them. We are born with brains that act as social sponges, sucking in our experiences of relating to others and using this to build templates that we take into adulthood.

A baby that is only hours old will orientate their heads to a rudimentary picture of a human face. Interestingly, they are so adept at this, they will even turn to look at a collection of shadows that have been assembled to emulate those seen on a face (Farroni *et al*, 2005). This ability to select and prioritise faces appears to be an inbuilt mechanism that encourages bonding and interaction from the word go. A child of only one year of age has a repertoire of tools to encourage and maintain interaction that is staggering: pointing, clapping, making vocal utterances, crying, smiling and laughing – the list goes on. All of this points to the importance of us engaging with the people around us to ensure our survival, as we are incapable of meeting our own needs for many years after birth. The need to interact and operate within social systems is hardwired into us and forms an important part of how we develop.

One of the central concepts in CAT is the idea that the roles we take in relationships are reciprocal, like the two ends of a rope. If I pull the rope, you are pulled; if you pull the rope, I am pulled. If I am caring, you are cared for. If you are valuing, I am valued. Some roles are more comfortable than others, meaning we are more likely to tolerate them, and some can be difficult to sit with as they provoke powerful emotions. If I am critical, you are criticised and may experience shame – a position you are unlikely to want to remain in for any length of time. As such, you must find a way to move out of that role, perhaps by becoming critical back, or placating and striving to please. Over time, these roles, and the way we move in and out of them, can become habitual, forming a 'dance' that we enact many times over until the steps become unconscious habit.

One of the most useful ideas from CAT, is that the reciprocal roles that we encounter in childhood become a sort of 'map' that charts the course of how we are likely to react to each other in adulthood. The way others interact with us in childhood becomes the way we learn to interact with ourselves, and then how we learn to interact with others. This might include the way you speak to yourself when you encounter difficulties, failures or obstacles. Or the way you respond when you receive criticism or feedback. It can include how you relate to authority and power, how you respond to the needs of others and yourself, and how you prioritise those needs. This also includes the way you relate to creativity and self-expression.

Understanding these relational 'dances' more closely can help us make sense of our habitual responses and gives us the chance to change the steps if the dance we are doing is no longer helpful. Becoming aware of a process allows you to be more careful about whether you continue to re-enact it or make a change.

A note to parents

Before I begin this section, I have to offer a note to parents. Every time I present this material during training, I am met with a sea of stricken faces as the parents in the room think back over the times that they have criticised their child or have commented in a way that has been experienced as negative, and are now panicking that they have set the relational tone for the rest of their children's lives.

The developmental psychologist Edward Tronick (2010) said it best when he encouraged us to think of early life experiences as including 'the good, the bad and the ugly'. The good is the normal everyday things we do with our children, such as going to the park, chatting in the car on the way home from school, reading a story before bed. The 'bad' refers to the times when things go wrong, for example we get angry and speak in an uncharacteristically harsh way, or we are stressed by work and cannot truly listen to what our child is trying to say. These moments occur when we are not at our best, but they sit within an overall experience of the world that allows the child to recover and develop a coherent, positive sense of themselves and other people. We can sometimes be guilty of underestimating a child's ability to do this, particularly if we, as adults, are able to hold our hands up, apologise and acknowledge when we have got things wrong.

The 'ugly' refers to when the negative experiences are persistent to the extent that there is no opportunity for recovery and instead the child must learn ways to survive and get through. If a child grows up in a home where there is ongoing neglect, rejection or abuse, and is not supported to make sense of what is happening, then they have no choice but to use their child-logic to draw conclusions about their situation and develop a survival strategy. The 'ugly' refers to the stuff that sits outside of everyday experience and inside the realm of trauma. Please do not beat yourself up for the 'bad' times in ordinary life, they are a normal and essential part of childhood and learning how to be a relational being.

Relating to creating

I would like you to imagine that a child of about four is sitting at a table doing a painting with their father or mother. As the child paints, the parent is asking questions and noticing the use of colour, 'Hey, I like that red', or, 'Tell me more about that shape'. The parent is being attentive and interested; they are showing value for the work of the child and care for their intentions and process. In turn, the child feels cared for and valued, and experiences the positive feelings this elicits. Imagine now that the child is several years older and is painting in class. They are taking care over their work and paying great attention to the process; they have taken the parent's role of being caring and valuing and they are now caring for and valuing themselves and their art. The teacher approaches and the child expects that they too will be caring and valuing, so they openly share and discuss their work, taking constructive pointers on how they might develop their technique without feeling overly attacked or ashamed. Imagine that same child is now working alongside a classmate and notices their painting. They comment on the colours and ask questions about what they have created – they are now being caring and valuing towards others.

Imagine another scene (and be mindful of self-care if this is close to your experiences): a child of about four is sitting at a table and painting with their mother or father. The parent is hyper-critical, commenting on the child's efforts with harsh words: 'No, it doesn't go like *that*', or, 'Why have you painted that blue? It looks ridiculous.' This mirrors a general relational trend where the child's attempts to play and explore is met with overwhelmingly negative feedback, scrutiny and criticism. The parent is being contemptuous and critical of the child's efforts, who in turn feels shame, anger, sadness, or whatever emotion arises as a result of the interaction.

Later on, the child is requested to do a painting in class by their teacher. They may refuse to do the task outright for fear of exposure. If they do venture to pick up the paintbrush, they begin internally sportscasting the process with harsh criticisms, feeling frustrated and angry when they cannot get the painting to match what they have in their mind's eye. When the teacher approaches, they expect the same harsh, critical perspective they themselves are taking, so are withdrawn, and closed off, or angry and volatile to protect themselves from the perceived attack. When the teacher offers feedback, it provokes shame as the child feels not good enough and contemptible. The child has taken the relational experience of being humiliated and criticised and has turned it inwards, using it to form the internal model for how they treat themselves and how they expect others to treat them. When they observe the work of their peers, they may defensively mock in an imitation of the contempt they are shown, or they might go to a completely different role, perhaps offering deferential praise. What the child is unlikely to be able to do is play, to risk uncertainty and failure in the aim of developing and exploring. They might shy aware from creative expression entirely, or may develop perfectionist standards which they then repeatedly fall short of – thus reinforcing that they are indeed deserving of criticism and contempt.

The story above involves only one part of a child's relational world of course; it might be that teachers, friends and other family members provide additional experiences that sit alongside, offering alternate 'reciprocal roles' from which the child can draw. This is not always the case however, and it is easy to see how a 'dance' derived in childhood can easily be carried into adulthood.

It is also possible that single, formative experiences can shape us in dramatic ways, despite otherwise positive relational experiences. For example, I had the privilege of working over a number of years with a wonderful teenager with a rich and expressive creative talent. She had created a series of paintings that depicted her internal experience as she transitioned into adulthood and grappled with her sexuality and gender; work that I found moving and profound but also challenging and confrontational. When she showed them to her art teacher, they responded initially by recoiling, and then in an apparent attempt to regain their composure, embarked on a critical diatribe about the student's insufficient use of shading. This was all done in front of the class, an experience that is sadly all too familiar for many. I can only speak for the UK, but it is my experience that our education system is not set up to teach art practice in its purest form within schools. Instead, we focus on measurable objectives that usually focus on technique. Luckily, this young person had done a huge amount of work exploring her identity and creativity and was able to show resilience and continue to practice, but for many, such adverse experiences in school can spell the end of their artistic endeavours for years, if not entirely.

Exercise 14: Mapping the dance

Float back in your mind to an early experience of being creative and having others interact with you and/or your work in some way. This could be at home or at school, or with friends. On a piece of plain paper, begin by writing what you hoped to achieve by making or showing the work at the top of the page. For example, you may have hoped that they would be valuing, and you and your work would be valued, or that they would be validating, and you and your work would be validated. If you were very young you might not know what your hoped-for outcome would be, so make a guess or use whichever word comes into your mind. Perhaps you wanted to be appreciated, praised, admired or cared for?

Now begin to write the words that best summarise your experience of the person involved in the story, and underneath write the impact it had on you and any feelings you become aware of as you remember the event. Don't overthink this but pick what the psychotherapist and writer Steve Potter (2020) calls the 'hot' words – the ones that jump out when you call to mind the memory. It might be that the person was praising, and you were praised and felt shy, or happy, or excited. Or it might be that the person was humiliating, and you were ➔

humiliated and felt rage, or shame, or sadness. If it works for you, you can depict these roles and feelings like this:

What did you do as a result? Did you stay in the 'bottom' role, or move into the top and become humiliating in response? Or did you go somewhere else entirely, for example abandoning the work and quickly changing the subject to deflect from the difficult feelings? You might want to add your reaction to the 'map' in whatever way works for you. If you experienced more than one reciprocal role, for example the person was humiliating and then became rejecting when you reacted, or they praised you and then moved quickly into criticism, then add these to your map.

If you find that this exercise calls to mind other experiences, then feel free to add the reciprocal roles that you encountered in these interactions onto your map.

Finally, step back and look at the words on the paper. Do any of the reciprocal roles bear any resemblance to patterns that you recognise in your life currently? Or do any of the feelings continue to resonate strongly? Consider the reciprocal role at the top of the page, how do you relate to that wished-for place in adulthood? Have you found ways to get that creative need met, or does this remain a place that you work towards but somehow cannot reach or sustain? Do any of the words on the page evoke qualities in the way that you treat yourself and your creative life?

Over the next few days, notice any times that you encounter roles or feelings that are central to your map, particularly with regard to your artistic work. Keep this map somewhere to hand as a useful resource to refer to at the end of the process. What has changed and what has remained the same?

Mapping your relationship with autonomy, spontaneity and self-expression

When we are considering our early relational experiences, it can be helpful to consider the wider lessons learned about autonomy, spontaneity and self-expression, as these are all central to the creative process. If you grew up in a home where you were corrected or shamed if you stepped outside of the accepted 'way things are done', then you might find it difficult to express yourself creatively, authentically and spontaneously if you are unsure how your work will be received. If your attempts at spontaneous expression were mocked, then you might find yourself producing work that is highly derivative of others. If you were constantly appraised and your early expressive acts labelled 'good' or 'bad', then you might find yourself judging your work in 'black and white' terms, disregarding anything that does not reach a good enough standard. If there were high levels of control within your family home, then you may find it hard to let go and really play. All of these things are likely to impact on your creative process and your work.

Consider the following questions. It might be useful to jot down your 'gut instinct' reaction to each one without overthinking or rationalising. We often find that our first response holds essential clues to our perspective, which we can quickly override as we apply an adult's logic to a child's experience.

- How much room was made for your autonomy, your thoughts, perspectives and preferences in your family home?

- How much was difference tolerated and accepted between family members?

- How did the people around you respond if you tried something and did not get it right immediately?

- How was failure talked about in your family home (yours and other people's)?

- How much of your time was devoted to unstructured play as a child?

- What was the impact of these things on your creativity as an adult?

If you find that any of these questions provoked an insight into something blocking your creative practice in adulthood, then it is helpful to think about what you needed as a child that you didn't receive, and actively plan how to offer that to yourself now. For example, if you experienced high levels of control, you may find it hard to be playful and spontaneous as an adult. You might find that you are able to create, but only in a planned and regimented way that results in work that you find overly formulaic or predictable. Use your daily creative time to experiment without fear of what others will say. Plan some unstructured time and devote it to listening and responding to the part of you that needs to play. Take that part of you to a forest and allow yourself to climb, or kick leaves, or just wander. If you can't hear that 'voice' because it has been neglected for so long, then 'fake it till you make it', and put yourself in situations that force you to be experimental. Buy some paints and devote time to making marks without any planning or intention. Walk around your neighbourhood in the early morning with a camera and photograph anything that catches your eye. Notice your emotional reaction to these activities – do you feel excited, frightened, foreboding, naughty, joyful?

Engaging in activities such as these may feel frivolous, or even silly, however they are a vital part of loosening up patterns in how we relate to ourselves that have become overly rigid and may have gone unnoticed since childhood. These patterns may have been extremely adaptive and even protective in early life, but, if left unchallenged, they can act as powerful and unnecessary limits in adulthood. By consciously stepping outside of the 'rules' and noticing, but not moving to change your emotional reaction, you can broaden your repertoire and begin to create flexibility which you can then apply to your work. Though this can be a challenging process, it can be profoundly joyful as you re-encounter childlike qualities that you might have feared were lost. Curiosity, playfulness, originality, humour, silliness, can all be invited back into your life and can express themselves in your creative work.

The power of narratives

As humans, we are socialised to exist in small groups such as families, but we must also operate within wider communities. One of the ways in which we do this is through the use of language and story to develop commonly held 'truths' that we subscribe to and orientate our lives around. These stories, when told repeatedly, start to make up the fabric of our shared sense of reality, even if they are dubious or downright incorrect. In the time I have been alive, the stories that my community tells about issues such as race, gender and sexuality have changed enormously, albeit slowly and incrementally.

An example of this is gender. As we have begun to realise as a society that the once-held 'truth' that gender is a binary construct is inaccurate and unhelpful, we have begun to change the stories we tell and the terms that we use, and therefore the way that we construct the concept. We now differentiate between biological sex and gender; we have ways to describe identities other than male and female and can now articulate a much broader spectrum of gender experiences. Our language creates our reality, and the way we negotiate that reality with each other.

In narrative therapy, we are curious about the stories that have become 'true' about individuals and are interested in how damaging or limiting stories might be renegotiated. Stories can ascribe strengths and impose limitations. They can attach us to roles within a family or friendship group which, over time, become non-negotiable expectations of each other. When working with families, I often hear these roles described: 'Tom is the musician of the family, he's always been musical', or, 'Oh, Phoebe is a natural writer; do you know she was writing stories from the age of two?' These stories might be helpful in giving us a coherent sense of our 'self', but they can also be limiting or downright damaging.

We can begin to view our identity as bound up in the words or stories that have been allocated to us, and this in turn can shape the decisions we make and the way we operate as adults. If you were called 'clumsy' as a child, you may be less likely to be taken to dance or gymnastics class, and may instead have been enrolled in extra language classes. You might not have been chosen for sports teams at school and therefore may have turned your attention elsewhere, concentrating on what you were 'good' at. Not given an opportunity to develop co-ordination skills, it is possible that you remained less co-ordinated than your peers, though you may have far surpassed them in your grasp of French.

These stories can be carried into adulthood, so when you walk past a dance studio, or watch a ballet, and feel a longstanding desire to move your body, you dismiss it immediately: 'I can't dance, I'm far too clumsy!' Now, I am not in any way suggesting that we are all created equal in terms of our strengths and talents, and it is entirely possible that you were clumsy as a child. However, the story that grew up and became 'true' did not allow for re-examination or renegotiation. Were you still clumsy as an adolescent, or did you grow into your limbs? Were there times when you weren't clumsy, but moved gracefully or nimbly? Did the environment make a difference? How tired you were? The activity, or the company you were with? As we discussed before, the human brain has to take shortcuts in order to function in the world and to make sense of other people. These shortcuts can be revisited, and if they are unhelpful or simply untrue, then we can begin to construct a different narrative.

Stories can also develop around to whom a talent or a skill 'belongs' within a group, and this can unconsciously set limits to how creativity is permitted to express itself. We might be allocated a certain skill or hobby which becomes 'ours', off limits to others in our family system. Other members may also be 'allocated' entire domains of self-expression, which then becomes off limits to you. For instance, you might have had a sibling who was the 'actor' of the family, and therefore any attempts on your behalf to show an interest in theatre may have been met with resistance. Or you might have had a parent who never quite fulfilled a childhood dream to be a musician but held on to it, to the extent that it became sacred territory into which you couldn't stray.

The roles that are allocated within our family can also contribute to how creativity develops; how liberated you feel to play, to fail, to make a mess, to experiment, to do something just for fun. If you consistently heard, 'You're the eldest, you should know better', or, 'You've always been the trustworthy one, such a good girl' as a child, how empowered might you feel to make art that is provocative, dangerous, or likely to offend? Or to try something that you might not be good at?

We give great attention to the things that reinforce these stories, and we ignore, deflect or rationalise anything that conflicts or challenges. For example, the 'good girl' is caught smoking and the parents make sense of this by blaming the friend they were with, even if the child protests and admits responsibility. The stories we attach ourselves to are designed to give us a sense of stability and coherence in a world that might otherwise feel frightening and uncertain. When we try and challenge or change these stories, the 'system' around us may organise itself to keep the status quo, as the alternative is unsettling and risky. If the 'clumsy' child enrols in a dance programme as an adult, they are likely to receive incredulous comments or scoffs, and may even be humiliated into returning to the familiar narrative. If the sporty child decides that they want to take up the cello, they may face a disheartening backlash from family members, teachers and coaches.

It is not just the people around us that do this, but our own internal systems can be complicit in organising against change. If you have always occupied a role in the world, then stepping out of it might feel very risky. Who are you if, instead of being the 'singer' of the family, you now want to be the 'writer' or the 'film maker'? If you make authentic, provocative art and are no longer seen as the 'good' girl, will people still like you? If you stop being the 'eldest' and allow yourself to wriggle free of some of your responsibilities to make art, will others judge you? If you make art that isn't considered 'clever' or 'excellent', but that you enjoy, will people think you are stupid? When we are attempting to wrestle free of unhelpful or outdated narratives, we need to be mindful of both the internal and external drives to keep us in familiar territory and notice any fears that arise.

It is important to name these fears and face them down in the quest for creativity, as, left unchecked, they can wreak havoc on our artistic lives. Let's take the example of Sarah, a talented singer and songwriter who came into therapy to address issues in her relationships and a sense of frustration in her creative life. As a child, Sarah was good at listening and found it easy to understand other people's experiences; she quickly became the person to go to with problems and dilemmas. When we met, she vividly recalled teachers discussing work or family issues with her when she was still in primary school, and as she moved into adolescence she was often found sitting on the stairs in the evening, clutching the phone (which back then was plugged into the wall) listening to the troubles of a friend. She was known as the 'responsible' one by family, teachers and peers, and was widely regarded as having her 'stuff' sorted.

Now, this wasn't inherently a bad thing, but it did become a dominant story about Sarah that left little room for alternative narratives (interestingly, she also became a psychologist). She was very aware that it felt good to be wanted, and to feel like she had her own stuff under control, and slowly she had learned to bury whatever was going on for her to fulfil this role. As she moved into adulthood, she began to realise that there was a darker side to this arrangement. She found it very difficult to speak up and share when she had a problem, or a difficult feeling, and when she did, she would be dismissed or placated as the system sought to re-establish the accepted narrative – 'You can't be having problems, *I* need *you!*'

Sarah came to see me in her mid-20s, halfway through her second doomed relationship with a man who was grappling with a host of complex issues and was using Sarah as a kind of residential therapist. In her creative life, she felt blocked, unproductive and frustrated. Most of her energy was being divided between a demanding job (in which she continued to fulfil the role of sage counsellor to others) and a host of personal relationships that centred on her offering support. She wasn't sleeping, and her creative output as a musician and writer was almost nil. Sarah realised that this pattern was something she needed to change and during our time together she began to experiment with an alternative story that made space for her vulnerability and humanity. She started to speak and tolerate being heard. She took support as she began the painful process of uncoiling the tight knot that had formed in her stomach and began to relinquish responsibility for the world around her.

This did not go unnoticed by the people in Sarah's life, and, as is often the case, the profound transformation in Sarah did lead to a shuffle and reorganisation of her relationships. Though this can be a painful process, it is my experience that once this reconfiguration had been completed, you are often left with a group of people around you that are far more attuned and supportive of the adult that has emerged, and far less invested in keeping you stuck in a pattern that no longer serves you. This was certainly the case for Sarah, who strengthened some of the relationships that had been pushed to the periphery by the loud and jostling needs of those close to her. She found that these friendships were just what she needed, mutually inspiring and supportive. Sarah began a new romantic relationship with someone who was also an artist and who encouraged her to write, offering thoughtful and constructive critique on her work and sharing his own art for her to do the same. Sometimes, relationships can withstand the transformation, and they change and grow along with you. Sometimes they don't, and there can be sadness and disappointment with the realisation that a longstanding connection no longer fits. I have never heard anyone say that they wish they hadn't made the transformation, however; a process that is essential if you are to renegotiate patterns, narratives and stories that are no longer working for you.

Sarah's experience is a very good example of how stories – even positive ones – can reduce flexibility, and it is flexibility that is the key to both psychological wellbeing and creativity (Kashdan & Rottenberg, 2010). Sarah was so busy listening to the experience of others that she lost contact with her own voice – literally and metaphorically – and experienced many years where her creative output was sporadic and confined to snatched moments when no one else needed her. She described half-writing songs that would remain unfinished for months, even years, or she would write nothing for a long time and then experience a torrent of creative energy when she finally took the time to check in with herself. This made her creativity feel unreliable and whimsical, to the extent that she genuinely believed that she couldn't create 'at will'. As she started to let go of the roles that she had assumed for so long, she began to listen carefully to herself and her experiences and used this as profound material and inspiration for her artistic work. She made space and time for her creativity and started writing music in a fluid and effortless way that no longer felt unpredictable and untrustworthy. She became unblocked.

Exercise 15: Retelling the story

Take paper and pen and write down all the words that are commonly associated with you, both now and in the past. You can do this in the first person, 'I am…' or the third person, 'Sarah is…'. Don't overthink the process, just write down whatever comes to you. You might find some of the words surprising as we are not always aware what we have internalised. Keep writing until you have exhausted the words.

Now sit back and look at the list of words. What do you notice? What feelings come up as you survey the page? How accurate is this portrayal of you? Are there any 'hot' words that provoke particular emotions?

Take a different coloured pen, and for each word add how that story, role or concept has impacted your creativity, either positively or negatively.

Look at the list of stories that have had a negative impact on your creative life. For each one, note down any 'unique outcomes' that come to mind. These are times that things have not played out as the story dictates; exceptions to the rule that fly in the face of the dominant narrative and challenge the 'truth' of the story. For example, if you ➜

have written 'reliable' and 'consistent', and have identified that this can impact your ability to play or experiment creatively, then note downtimes when you weren't reliable. When have you behaved in a spontaneous or unpredictable way, even if that moment was in childhood? Are there times when you are inconsistent or unreliable? Times when you don't follow through on plans, even if these are only plans you made inside your own mind? What was it like to behave in a way that others would consider unusual for you?

What do you notice about these 'unique outcomes'? What is your emotional response to them? Do they feel exciting, risky, shameful, energising?

Over the next week, notice times when you behave according to the 'stories' that are told about you, and times when you don't. Use your daily creative time to experiment with ways of behaving that are unusual for you. If you are known as a rebel, try a 'paint by numbers' that forces you to ascribe to certain colours and stay in the lines. If you are usually organised, then use your materials to create something on the spur of the moment with no planning. If you are known for being polite, try painting a large swear word and see how it feels. What bits are comfortable, or uncomfortable? What anxieties come up as you step outside of your allocated space? What thoughts come up, and what feelings? You are always free to go back to what is comfortable for you; we are merely experimenting and seeing how it feels.

Narratives about art and artists

About two years ago, I began working on a project focusing on supporting working-class artists into art education, and then into practice. I come from a working-class family and was horrified to read that only 7.9% of practicing artists in the UK come from this background; no wonder so little of what I encountered in the art world resonated with my experiences. As I began to talk about the project, I was amazed by the opinions and narratives I encountered from the other working-class people around me. Hearing their reactions gave me some insight into the deeply ingrained beliefs about art and artists in my culture: 'You'll never make a living doing that', 'What do you want to do that for?', 'Art is for wankers', 'How will you deal with all the mental health problems?' These comments point to societal attitudes towards creativity that somehow making art is indulgent or luxurious and therefore not considered a worthy use of time; that all artists must be poor, or 'tortured' individuals that likely experience mental health difficulties; that artists cannot make a living from their work and will therefore end up poor. These narratives are maintained by the way we teach art, portray artists and the stories we choose to tell each other about creativity.

It is very likely that you will have internalised whatever the dominant narrative is about art in your culture, and it is probable that this impacts the way you approach and think about your own creativity. In the same way as it can be useful to revisit the narratives and stories about the 'self' that have become truth, it can be important to step back and accurately appraise the stories about art and creativity that surrounded you, being curious about what impact these had on the way you think.

Exercise 16: Renegotiating the narrative

Take a pen and write down what words come to mind when you think about how art and artists were talked about in your family home and community. How was art taught in your school? Who and what did the teachers choose to focus on? Were art and artists discussed in the family home, and if so, how were they spoken about? What was your parent's relationship to their own creativity – were they creative?

If so, did they prioritise their art or was it side-lined in favour of other activities and responsibilities? Was there a practising artist or creative person in your family, and if so, how were they talked about?

Sit back and look at what you have written. Circle the words that summarise your early impressions of art and artists. How have these stories impacted your relationship with art and creativity and the choices you have made in relation to these? Now look at them again and deliberately engage your wise, 'adult' self. What do you think about these stories now? How valid are they? What are the 'unique outcomes' in relation to these, for example, artists you know that are neither poor nor tortured? What do you believe about how creativity was spoken about from your perspective as an adult, how have you arrived at these different perspectives?

Conclusion

In this chapter, we have begun to think about the early development of patterns in how we relate to ourselves and others, and how we use stories to shape and negotiate our experience of the world, both individually and as a culture. These formative experiences can have a profound impact on the development of creativity and your relationship with your internal artist. It is not uncommon for these things to go unexplored and to sit outside of your awareness, quietly governing how you navigate the world as an adult. Renegotiating these can be painful, exciting, fraught or simple; it can change your relationship with yourself and others and can be challenging or liberating for the people around you. However you experience it, the renegotiation process is part of change. Though the process can be challenging, I have never known someone come out the other side and express a wish that things could go back to the way there were. That is not to say this doesn't happen while on the journey – it is perfectly normal to get halfway through a process and think 'Stop the ride, I want to get off!' If you follow the transformation to the end, usually things become clearer, and you are closer to getting your needs met.

When looking back on early life experiences, you might encounter difficult thoughts and feelings about people who remain important and central to your life. This could be family members, but can also include friends or teachers. Again, I urge you to see the process to the end before taking any action or sharing these emotions in a way that might cause lasting change to your relationship. It is normal to feel disrupted, unsettled and uncertain as you begin to explore things that have been on the ocean floor of your consciousness. I always liken it to a snow globe. All the glitter or snow is settled on the bottom of the globe, then you shake it and it flies all over the place in a seemingly chaotic way. Eventually, though, it settles again, but the configuration is different. If possible, do not act while the snow is swirling, but wait for it to settle and survey the new landscape before taking action in relationships.

I wanted to conclude this chapter with another note on envy, as this is something that can rise up in ways that can sabotage your process. If there are people around you who have experienced blocks or frustrations in their own creative life, then they might find it difficult to tolerate watching you become unburdened and making changes to the way you navigate your artistic practice. This can give rise to envy, which is distinct from jealousy in its drive to destroy that which provokes it. Be wary of subtly undermining comments, clear attempts at sabotage, and both subtle and overt attacks. Holding in mind the possibility that these may be derived from a place of envy can help you navigate them differently. Rather than derailing your process, it might be a sign that the person has a process of their own that needs attention. Where possible, surround yourself with people who have done, or who are doing, their own work and can support you in yours.

Exercise 17: Review

Let us turn out attention to your daily creative practice for a moment. How are you finding the process of creating each day? How easy or hard is it to commit to something in this way? Have you noticed any changes in how you are using the time, or the materials? What about the morning pages? Are you continuing to complete three pages each morning? Are there things that interrupt or impact either your daily creative time or your morning pages? Are there any ways that you might pre-empt or overcome these?

Keeping a daily commitment is challenging, but both the morning pages and the daily creative practice are spaces where you can process what you are exploring in this book. Getting into the habit of both creates a platform that you can build on once you finish this book to ensure that any changes you make are lasting and are not so easily swallowed up by the demands of life. If you have fallen out of the habit of either exercise, I invite you to pick them up again. It is fine to feel resistance, irritation, boredom- whatever comes up. Thank these emotions for giving you information, and then move straight into doing the work.

References

Farroni T, Johnson MH, Menon E, Zulian L, Faraguna D & Csibra G (2005) Newborns' preference for face-relevant stimuli: Effects of contrast polarity. *Proceedings of the National Academy of Sciences* **102** (47).

Kashdan TB & Rottenberg J (2010) Psychological flexibility as a fundamental aspect of health. *Clinical Psychology Review* **30** (7) 865-878.

Potter S (2020) *Therapy with a Map: A Cognitive Analytic Approach to Helping Relationships.* Pavilion Publishing

Ryle T & Kerr I (2002) *Introducing Cognitive Analytic Therapy: Principles and Practice.* Wiley-Blackwell, London

Tronick EZ (2010) Things Still To Be Done on the Still-Face Effect. *Infancy* **4** 475-482.

Chapter Four: The role of emotions

A gentle warning

We are going to be exploring the role of emotions in this chapter, both how you can tune into them to gain inspiration and insight for your creative work, and how can you move away from them again and ground yourself. If you have experiences of trauma or negative life experiences that you have not had the chance to explore in therapy, then some of these exercises might not be helpful for you; they may be destabilising and bring up emotions that are hard to shut down again. If in any doubt, it is always worth talking this through with a trained therapist or psychologist, who will be able to offer a safe space to encounter your emotions together. Of course, I am biased, but it is my opinion that it is always better to venture into unknown emotional territory with another person; someone who can sit next to you and peer over whatever chasm you encounter and can accompany you on the journey back. If you do decide to look for a therapist, then there are resources at the end of the book.

Introduction

Human emotions govern our experience of the world and direct our behaviour. They give us information about the world around us and communicate our response to others. They can be beautiful, terrible, fleeting, or all-consuming. They can inform our creative practice and derail it entirely. They can come like waves, and leave just as quickly, or sneak up just on the edge of our awareness. Whatever your attitude towards feelings, these capricious creatures are essential to our lives and our ability to make art.

Like many things, our relationship with emotions is formed early and within the context of our relational experiences and the culture we are immersed in. Some cultures have a far more tolerant attitude towards emotions, while others deem them unnecessary, uncouth or embarrassing. Some families have 'high expressed emotion' (ie they demonstrate their feelings very clearly) and others rarely demonstrate any emotional response at all. If you come from a family of shouters, whose emotions burn brightly but quickly, then you may find environments where emotions are not openly acknowledged alien and threatening. Inversely, if you come from a world where feelings were never spoken or were kept at bay with alcohol or work addiction, then you may find open expression of emotion terrifying or overwhelming.

There is a close, two-way relationship between creativity and emotion. Most of us have first-hand experience of emotions directly inspiring creativity, for example, times when you have felt sad or angry and this has prompted you to write, paint or draw. Emotions can inspire us to start a piece of work, can shape the process of how and what we create, and ultimately can become integral to whatever we produce. If we create from our emotional world, then the work becomes imbued with the feeling and acts as a powerful point of connection for others. If we can tolerate the experience of whatever it is that we are feeling, we can create work that speaks of common human experience and transcends our specific context. When I look at 'Birth' by Frida Kahlo, I feel the complex, messy and powerful emotions that both birth and death elicit, despite living on the other side of the world, almost 80 years after it was painted.

Both positive and negative emotions have the capacity to contribute to higher levels of creativity (To *et al*, 2012), the important thing appears to be that you feel *something* and use the activation that this gives you to make work. Contrary to the well-trodden trope of the 'tortured artist', it appears that different emotions, both positive and negative, can contribute in different ways throughout the creative process. For example, positive emotions can help us get started, but more complex emotions like frustration or anger can help us persevere and get the task done as it nears completion (De Dreu *et al*, 2008).

The relationship between creativity and emotions can also work the other way, where the act of creating evokes an emotional response which may be unpredictable. Sometimes when we make a creative work, we encounter powerful feelings that we didn't know were there but that were brought to our attention through the process (Averill *et al*, 2001). For example, you might find profound feelings of anger or sadness surfacing as you paint, or notice a sense of longing or regret as you write an account of an experience. There is also a huge body of research that shows creative activity has a positive impact on mood and many mental health programmes now include art, writing, dancing and other creative acts as tools for wellbeing. Making art can improve how autonomous you feel and how able you are to express yourself, and this has a positive impact on your emotions (De Petrillo *et al*, 2005).

If you are going to use emotions as essential tools in your creative practice, then you need to be able to experience them enough so that they act as information and energy, but not so much that they engulf and derail you. The good news is that this is a set of skills that can be learned and developed throughout adulthood.

Using emotions as an effective aid for creativity requires two skills: the ability to notice what you are feeling and the ability to move towards and away from the experience depending on what the situation demands. In psychology, we call the latter 'emotional regulation'. This is a useful term in some contexts but flawed in the sense that it conjures up the image of a somewhat effortless process that can be employed to deal with whatever feeling a person encounters at whatever amplitude. In my experience, there are times that our emotions hit us like a truck and we lose the ability to engage the skills to regulate them – we are immersed and have to find something or someone to brace against while we wait for the experience to pass. These extreme moments are not what I am referring to here, what we are concerned with is the everyday ebb and flow of feelings and states that can be dialled up or down depending on our responses.

How do we learn about emotions?

We experience emotions from birth and rely on the people around us to teach us how to notice, name and ultimately to manage them in ways that are acceptable by the standards of the culture in which we live. If you watch a caregiver with a child, they will often 'sportscast' what the child is feeling, 'Oh, that made you angry when Stacey took your toy', 'You look so sad', or, 'Look how happy you are!' These encounters take the subjective experience of our internal emotional world and code them in language, which we can then begin to use to communicate our state to the people around us. From a developmental perspective, the role of adult caregivers is to model how to respond to emotions and to teach ways to regulate them. For example, the child whose toy was taken will need some adult support to problem solve how to resolve the situation. The child who is feeling sad might need comfort and care. The child who is happy may need to see the people around them mirroring back their smiles and enjoyment. Over time, the child internalises these experiences and, with some helpful brain developments along the way, becomes more able to respond to their feelings independently as they move into adulthood.

Many people do not have the experience of others noticing, naming and supporting emotions during childhood, and can reach adulthood with feelings that remain mysterious and outside of language. Others have learned to regulate their emotions so tightly that they rarely notice what they are feeling, or quickly move away from emotions as they arise. You may have had caregivers that struggled to deal with your feelings and gave you explicit cues that being angry, sad, jealous, or scared was not okay, leading you to conclude over time that they must be harmful, frightening or shameful. Inversely, you may have watched other people respond to their emotional world in ways that felt out of control and explosive, leading you to fear being caught in the grip of a powerful emotion or oscillating between being engulfed by feeling, or feeling nothing at all. These formative experiences can be compounded by events in childhood, particularly trauma, and can result in overwhelming emotional experiences or numbness and dissociation.

What we are interested in is how these formative lessons impacted your ability to engage with your feelings now, and what impact that has on your creative work. Are you able to connect with your emotions when you work, or do you mainly refer to thoughts? If a piece of work brings up a feeling, do you feel able to experience it in the moment, or do you quickly move to distraction, or find a way to push it away?

Exercise 18: Exploring your relationship with emotions

Take a pen and paper and note down all the words that you have for feelings. For some this might be a huge list, and for others it may consist of a concise few. Just get down on paper any 'feelings words' that come to mind.

Now look at the list you have created, and for each one note how comfortable or uncomfortable you feel when you encounter this emotion. You might want to rate them 1 to 5 with 5 being the most comfortable and 1 being the least.

What emotions bring up real discomfort for you? Do you have a sense of why? How were these emotions experienced and expressed by those around you in your childhood? What about in your life currently? Have there been times when you have expressed this feeling? How did the people around you respond? How do you react when you encounter this feeling now?

Lastly, complete the following sentence with whatever feelings make you uncomfortable:

- *If I allowed myself to feel X, ... would happen.*
- *If I allowed myself to feel X, other people would think ....*
- *If I allowed myself to feel X, I would be ....*

Over the next few days, begin to notice whenever an emotion that you are uncomfortable with starts to arise, and pay attention to what you do in response. Do you push it away, distract from it, immerse yourself in it, use alcohol, drugs, or sex to numb it? Where do you notice the feeling in your body and how does your body respond, for example do you hold your breath, or tighten your muscles? If you don't experience uncomfortable feelings at all, then be curious about other emotions that may arise in their place, for example becoming anxious instead of angry, or angry instead of sad. If you aren't aware of any emotional experience, then what do you notice in your body? Is it numb, disconnected, or dissociated? Are any parts of you alive to sensation, or do you experience a 'blanket' numbness that encompasses your whole body? →

Try not to make value judgements about what you encounter. Whatever relationship you have with your emotions has developed in relation to your experiences and has helped you to survive. If you feel like you to want to change any of these relationships, then try and do so with a great respect for whatever adaptations and coping strategies you used in the past.

The myth about emotions

There are many cultural myths about emotions that sit at odds with our experience of being human. The first and most pervasive one that many therapists encounter frequently, is the very Western ideal that you *should be happy*. If not all the time, then much of the time. Somehow, happiness has become the state to strive for and anything outside of this has been increasingly pathologised to the extent that even perfectly normal human reactions such as grief can be seen as a mental health problem.

Emotions, in and of themselves, are not mental health problems, and you are not 'designed' to just be happy all of the time. In fact, you are primed to experience a wide range of emotions that give you vital information about the situation you are in. For example, if you are in a job that constantly treats you badly, drains you of your energy, gives you unrelenting deadlines and little support, then you might find yourself feeling snappy, irritable and angry at the people around you. This is not a sign that you are becoming mentally unwell, though of course that can be an unintended consequence of chronic stress, but instead is a sign that you are in a situation that is not okay, and something needs to change. If I had a pound coin for every referral I receive from GPs that start, 'Please see this very angry man/woman', I would have enough money to retire very comfortably. What is interesting is that, when I do in fact see the 'very angry' man or woman, the work inevitably focuses on whatever unresolved situation they are encountering in their lives that is resulting in anger. This can include situations from the past, which require a different form of resolution, or current situations that have become untenable and destructive. What is always the case, is that the anger is a symptom of something in their environment that is not okay and needs the person to take action.

The same can be said for other emotions. Sadness often alerts us to loss and longing that we have not paid attention to and have not found a way to resolve. Jealousy will poke its finger at the thing we wished we were brave enough to go after in our own lives. There is no such thing as a 'right' or 'wrong' feeling; we feel what we feel, and this gives us information about what we need.

The second myth that I feel is at the centre of much of the distress that I encounter, is that emotions must be acted upon in some way and must inevitably be resolved or numbed. Now, in some circumstances such as the example of the person with the untenable job, that might be the case. It may be that the person is being galvanised into action and needs to harness the power of their anger to do so. However, there are those feelings that just need to be experienced, without a move to numb or avoid them. This is something that we are increasingly struggling with in the Western world, and many of us have never been taught the skills to merely sit with and observe an emotion as it rises and falls. Instead, we are sold ways to make these pesky feelings go away or are given drugs to create a sort of 'plateau' that limits their intensity. This perpetuates the idea that anything other than happiness is an undesirable state that must be rectified.

If you have lost something or someone that is precious to you, you might need to feel the sadness and the grief that this loss elicits before you begin to adjust to a world without whatever or whoever you have lost. The sadness serves a function: it points to the importance of what has gone and your feelings about them and the role they played in your life. It may also speak to a grief about what this person did not do. Sadness encourages us to retreat inwards, to get smaller and stiller while we come to terms with what has befallen us. If we run from it or act to avoid it, we are likely to destabilise ourselves further or end up pushed into a situation in which we have even more to be sad about.

The same can be said for anxiety. If you are about to play a large concert or attend the opening of your first solo exhibition, then you might experience anxiety as a clear message about how important the event is for you and how much you care about it. One response would be to avoid attending to mitigate the anxiety, but you risk missing out on something that is important enough to make you anxious. You could medicate the feelings with alcohol or drugs, or distract from it by creating a bigger, more anxiety-provoking drama, or you could mentally run through the endless list of things that might go wrong to give yourself a sense of control over the situation. All of these things are likely to cause secondary problems in addition to the question of how to deal with the original anxiety. The mistake we so often make as humans is to find ways to push away perfectly healthy but potentially challenging emotions, in ways that then cause us even more difficulty.

I once knew a very talented songwriter who was easily as gifted as any of the great performers in his genre. He had a rich, deep voice and an observant eye that he translated into thoughtful, witty lyrics. He also experienced crippling stage fright and would get so anxious before taking to the stage that he would drink several pints of beer very quickly as soon as he arrived at the venue. This would usually escalate into a few more, and often he would be barely able to stand by the time it was his turn to perform. Of course, this was an effective way to deal with his anxiety as he felt very little through the haze of alcohol, but it also meant that he often made mistakes, and was increasingly treated more as a novelty act than the wonderful performer and talented writer that he was. By finding ways to drown his anxiety, he inevitably ended up feeling much more anxious the morning after when he relived the gig and the many things that he said and did when drunk, which he might not have done sober. This made it harder to face the audience the next time around and made the need to drink even greater. Rather than understanding anxiety as an indicator of the importance of music and performing, my friend viewed it as an enemy that needed to be pushed away and avoided at all costs. In missing what his anxiety was trying to tell him, namely that his work was important to him, he inadvertently focused on managing his anxiety to the extent that he devalued his music. On top of that, there was also the impact on his health, his finances, and his relationships.

Now, I am not going to pretend that I have never downed a beer before stepping on stage (there are far too many witnesses to attest otherwise), but this is a good example of how our quest to not feel something can ultimately derail our creativity.

Tuning into emotions

The first step in being able to recognise what we are feeling is to tune in to what is happening in our bodies. Emotions are mental events with physical indicators, which, if you look for them, can alert you that a feeling is building before it becomes overwhelming. If you build this skill, you will sensitise yourself to the subtlety of your emotions and can integrate this into your creative work. Identifying what you are feeling as you begin a piece of creative work might offer inspiration, noticing what emotions arise as you continue might offer insight and further direction, and paying attention to how you feel as you look at the finished piece will let you know if you have achieved what you set out to convey and give you a glimpse of how other viewers might experience what you have created.

'Tuning in' to your body may sound straightforward, however many of us tend to focus on what is happening inside our minds and treat the rest of the body like a vacant hotel. Now this might not resonate for you at all; many people who have played sports or danced or been gymnasts as children have highly developed interoception (the ability to notice and respond to internal body signals) and proprioception (the ability to know where your body is in relation to what is around you). However, there are others, like me, who are less aware of their physicality to the extent that, when I first started to practice yoga, it was genuinely something of a revelation that I had feet. Of course, I knew that they were physically there, but had all but dissociated from their incredible capacity to sense and respond to the ground underneath me. In the early days, I would have to purposefully direct my attention to my legs and feet to get a sense of where they were and what they were doing, as my focus was so instinctively on what was happening inside my brain. If you are similar, then you may only notice physical events when they become unavoidably intense, for example you only realise you are hungry when you are ravenous or need to use the bathroom when it is urgent. If this is the case, then it is important to get into the habit of regularly 'checking in' with what is happening in your body and learning to de-code what this is telling you about what you are feeling.

One of the best ways of increasing your awareness of what is happening in the current moment is to cultivate the art of 'Mindfulness' – the ability to attend to whatever you are experiencing without judgement. Mindfulness has become increasingly popular as an effective treatment for a range of difficulties including pain management and depression, however its origins predate Western psychology by several thousand years. Up until the 1980s, mindfulness was practised as part of religious expression to gain spiritual separation from the impermanent elements of life, which include thoughts, feelings and even mortality.

Jon Kabat-Zinn (Professor of Medicine emeritus at the University of Massachusetts) founded the Mindfulness Based Stress Reduction Clinic in 1979, which was the first treatment programme to specifically use mindfulness as an intervention. He pioneered the idea of mindfulness as a psychological tool that sits outside (or alongside) religion and teaches the radical skill of observing all things without becoming embroiled in the encounter and without moving to judge or appraise what is experienced. He began to experiment with its utility for dealing with chronic pain and physical conditions such as cancer, and quickly developed a convincing evidence base. Mindfulness continues to be used routinely in pain management and is now recommended by the National Institute for Health and Care Excellence (NICE) for the treatment of depression and as a method to improve workplace wellbeing.

Kabat-Zinn defined mindfulness as 'the awareness that emerges through paying attention on purpose, in the present moment, and nonjudgmentally to the unfolding of experience moment by moment' (2003). This sounds straightforward in theory but can be one of the more challenging techniques that I use in therapy, as it sits at odds with the way we are conditioned to think and feel in modern society. Rather than moving to respond to or fix a feeling, mindfulness teaches you the ability to encounter your feelings and to allow them to ebb and flow without interference. This approach has an added bonus for creative artists in that it has been shown to improve creativity and promote a 'flow' state as well as improving mood (Chen *et al*, 2022).

It is important to note that the modern practice of mindfulness is only part of the much richer and wider approach to living laid out in Buddhism, and that it is often applied in ways that are incongruent with the original philosophy. In this book, we will explore its utility as a way of increasing sensitivity to and tolerance of emotions. However, if you find these exercises useful and want to explore this approach further, there are suggestions for further reading at the end of the chapter.

Exercise 19: Body scan

This exercise comes from mindfulness tradition and focuses on becoming aware of what is happening in your body, moment to moment, without judging or moving to fix it. If you have experienced trauma in your life, then I strongly suggest you begin this practice with a professional who can guide you and help you respond to whatever you encounter in your body. You do not have to be sitting or lying down to do this, and you do not have to close your eyes. If you are new to this, however, you might find it easier to build this skill somewhere comfortable and quiet before practising in louder and more distracting environments. If you prefer to have someone guide you, then you can find an excellent recording by one of the most influential mindfulness practitioners, Jon Kabat-Zinn here:

www.youtube.com/watch?v=_DTmGtznab4

The most important thing during this exercise is just to notice what arises and let it come and go without attaching a whole thought process to it or moving to make it different. You are observing what is happening without judgement, it is what it is. There is no 'right' way of doing mindfulness, you are just concentrating on being and letting whatever happens, happen.

Begin by noticing how your body feels against whatever surface it is in contact with. If you are sitting, notice the places where your body makes contact with the chair. If you are lying, take your attention to the places that you can feel the floor or surface underneath you. Allow yourself to settle.

Take your awareness to your breath and just notice how you are breathing without moving to change it. Are you taking deep or short breaths? Is your breathing rapid, steady, or slow? Are you taking air all the way down into your diaphragm or are you holding it somewhere up in your chest? What parts of you rise and fall as you breathe?

Take your attention to your feet. Notice any sensations in your toes, your heels and into your ankle. Notice the points of contact with the ground underneath you. If you are wearing socks and/or shoes, then notice how your foot feels inside them. How warm or cold are your feet? ➔

Shift your focus up to your legs and 'scan' slowly up towards your body, taking note of any sensations you encounter along the way. Do you notice any tension, heaviness, or points of discomfort? If you notice any feelings arise, then allow yourself to observe them without moving to respond or push them away. If you get distracted by thoughts, then gently guide your mind back to the exercise without judgement – the goal is not to get your mind to stop but just to become aware of mental events and gently refocus on your physical self.

Take your attention to your pelvis. Notice where your buttocks make contact with the floor or chair and become aware of any accompanying sensation. How does your lower back feel? What do you notice as you take your attention to your stomach? Do you notice any sensations or emotions, and if so, can you stay with them and let them happen?

Move your awareness up into your chest and notice what you find there. Has your breathing changed or stayed the same? How do your ribs and back feel? Notice any points of contact between the back of your body and the chair or floor. What is your mind doing? Notice any story it is telling about this exercise, then bring your awareness back to your body.

Take your attention up through your neck and into your head. Notice the back of your head and any sensations you encounter there. Take your awareness to your face. Begin to notice the sensation of breathing and the points where the air enters your body, how does it feel? Begin to notice the very top of your head and experience any sensations you find there.

Lastly, take in your body as a whole, the front and the back. Where is your attention drawn? What sensations or feelings do you become aware of as you do this? Do you notice any urge to move or to fix any of the experiences you encounter?

Allow your awareness to come back to the world around you, notice the things you can see, hear and feel. Give yourself a moment before moving back into action.

Please don't worry if you spent much of that exercise feeling bored and wishing it would stop, that is totally normal. The goal is not to change, it's just to notice without getting frustrated with yourself or wishing it were different. The aim is to learn how to tune in to the 'what is' and to get familiar with encountering yourself in all your changing, nuanced, constantly shifting glory. If you do this regularly, you will become better attuned to your emotions as they rise and fall and will be able to use what you uncover to inform your work.

Research suggests that practising mindfulness regularly can support creative artists to get into a 'flow' state, the sort of focused attention that allows creativity to literally 'flow' freely. There is a commonality between a mindful state and a flow state in that both are concerned with the here-and-now and allow you to become immersed in whatever task is at hand (Schutte & Malouff, 2020).

Mindfulness can also improve creativity by promoting 'divergent thinking'. As you become more accustomed to sensing and accepting what is happening in and around you, you become more sensitised to insight and possibilities that might have otherwise lingered outside your awareness (Henriksen et al, 2020; Richard et al, 2017). The upshot of all this research? If you want to improve creativity, then a regular mindfulness practice is a good place to start. Try taking ten minutes to do a mindfulness exercise before you do your 30 minutes' creative time for the next few days and see what happens.

Dialling down emotions

Being able to notice what you are feeling is important, but so is being confident that you can respond to what you encounter and can step away when you need to. People often tell me that they are scared to 'dip in' to a feeling in case they are engulfed and can never get out again. It is true that whenever you make a psychological change, the 'pendulum' can swing a little too far the other way before finding a comfortable resting place, however there are some ways that you can dial down emotions and prevent feeling overwhelmed.

There are other reasons you might want to step back or switch emotional states. Emotions can inspire and maintain creativity, but some can block and inhibit it, particularly if they are chronic or consuming. For example, you may have experienced times when your mood was low and motivation hard to come by, and therefore experienced a 'dry spell' in your creative life. Or you may have had periods of high anxiety during which it became hard to settle to paint or write. As we explored in Chapter Two, shame is also a great example of a feeling that can inhibit authentic expression as it creates a sort of paralysis to protect you from social exclusion. It is important to learn the skills to shift or get distance from emotions that are hindering your work. The following exercises come from dialectical behavioural therapy (DBT), a therapy that we most often deliver in groups and that focuses on building emotional tolerance and skills for emotional regulation. This therapy was developed by Marsha Linehan in the early 1990s, and since this time has become a widely available, well-evidenced approach to managing emotions.

Exercise 20: Utilising your senses

One of the flaws in human thinking is the tendency to go back through the past and ruminate on things that have happened over which we have no control, or to project forward and worry about things that have not happened yet and may not happen. Both of these processes can give us the illusion of control or safety, but in actual fact, both serve to increase our anxiety in the here-and-now and do little to change the past or safeguard the future. Our brains are not capable of differentiating between 'real' and 'perceived' or imagined threat, and therefore we experience an emotional response to our thoughts as if they are really happening. One of the most effective ways of bringing yourself out of a difficult feeling and back into the here-and-now is to use your senses:

List three things you can see in your environment (we are primarily visual animals, so start with your sight), then list three things you can hear, then three things you can physically feel. You can either list them out loud or inside your mind. Keep repeating this until whatever feeling you were experiencing has calmed.

If you just take a minute right now to do this, you will see how rapidly this exercise focuses your attention on the world around you and how this can act to stop unhelpful thoughts and calm whatever emotion you are experiencing.

The above exercise is a quick grounding strategy but you can build on this premise to create a sort of emotional 'first aid kit'. Attending to your senses and using these to deliberately soothe a feeling gives you influence over your emotional world and can act as a safety net if you find yourself in distress.

You can also build a kit to deliberately evoke a particular mood or emotion that you know primes you for creative work; for example, the smell of poster paints immediately transports me back to primary school and makes me want to don an oversized overall and paint. You might find that the smell of your mum's perfume makes you feel safe and comforted, and this helps you to write, or that taping up a picture of a favourite space in nature helps you feel inspired to make music.

I am currently taking a few days out of my busy life to write, a great luxury that I am grateful for, but the initial 'out of place' feeling upon entering my impersonal, cold hotel room was less than inspiring. Rather than feeling led to write, I felt led to flee and return to my loud, boisterous house where writing is often next to impossible. Reminding myself to practice what I preach, I took some time to take out and arrange my notebooks and favourite pen, and put some comfortable, familiar music on. I repositioned the desk by the window and brewed a cup of tea. The room hasn't changed, but my mood has, and I am now happily typing looking out of the window over the Yorkshire countryside. This is a small example, but taking time to attend to your environment can pay dividends in allowing you to move out of 'threat' or 'drive' and into the soothed, 'oxytocin' space that is sometimes needed for creativity.

Exercise 21: Evoking emotions

Create a self-soothe box full of smells that have positive associations, pictures (either photographs, cut-outs from magazines or even flyers) that provoke memories or a sense of possibility, soothing fabrics or tactile items (I love the wooden 'rib' I use when throwing pots, it is tactile and fits perfectly in my hand) and objects that are associated with whatever emotional state you are trying to evoke. Don't forget your sense of taste, include strong, evocative tastes such as the spiced tea you drank on a warm holiday or the 'Fisherman's friend' sweets that your grandmother used to give you. You can also make an accompanying playlist of music that you find inspiring, soothing, motivating, or evocative. Put the box somewhere close to where you usually create, maybe under your desk or on a shelf in your studio. If you find yourself struggling to get going, take some time to delve into your box and notice what objects or elements have the most profound impact on your mood.

We have talked before about the role of shame in creativity and the importance of being able to find ways to respond without shrinking into ourselves and becoming paralysed. Making art that is novel or that speaks to your experiences can be exposing and risky; shame is intended to limit that risk, to get you to conform again and avoid any of that nasty social rejection that might get you ostracised. Going back to the social function of emotions, in the past your very survival would have depended on your ability to ingratiate yourself into a social group or tribe, so no wonder you have inbuilt mechanisms to ensure this. These mechanisms are adaptive in many contexts, but when it comes to creativity you want to be able to choose the moments that you conform and the moments where you get radical and express yourself.

One way to respond to shame is with compassion; not a wishy-washy nod to kindness but a proper, deep empathy for yourself and your work. There are several ways to achieve this, all of which take practice and conscious effort to make them second nature. The first step towards self-compassion is to change your relationship with perceived failure and setbacks and to learn how to speak to yourself with empathy when a project or piece of work does not go your way. It is sometimes easier to imagine how this might sound by applying it to someone else, particularly someone you care about. If a close friend received harsh criticism over a painting she placed in an exhibit, how would you respond? Would you take the opportunity to point out that she is probably a fraud and should stop painting before she embarrasses herself? Or would you offer empathy, acknowledge how much criticism can hurt, offer encouragement to persevere? Would you remind them how subjective critique can be, and think with them about how they might move forward, or suggest that perhaps she might want to think about a different career? In my experience, it is much easier to imagine what you might say to another person than to focus that level of empathy and thoughtfulness towards yourself.

Another way to practise this is to think about your situation from the perspective of your compassionate figure from Chapter Two – this can be a real or imagined person, or even a pet. My Newfoundland dog, Marley, is somehow able to offer me a level of quiet solidarity that few humans can. When I have encountered failure or setbacks, and have thrown myself into a chair in despair, he will come and lean his weight reassuringly against my leg and just sit until I am finished experiencing whatever it is that I am feeling. I will often bring him to mind when I need to offer myself compassionate solidarity. Perhaps you chose a mentor or teacher that gave you a balanced, truthful but kind perspective, or a family member who showed great wisdom coupled with love. If you notice yourself feeling shame, then bringing to mind these individuals and asking yourself what they might say about the situation can offer you a compassionate viewpoint to start from.

Another way of showing yourself compassion is to locate whatever experience or situation has provoked shame within the common experience of humanity. It is unlikely that you are the first or last person to ever have a manuscript knocked back by a publisher, or have a screenplay that is not picked up, or a poem that is deemed immature or underdeveloped. You will not be the first or last person to experience the sting of public humiliation when you put work out there and for whatever reason it is not received in the way you want it to be. You are standing within an unseen community of creative people that stretch right back to the earliest days of humanity and flow out in front of you to include all the artists that are yet to come. You are grounded and held in a community who know all too well the risks and joy of a creative life. Calling to mind all those that went before you and all those that will come after can help to locate whatever situation has led to your shame within a framework that makes the impact much less great and much less personal. Failure, criticism and disappointment are all par for the course if you are to make work that means something to you and that matters. You are not alone in this and deserve the same compassion and understanding that everyone else does. Your failure is not somehow worse than another's, or more catastrophic, and you are able to pick yourself up, feel compassion for yourself for a time, and then get back on with the important work at hand.

A word on thoughts

We cannot spend an entire chapter exploring feelings without also giving some attention to the tricky subject of thoughts. Thoughts and feelings interact in a causal way and learning how to observe this gives you far greater control and choice about how you then behave. In cognitive behavioural therapy this relationship is shown like this:

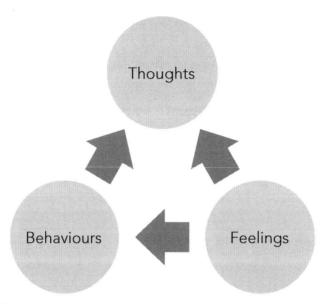

(Beck, 2011)

When I am exploring an incident with a patient that involved a powerful emotion, we can often trace the emotion back to a thought. 'He doesn't love me anymore' gives rise to a wave of despair; 'I am never going to be good enough' opens the floodgates of hopelessness; 'I am quitting this job as soon as I find something better' invites relief. Thoughts are the internal monologue that gives language and meaning to our experiences. Most thoughts float in and out of our minds without too much conscious interrogation, or at best provoke a brief pondering: however, thoughts that are troublesome, worrying, or that provoke a strong emotional reaction get our attention and can start a vicious cycle which can derail creativity and stop you working. If you think 'everyone is going to laugh at me', then you will quickly feel anxious and self-conscious and will stop creating. If you think 'so many people are better at this than me', then you will quickly feel despair and may give up.

Let me give you an example. Sarah is a successful woman living in the north of the UK. She came to see me amidst a relationship breakdown and a crisis in her sense of who she was and what she wanted. Sarah has spent much of her youth singing in various choirs or performing solo in musical theatre or at events. She had always enjoyed performing, but as medical training became more demanding, she found she had less and less time to dedicate to music. Sarah met and married her then-partner in her late 20s and by her mid-30s she was qualified as a paediatrician with a busy job and had two young children. She described finding those years disorientating as she worked harder and harder but felt less and less satisfied with her life – an experience that frequently provokes the decision to come into therapy. I met Sarah in her early 40s; she was still enjoying her work but no longer wanted to dedicate her entire life to her job as she was not finding the sort of fulfilment she was looking for. Her children were growing and were developing relationships and hobbies of their own, and she and her husband had mutually agreed to separate.

In therapy, Sarah and I explored her sense of identity outside of work and motherhood and stumbled upon her latent love of singing. She shared that she often found herself singing in the shower or in the car and missed the connection and joy she felt when performing in a group. Sarah and I agreed that she would research local choirs and enquire about joining, and I was pleased to learn that there was a fantastic all-female choir in her neighbourhood that were looking for new members. She planned to attend but found that she made it as far as the door and could not make herself go inside. She described it like a 'freeze' response that resulted in her returning home without saying a word to anyone.

We explored the feeling as she placed her hand on the door and she talked about a wave of desire and longing, followed by a powerful wave of hopelessness and despair. The feelings shocked her, and she had thought about them many times in the days between the incident and her next session. It transpired that, as an adolescent, Sarah had hopes of becoming a professional singer and had shown great promise – she had won every talent contest at school, had sung at local events, and was well known in her local area. Though Sarah had greatly wanted to pursue music, she had been concerned that she would not be able to earn a steady income as a singer, again, a common worry that can derail many artists, and had instead enrolled on a medical degree. She continued to find ways to sing until the demands of her life made it impossible and had then quietly packed away the dream until she stumbled across it in therapy.

I had not realised the longing and loss associated with singing for Sarah, and had meant the exercise as a benign promotion of self-care. However, in that moment, she confronted the loss of not just her musicality but of her identity outside of the confines of her demanding roles as wife, mother and doctor. As she placed her hand on the door, she felt initial hope which was quickly followed by the thought 'It's too late, you're too old'. This brought the crushing sense of hopelessness and despair that resulted in her leaving.

Sarah's responses to her feelings are absolutely understandable and revealed important information for us to work on in therapy. We were able to sit with the grief about some of the choices she had made and the years where she felt she had lost herself. Music was a large part of this; an emblem of her spirit that she had set aside to attend to the practical matters of life. The importance of reclaiming that part of her was clear: however, the thought, 'It's too late, you're too old', provoked an emotional response that paralysed her and kept her locked in that lost place. The longer she did not reclaim her musical self, the more she confirmed her deep fear that it was indeed too late and the more hopeless she felt.

The lovely thing about a cycle is that you can approach it from any angle, and you will inevitably break the chain. We decided to approach it from several angles; we gave space for the emotions of despair and hopelessness and then agreed to experiment with a different behaviour to see whether the thought would remain or not. Sarah returned to the choir, and when she got the (now familiar) thought 'It's too late, you're too old', she noted it but pushed the door open and entered anyway. What Sarah found behind that door was not only her reclaimed musicality, but a warm, creative community within which she found meaningful friendships and connection. She continues to sing, and learned first-hand that it is never too late, even if you have to grieve for the lost years.

Thoughts are information, just like feelings, however we tend to experience them as 'true' in a way that can leave little room for negotiation. On many levels this makes perfect sense – our reality is the only one we have and so of course we rely on it to make sense of the world. However, the evidence is conclusive that our brains take shortcuts, make assumptions, create and maintain biases and apply previous learning to unrelated situations. Our thoughts are not the logical and trustworthy source of information that we wish they were. There are times when our thoughts are distorted or are based on outdated information or experience and therefore require flexibility and negotiation. When we truly stop to evaluate our thoughts, we are often surprised by how little evidence our brain has relied upon to make such a conclusive leap. For the most part, this is an adaptive process that allows us to live with and make sense of remarkable amounts of information. However, if a thought is standing between you and creativity then it requires attention. As we discussed in earlier chapters, if you have a critical 'voice' that chirps up every time you try to create something, then this could be considered a thought pattern that needs renegotiation. If you experience the thought 'I am never going to finish this work' and this results in anxiety that stops you working, then this thought needs some attention. If you think to yourself 'I am being so self-indulgent' every time you set aside time to devote to creativity, then this thought needs some interrogation.

The rapidity of some of our 'negative automatic thoughts' (essentially, thoughts that have become so ingrained and established that they are barely perceptible) can make them stealthy and difficult to do business with. They can occur instantaneously with a conviction that makes them very difficult to differentiate from 'truth'. This means we are far less likely to test them for accuracy and can end up reinforcing them, sometimes for many years. For example, if every time you see a paintbrush you think 'I can't paint' and therefore never pick it up, then the 'truth' that you can't paint remains 'true'. This thought may be grounded in early experiences of finding it hard to master painting, or in clumsy feedback given at the wrong point in your artistic development, but the consistency of it over time has meant that you have not revisited it to see whether the 'truth' still holds. Can you paint? How do you know? The reality is that everything is changing, all the time, and even if something has always been 'true' to date, it does not mean that it is 'true' now.

Just like we can gain distance from our emotions, we can also gain distance from our thoughts and begin to notice them as mental events, not indicators of absolute 'truth'. For Sarah, understanding that the thought 'It's too late, you're too old' was a mental event that could be tested, negotiated and ultimately challenged, meant that she was able to push that door open and find out.

When practising your body scan or other mindfulness exercises, be interested in the thoughts that come up. Practise watching them without getting embroiled in a story or a process, or if you do find yourself going down a line of thought, gently escort yourself back to the task. You can also use the values that you identified in Chapter Two as a sort of measure and can check whether a thought is congruent or incongruent with a value. If you notice a discrepancy, then you can follow the value as a consistent guide to where you want to be. For example, if Sarah had identified an underlying value of 'using creativity freely and to the best of my ability', then the thought 'It's too late, you're too old' sits directly at odds with her values. As such, she can thank her brain for the input but disregard the thought and move ahead with her value-driven action, to push open the door to the choir.

Emotions as inspiration

Research suggests that emotions, both positive and negative can help improve creativity if we can utilise them at the point where they give us energy and 'activation'. One way to work with this is to deliberately cultivate an emotional state that is conducive to work. Another approach is to listen out for emotional signals and be willing to act and make work at the point that we are feeling something. This will probably involve stepping out of the expected pattern of behaving and pausing whatever it is you are doing to make work, but this flexibility will pay dividends.

Sometimes is it essential to create from a place of raw, unfiltered emotion. In fact, I would argue that the way to respond to any challenging, painful or heartbreaking moment is to *make*. When we make work, we give voice to our experiences and allow ourselves to hear how we feel about it. We give it due attention and allow it to speak to us and through us, and often that is enough to allow us to process and find a way through what has happened. However, there are also times when whatever state we find ourselves in is not conducive to work, perhaps when we have a deadline looming and become paralysed by anxiety, or when we experience a loss or pain so immense that it cannot be immediately filtered into work but needs time to settle. At times like this, it is important to be able to coax out your creativity by creating a safe, inviting environment that is almost like that required by someone convalescing from an illness. It is the feeling of safety and care for the bruised, frayed part of yourself that is evoked by chicken soup or tea made by someone who loves you. Allowing ourselves this sort of care, we bring forward our creative self to do what it can, even if that is only to write a few words, play a few lines of music that you love or sketching whatever is on the table in front of you.

As I have been writing this chapter, I have realised that I have different creative mediums for different states. For me, right in the middle of an emotional maelstrom is where I write music, or at least the music that has punch. Outside of these times, I might play a bit of piano or even note down some lyrics, but the music comes in little bits, unlike the fully formed birthing that happens when I'm emotionally wrought. The opposite is the case for ceramics, I find that I cannot throw a pot until I am fully present in the moment and can be reciprocal with the clay. The emotional landscape of these two places could not be more different; music allows me to crash along with the waves of feeling, channelling the energy into sound. Ceramics feels more like floating peacefully, bobbing gently with the whims of the waves. This means I have to set the scene for throwing in a way that is different to my often late-night musical sessions.

When I go to work in my studio, I first make a pot of my favourite tea. I have a rustic and beautiful mug made by the person that I bought my pottery wheel from and take that, along with a tiny ceramic jug full of milk, on a tray that is painted with cherry blossom. I light a candle that fills the air with the most wonderful fragrance, and I will sometimes put on music, depending on my mood. This little ritual means that I start ready to create; I have given myself little bits of care that create an environment of warmth and support and which mean that, whatever happens with the clay, I can receive it with good humour and perspective. If I flew into the studio harassed and berating myself for not having made enough work recently, then my body and mind would be tensed like taught wire. My tolerance for mistakes would be low and my willingness to experiment vastly reduced. That tension would be communicated to the clay as I worked and inevitably it would respond by flying across the room, thus darkening my mood and increasing my irritation. I do not hold myself up as a perfect example of how to be a creative person, and have definitely had times when the writing is not flowing or the clay is flying, but paying specific attention to how I approach the work means I stack the odds that I can be present and can create something authentic and playful. I urge you to spend some time thinking about what creates an environment of warmth and safety for you, and then to implement this into how you prepare to make work.

I just came off the phone to my friend who is an extremely gifted photographer and has overseen the fine art degree programme at a local college for the last 15 years. His department is being demolished as part of a short-sighted, government-driven push towards education only for the sake of employment; a move that is seeing many thriving art courses being decommissioned and destroyed. I have watched this process over a number of weeks as priceless equipment becomes buried under tools and dust, and important work is stacked in the corner by people who genuinely have no sense of what it is they are dismantling. After I wrote the last paragraph, we spoke briefly on the phone about practicalities and what is going where, and then, after we hung up, I sent him a flippant message along the lines of 'don't let the b***ers get you down'. I realised the irony as soon as I sent it. Of course, he needs to let it get him down, or enraged, or hopeless and despairing, or grief-stricken, or whatever it is that the destruction gives rise to.

I rang him straight back and urged him to make work. Now. In the middle of the rush to save what can be saved, and to vacate before the building falls in on top of him. Just for ten minutes, to take the moment to look, to feel and then to *make*. What is flowing back into my inbox is work that is making my eyes sting and my blood boil. Images of half-demolished ceilings and trailing wires reaching down onto kilns and buckets of home-mixed glazes. A sign with the college logo on it that says 'It's all in how you look at things :(:' hanging on the wall above a pile of hastily moved canvases and coffee mugs and a stage, now laying half demolished. He took the radical act to step out of 'doing' and into 'being', and to let his camera speak from that place, and the work carries the impact of a thousand bulldozers. It captures a department that took decades to build, that he took decades to build, being destroyed in days. The work is powerful and unavoidable and is a pressing and immediate example of what can happen when we stop, allow ourselves to feel, and then urge ourselves to make. To write, paint, draw, photograph, sing, move… whatever form the expression takes.

If we speak from a place of authenticity and unfiltered emotion, we can connect with the parts of others that have encountered these places, too, even if the specifics are not the same. All of us know the feeling of looking upon the destruction of something precious and sacred, even if we have not all built and then lost an art department. We can all connect with the impotence of rage against an unstoppable and ignorant force, and grief for something that cannot be easily undone or replaced. You do not need to know the context to feel the salience of the stained coffee cup bearing the name of a teacher, now made redundant, just visible on a desk covered in detritus and dust.

Exercise 22: Speaking from your emotions

Before you begin this exercise, please have some paper and either paints or pastels to hand. You don't need any particular type or quality of paint, a simple watercolour set will do fine.

Take a moment to check in with your body, beginning at your feet and moving up through your legs, abdomen, chest and finally into your head. Notice any physical sensations and then direct the spotlight of your attention there. Perhaps you notice a heaviness in your chest, a knot in your stomach, a lightness in your legs or a tension across your forehead. If you cannot sense anything, then take a short walk without any other distractions before trying again.

Without filtering or censoring, ask yourself, 'If this part of me could speak, what would it say?' Notice the first thing that comes into your mind. Keeping your awareness there, ask yourself, 'If this part of me could paint, what would it paint? What colours, shapes and textures would it use? Would the marks be large and sweeping, or small and delicate? Would the image be imposing, or subtle, unmissable, or almost invisible?' Without overthinking or planning, begin to paint whatever you see in your mind's eye. If you find yourself feeling lost, take your attention back to whatever part of your body you tuned into at the beginning. Don't stop until the feeling relaxes and diminishes, or until you feel you have captured something of the essence of what you felt.

Stand back and look at what you have made. How was it to do this exercise? Did it feel easy or challenging? Did part of you feel silly, or anxious without a plan for what you were going to create?

Try this exercise again but using whatever medium you usually work with. If you are a ceramicist, try focusing on a sensation in your body and then ask, 'If this part of me could express itself in clay, what would it create?' Then see where that takes you. If you are a writer, ask yourself 'If this part of me could write freely, what would it write?' and then let whatever comes to you flow out onto the page. The key is not to censor, evaluate or critique what is coming up, but just to let it happen. You can always go back with your 'thinking mind' once the work is done.

The importance of a space

The importance of emotions to creativity are clear and unequivocal, which leads us to think about the space we work in as a potentially powerful conduit for feelings. A cluttered, poorly organised space will result in stress and distraction; a space full of the things that you love and that inspire you will put you in the mood to create as soon as you open the door. For me, even the smell of my studio makes me want to don an apron and throw pots or to open my laptop and get writing. I am in the very privileged position of having a space at the end of my garden – a repurposed shed with a polyurethane roof that I believe once housed a hot tub. When it is raining, the noise on the roof is calming and comforting, when it is sunny, the space is illuminated and warm. Even on a grey day, the light settles on carefully curated objects that I love and wills me to make work. Now, I am aware that not everyone has a garden, or the funds to repurpose a shed. Not everyone has a whole room that they can dedicate to the art of making, but that really doesn't matter, it is still perfectly possible to create a dedicated space for creating.

Before the 'studio' was built, I picked up a beautiful, antique desk for £70, which I painstakingly sanded to remove the orange pine wax and to reveal the beautiful wood underneath. I placed it in the tiny bedroom in our home, right by the window. It is one of those lovely, ancient affairs with tiny shelves, nooks and drawers on top in which all manner of beautiful and creative things can be stored. I carefully selected a plant that could not easily be killed, and photos of my dog and family, as well as postcards and memorabilia from events and friends, and placed them around the space. I painted a brightly coloured picture of my favourite flowers in my garden and placed it directly in my eye line. Even though the whole space is less than a square metre, when I sat down in the chair, I was immediately calm, happy and ready to create. If you don't have the space for a desk, then find a beautiful box and paint it, or allocate just one shelf and arrange it with objects that you love. The important thing is that the space is yours and that you are able to create unobserved.

There are very few people or approaches that I can say have genuinely changed my life, but the Marie Kondo approach to tidying is an exception. As a person that moved around a lot as a child, I had a great attachment to things as the one constant that accompanied me wherever I went. As an adult, my home was thoughtfully arranged but always contained a lot of stuff that would quietly stress me out. Books I meant to read, clothes that no longer fit, objects that other people had given me that I didn't quite love but felt compelled to hang on to. My world was a riot of things that vied for my attention and clamoured for space. The situation came to a head when I moved house while pregnant and had to enlist help from family and friends. My long-suffering and extremely generous brother quietly inhaled, 'I really don't like you right now', as he staggered under the 100th box of pottery and books and loaded it into the back of a heaving van. To be honest, he had a point.

Quite by chance, I stumbled across Marie Kondo on a television programme in which she visits the homes of people also beset by 'stuff' and humbly and quietly changes their entire outlook by getting them to sort through their belongings by category, holding each item in their hand and asking, 'Does it spark joy?' Anything that no longer sparks joy is respectfully thanked for its service before it is donated or recycled. I was struck by her respect for 'stuff' and for the attachment people have to it, and also by the apparent effectiveness of her approach. I subsequently bought both of her books and did the method from start to finish, exactly as outlined, and I can genuinely say that it changed my space (and life) entirely. I went from being besieged by things, to existing in a space where everything my eyes alight on is an object that 'sparks joy', either for its usefulness and role in my life, or for its beauty. The impacts on my ability for creativity were numerous; I had more time, more physical space, more mental space, and more inspiration. I did this six years ago and am yet to return to my errant ways.

Now, I am not suggesting that you revamp your entire living space (unless you want to), however, I am suggesting that paying close attention to your creative space is likely to benefit your creativity immensely. Your mind is always scanning your environment and processing what it sees, even if this is out of your awareness. Holding unfinished work in your hands and genuinely asking yourself 'does it spark joy?' might identify work that is no longer serving you or that you have moved on from, but that is quietly bothering you. Holding materials and even bits of furniture in your hands and feeling for your reaction will tell you if you need to thank them, then let them go as they are causing unnecessary frustration. That stool that squeaks every time you sit on it, the desk that is fractionally too low, that wedging block that is just too large, can all be respectfully thanked and then moved on. If you are able to surround yourself with things that 'spark joy', then your mind has ample access to inspiration and beauty and will not be irked by a reminder that you are yet to finish your invoices or file your tax return.

Exercise 23: Priming your creative space

This exercise might require some preparation and planning, and even a Pinterest board if the mood takes you. However, don't allow yourself to get so caught up in planning that you don't move into action and actually make the necessary changes; if needs be, allocate a certain amount of time to day-dreaming and creating the vision, and then strike out into action whether you have all the resources ready or not.

Take a look at the space you use for creating work – this might be a dedicated studio or a corner in a room, or even just a box that you use to convert the kitchen table into a workspace. If you do not have an allocated space, then this is where you will begin. Even in the smallest of rooms, it is possible to use fabric, or position furniture in such a way as to carve out a small corner just for creative pursuits.

Stand in the middle of the space and pay attention to how it feels to be there – do you feel led to write, paint or draw, or do unfinished jobs catch your eye? How inviting is the space that you have allocated? How easy is it for you to access all the things you need? Are there any tasks that niggle you every time you enter the space? Any piles of items that are asking to be organised or shelves that are desperate to be fixed? Do you find every object in your space either beautiful or essential? Are there any things that could be moved or made more aesthetically pleasing? What mood does your space evoke? If you notice that you feel frustrated, irked, morose or hopeless, then what changes do you need to make in order to create a positive space where creativity feels possible? Do you need to let in more light or change pieces of furniture that do not (as Marie Kondo so wisely put it) 'spark joy'.

Conclusion

Emotions are immensely powerful things that shape our experience of life and are often at the root of our behaviour. Both positive and negative emotional states provide 'activation' that support us in different parts of the creative process. Being able to tune in to what we are feeling makes it more likely that we will create work that taps into our common human experience and resonates with others. I would argue that this ability to transcend context is what we are trying to describe when we use the term 'fine art'.

There are many well-researched methods for drawing closer to, or gaining distance from, feelings that make them less mysterious and out of control, but they take practice and openness to experience. By getting familiar with our emotions and learning how to work with them, we increase our sensitivity to inspiration and ensure that we are able to respond to whatever our art provokes or uncovers. We can also buffer ourselves against the emotional impact of putting work out into the world and ensure that we remain resilient, regardless of how it is received.

References

Averill JR, Chon KK & Hahn DW (2001) Emotions and Creativity, East and West. *Asian Journal of Social Psychology* **4** 165-183.

Beck JS (2011) *Cognitive Behaviour Therapy, Second Edition*. Guildford Publications, UK.

Chen H, Liu C, Zhou F, Chiang CH, Chen YL, Wu K, Huang DH, Liu CY & Chiou WK (2022) The Effect of Animation-Guided Mindfulness Meditation on the Promotion of Creativity, Flow and Affect. *Front Psychol*.

De Dreu CK, Baas M & Nijstad BA (2008) Hedonic tone and Activation Level in the Mood-Creativity Link: Toward a Dual Pathway to Creativity Model. *Journal of Personality and Social Psychology* **94** (5).

De Petrillo L & Winner E (2005) Does Art Improve Mood? A test of a Key Assumption Underlying Art Therapy. *Art Therapy* **22** (4).

Henriksen D, Richardson C, Shack K (2020) Mindfulness and creativity: implications for thinking and learning. *Thinking skills and creativity* **37**.

Kabat-Zinn J (2003) Mindfulness-based interventions in context: past, present, and future. *Clinical Psychology Science and Practice* **10** (2) 144–156.

Richard V, Halliwell W, Tenenbaum GJTSP (2017) Effects of an improvisation intervention on elite figure skaters' performance. *Self Esteem Creativity Mindfulness Skills* **31**, 275–287.

Schutte NS & Malouff JM (2020) Connections between curiosity, flow and creativity. *Personal. Individ. Differ.* **152**: 109555.

To ML, Fisher CD, Ashkanasy NM & Rowe PA (2012) Within-Person Relationships between Mood and Creativity. *Journal of Applied Psychology* **97** (3).

Chapter Five: Inspiration

Exercise 24: Check in

Before we get started on the concept of inspiration and how we might deliberately put ourselves in its path, it would be helpful to check in with how your daily art time is going. How have you found making consistent, predictable space to show up and create each day? Has it become second nature now, or is it still something that requires work and effort? What are you noticing about the process of creating? Is it fairly predictable, or does it fluctuate depending on the day and whatever else is happening in your life? Are you finding it a safe place to experiment and play, or do you notice intrusive thoughts about the quality of what you are creating? Have you felt able to keep your practice private, or have you been tempted to share your work?

How are you finding the morning pages? Are you still writing each day? Do you notice now if you miss a day? What is the impact of this?

Over the next few chapters, keep your commitment to your daily creative practice and your morning pages. It is this act of repetitive 'doing' that creates habit and lasting change. Just as we explored in Chapter Four, our thoughts, feelings and behaviour are inextricably connected, and if we alter any one of them, the others will follow. By radically altering our behaviour in a sustained way, we are creating the space for a transformation in the way we think about our work, and subsequently the way we feel about it.

Inspiration and creativity

When I was a student, I worked as a waitress in a very uninspiring chain restaurant to fund myself through education, and often worked Sundays as this fitted with my university timetable. There were not a lot of perks to this job, and I don't mind admitting I was exceedingly poor at it. However, one definite perk was getting to spend most Sunday lunchtimes with a long-term customer, Glynis. She would arrive somewhere very close to 12:00, just after we opened, and would often be seated in my area of the restaurant. I looked forward to her arrival to the extent that I would watch the clock if it went much past 12:00 and would feel cheated if someone else was allocated to serve her. Glynis was in her late 90s when I met her and would openly boast that she continued to be the local university's oldest student (a fact I have not checked but which I have no reason to doubt). She enrolled on adult education courses every term, and would tell me about mushroom identification, medieval architecture or 'literature of the English country house' as I waited on her. She would ask me about my psychology studies and my perspective and thoughts about what I had learned, and she was quick-witted and perceptive in her replies. I sometimes regret that I didn't ask her more questions about herself, particularly why she chose this seemingly faceless restaurant upon which to bestow her loyalty. I did ask her why she continued to study, though, and she told me that she was endlessly bored by the people she lived with, who seemed to have given up and had certainly run out of topics of conversation. She told me that she found inspiration from the teaching but also from being around interesting and interested people. During the first year that I knew her, she still got the bus to the university to attend classes, joining the throng of other students on their way to lessons.

Glynis died just before I left to begin my first job as an assistant psychologist. I heard no details of what happened or how she died, just that she had gone, and I still feel the sadness as I write this. As far as I know, she died halfway through completing a course in forensic science, or botanical illustration, that she attended because she needed to open her mind to new and interesting things right to the end. She was close to 100 when she died and was easily as engaged and inspired as I was in my early 20s, arguably more. I mention Glynis because the subject of inspiration always brings her to mind; she was the best example I have ever known of the lifegiving power of putting yourself in the path of the novel and inspirational and being open to experience. The fact that she was still eating an entire pizza for lunch in her late 90s is an inspiration in and of itself.

What do we mean when we talk about inspiration? This appears to differ depending on whether you are talking to an artist, a lay person or a researcher. If you read the academic literature, this term covers everything from a 'bolt from the blue' idea, to an 'aha' moment of insight, to the feeling of being moved to create by an object or person (Oleynick *et al*, 2014). In research, it has proven difficult to 'operationalise' inspiration, that is, to turn it into a well-defined construct that can then be tested and measured. However, most of us are familiar with the experience of feeling inspired and recognise its importance in our own work and the mark of it in the work of others. If someone says, 'I was so inspired', we seem to understand what they mean on an intrinsic level, even in the absence of an agreed definition. Most of us will be able to identify times that we have observed something so moving, so beautiful, or so perfectly articulated that it has changed our idea about what is possible and has maybe even inspired us to make work in response. I remember so clearly the first time I saw my friend Nat sing – it felt like the incredible sound that emanated from her was resonating inside my own chest; it was impossible to look at or think about anything else. It was a lesson in what the human voice is capable of when loosened from convention, and it served as a profound inspiration to me in the developments I was making in my own vocal style at the time.

I had the same experience the first time I visited the Musee d'Orsay, most famous for its collection of paintings by artists such as Monet and Renoir, but also home to some remarkable sculptures and statues. I enjoyed the immensity and beauty of the paintings, but as I was leaving, I came face to face with a marble woman, peeking mischievously from underneath a curtain of hair in a way I just could not look away from. It transpired that she is a depiction of Aurora, the Roman Goddess of the dawn, created by Denys Puesch. In that moment, she changed my entire concept of the life, movement and spirit that could be communicated through inanimate material. I genuinely felt as if she was leaning out at me and I couldn't tell if she was mischievous, playful or malevolent. I attribute my subsequent foray into and love of ceramics to this encounter; it was my first initiation into what is possible.

Both of these moments are memorable and led to a marked change in the path of my creativity. I am aware of countless other bits of inspiration that perhaps don't sit so close to the front of my mind, but nonetheless had a significant impact on my work and have continued to shape how I have developed as an artist and a musician. For the sake of this chapter, we are going to be exploring inspiration in the context of these moments, the big and the small encounters that help to generate ideas and insight, and that move us to make work.

This book is not just about setting you up for a short-term spike in your creativity, though that is of course encouraging and exciting, but developing habits that will sustain your creative practice over time and ensure that you are able to keep creating for as long as you want to and are able. A creative life that endures needs fresh energy and ideas and therefore requires you to keep taking proactive steps to put yourself in the path of inspiration. The things that inspire you are profoundly personal, so this chapter will not contain a set of rules or procedures to follow, but instead some directional arrows to begin to explore or to reinvigorate your relationship with inspiration.

But how amenable to change is our relationship with inspiration? There are well-defined personality traits that appear to be synonymous with the ability to create; these include 'originality, independence, risk taking, personal energy, curiosity, humour, attraction to complexity and novelty, artistic sense and open-mindedness' (Plucker *et al*, 2010). Of all of the traits that have been examined, however, the most strongly related to creative behaviour and performance appears to be openness to experience, that is, how willing and able we are to open ourselves up to that richness of the world around us and be curious about our interaction with it (Beaty *et al*, 2014; Kaufman, 2016). I suspect that one of the mechanisms that underpin this relationship has to do with inspiration and our receptivity to it. If we can be open to experience, then we can be open to ideas and insights as they occur and are perhaps more likely to act on them. We have little control over some of the more 'fixed' attributes of a creative personality, but some are amenable to being consciously fostered and developed. In this chapter, we are going to look at how you might begin to increase your openness to the world around you and your sensitivity to the 'voice' of inspiration. I hope that by the end of the chapter you will have experimented with different techniques and be well on the road to a set of practices that will keep your creative 'well' flowing for years to come.

Threat, drive and self-soothing

In Chapter One, we began to think about the threat, drive and self-soothing states and their implications for creativity. The threat state primes us to scan for and respond to danger; it prioritises only that which promotes our survival and prompts a whole host of physical responses to ensure we stand the best chance of facing down whatever danger we have encountered. The drive system helps us to acquire what we need by plying us with a satisfying chemical hit every time we gain something, whether that is material or imagined (Gilbert, 2014). Both of these states are biologically arming us with the best chance of survival: however, modern life has hooked into them in a way that can leave us wired, anxious, compulsive and distracted. In many ways, capitalism is built on these systems; you are informed of a threat (you're getting older so will be perceived as less attractive, you are not built like a racing snake, therefore you will not be as successful as your thinner counterparts), and then you are sold a solution. This is a double whammy as it not only activates your threat system, but also gratifies the very rewarding drive system once you acquire whatever it is that is going to solve your problem.

Both of these systems can make it harder for us to spend unstructured time alone with our thoughts in the way that is necessary for inspiration and insight. It is virtually impossible for most people to sit without an activity for more than a moment, and very rare that we now encounter boredom for any length of time. Of course, there are some great positives to these advances in technology; we have a world of information that can be accessed immediately, we can connect and check in with the lives of others in a way that was impossible only 20 years ago, and we have access to images of places that would once have been the territory of only the most adventurous. But – and it's a big but – the clamour and noise can drown out our thoughts and our feelings and makes the 'voice' of inspiration and ideas so much harder to hear. It is fine to use and enjoy these tools of the modern world, but it requires that we work harder to hear ourselves and our creativity.

One of the most important things in countering the threat and drive system is to purposefully induce a soothed state by enlisting the power of oxytocin. Oxytocin allows us to enter a calm, alert state that makes it easier to pay attention to our thoughts and feelings and to notice the world around us. Treating yourself with compassion and creating an environment of warmth and safety allows us to attend to our creative work in a way that encourages experimentation and play, which in turn is shown to increase the originality of ideas (Hoffman & Russ, 2012).

We can also use the soothing system to bring us into a state where we can tolerate doing 'nothing', that is, spending time pottering and listening to our own thoughts. This is very much part of the creative process but is less demonstrably productive than making work, meaning we can struggle to justify it to ourselves and to others. Allocating time, even in the middle of busy lives, to 'mulling', inevitably ends up being time well spent as it can serve as space to review work that has been made or dream up work that is yet to come to fruition. When I think about the times I have received most inspiration for writing this book, it is the unstructured, unplanned moment of 'mulling' such as being in the shower, sitting on a train, driving to a meeting or walking to meet a friend. These snatched moments of alone time with my thoughts have resulted in a seemingly endless list of 'notes' to myself which I usually have to capture on my phone as I am away from my desk.

But where do these moments come from? Inspiration can be gained both by going inwards and letting our minds process what they already know, and by turning our attention to the world around us in a way that is mindful, purposeful and receptive. When we slow down and tune in, we find things in both our external and internal worlds that can be brought forward and expressed. So many people talk to me about feeling uninspired and unmotivated, but when we come to look at how much time they spend looking for the voice of inspiration, it is often next to none. The reason is usually competing demands for time that are so numerous and consuming that every moment is accounted for, and the 'voice' of inspiration would have to be a bellow to get noticed over the din.

If you look back at the past week, how much time would you consider to be unstructured, ie, that is not already allocated to a task or activity? Did you find yourself borrowing time that was allocated to another activity for mulling things over, for example did you find your mind wandering in a meeting or use the drive to work to think back over the last piece you wrote? What would it be like to actively allocate small pieces of time to pottering, with a view to letting your mind wander and alight wherever your attention is needed?

Cultivating inspiration

Our brains tend to favour information regarding threat and drive, as that gives us the best chance to survive, and does not naturally lean towards inactivity and silence. The society we live in compounds this by valuing *doing* far higher than *being*, to the extent that we have monetised time. Time spent 'mulling' or thinking is seen as wasted or unproductive, and success is often measured in terms of direct output. As a creative artist, you need to find ways to purposefully seek out inspiration and insight by protecting time to *do* nothing and just *be*. This is easier said than done, but there are tools that can support this process.

Bilateral stimulation

One of the great ways to tune into the 'voice' of inspiration is to move your body to release what insights, experiences and emotions might be lurking there. By loosening and mobilising our physical self we become more sensitised to the sensations and emotions that may normally be outside of our conscious awareness and may be more receptive to inspiration and ideas. When I first began a serious yoga practice, I was shocked about what I found inhabiting my muscles, particularly my legs. As I stretched, what was released was seemingly years of unfelt, unprocessed, unknown stuff that had been worked into the fabric of my muscles and was just lying their waiting.

Not all types of movement are created equal when it comes to inspiration and connecting with what you think and feel. Bilateral stimulation refers to activities that activate the left and right side of your body and brain in a rhythmical way, for example watching a tennis ball going back and forth across a court or drumming in a way that utilises each hand in turn. This type of stimulation impacts how we process memory and is deliberately used in eye movement desensitisation and reprocessing therapy (EMDR) to process and treat trauma and to address other mental health issues such as phobias, addiction and even depression (Abel & O'Brien, 2010; Hase *et al*, 2015).

The mechanism by which bilateral stimulation works is unclear, but several theories have been posited which include drawing connections between this sort of stimulation and the state of REM in sleep. Shapiro (2001) developed EMDR when she was walking through a park and was contemplating a situation that she was finding challenging. The story goes that she noticed that the way she was moving her eyes side to side appeared to alleviate some of the distress that she was feeling. This most unlikely of scenarios resulted in swathes of research that support this observation – something about bilateral stimulation does indeed impact the way in which we process.

When bilateral stimulation is used in a therapeutic context, it is mainly to process specific, usually traumatic memories that are continuing to cause distress. Shapiro believed that some memories are stored outside of context, i.e., they are not connected to the network of memory in the same way as benign experiences but are held in a sort of 'suspended animation' that can be triggered by situations that remind us of the original event. When these 'pathogenic' memories are activated by smells, sensations or events in the world around us, we experience the same feelings as if the event is happening in the here-and-now (Centonze et al, 2005) in a way that does not always feel like remembering. The benefit of this system is that you can respond to perceived threats quickly and without having to scroll through your autobiographical memory; a process that would be inefficient and would likely get you eaten if presented with a tiger. The problems start when the memory gets stuck and is retriggered over and over in situations that are not actually risky. By bringing the memory to mind while engaging in bilateral stimulation, the brain appears to be able to reintegrate it into the wider network and can 'reprocess' it (Haze et al, 2017) in a way that is difficult to achieve outside of these conditions. Something about that movement helps us to move a memory from 'suspended animation' to its rightful place in the neural networks that form general memory. This seems to deactivate its emotional potency and allows the event to feel more balanced by events that happened before and after it.

So, what has this got to do with creativity? It appears that there is something about bilateral stimulation that allows our minds to heal themselves, to put things in their 'right' order and to make links and connections between things that were not initially obvious. Let me give you an example. As a relational therapist with an aversion to manuals, I entered my EMDR training with a high level of scepticism and a mind that was not as open as I would like to believe – I'm ashamed to admit I used the word 'voodoo' on more than one occasion in the run up to attending. During the training, we had to use real-life examples as we practised the techniques on each other. I chose a relatively innocuous but vivid memory that occurred in the early days of learning to snowboard, a skill I acquired well into adulthood, and which did not come naturally to me. At the outset of the exercise, the memory was like a snapshot, an apocalyptic postcard consisting of a bleak, sunless morning and the 'tunnel-vision' perspective of a slope covered in ice the size and shape of bowling balls. I rounded the corner from the ski lift to be greeted by this sight, in the full knowledge that the lift was one-way, and the only way down was through. The moment remained frozen in my mind, accompanied by a sort of horrifying, paralysing clarity that this was going to really hurt. My board made a rasping, scratching sound as it moved over the ice, and I fell and fell until both sides of my legs and hips were covered in saddle-bag size bruises. It was brutal and miserable and inescapable. Somehow, I persevered over the coming days and eventually could get down a mountain in a vaguely passable way; however, every time I hit ice and heard that tell-tale rasping noise my body would tense up and I would lose my balance and fall.

When I recalled that image in training, it was as static as ever and brought with it the emotions as vivid and clear as I had experienced them at the time. However, as my partner waved her finger in front of my eyes, the image began to expand and widen to include the view across the valley and down to the village below. I began to remember who I was with, and what they were doing and could recall the sight of the lift rising next to me and the restaurant at the bottom of the slope, which I eventually staggered into when I finally reached the bottom. As we continued, I remembered the dinner we had later that evening, the people I met and the very memorable – but, until then, forgotten – conversation we had. Eventually, my mind threw up another memory of the next day, a crisp and sunny morning that dawned to reveal fresh (soft!) powdery snow which forced the party I was with to remain on easier, more forgiving slopes. It was the day that I really understood why being up a mountain can be magical, and every time I fell, I was delivered into an armchair of soft, powdery white.

My brain had instinctively known how to place this memory in context and when given the opportunity had connected it with other experiences that balanced the negative. Most importantly, several months later when I was back up a mountain and hit ice with my board, my body did not respond by stiffening, but by loosening to absorb the impact and I was able to keep my balance and enjoy the moment. By integrating the memory, I had deactivated its ability to provoke a threat response and was able to hold it in a sequence of other good and bad experiences. What also struck me was how other, seemingly unrelated concepts, thoughts and experiences had sprung up in relation to this 'touchstone' memory. Associations were formed in a way that I don't think I would have been able to consciously emulate.

If bilateral stimulation allows us to make associations and connect previously disconnected material, perhaps it may serve as a usual tool for creative thinking and inspiration. So far, the implications of bilateral stimulation for creativity have not been studied and the technique is only used in a therapeutic context. There is, however, research exploring the impact of brain stimulation using Transcranial Direct Current Stimulation (tDCS) (Nasseri *et al*, 2015) which clearly demonstrates that the old assertion that only one hemisphere of the brain is involved in creativity is false. In fact, creativity arises from activity in both halves of the brain and requires an interplay between the two (Zmigrod *et al*, 2015). Bilateral stimulation appears to allow our brains to process information in ways that we don't yet fully understand, and this might have important implications for creativity. Cultivating this state may give our brains a chance to process unimpeded and associate freely, which may then give rise to moments of insight, inspiration and clarity.

In therapy, we artificially create bilateral stimulation by either moving our finger from side to side while the person follows with their eyes, or by placing alternating buzzers in the hands or on the wrists. However, we encounter less deliberate forms of bilateral stimulation every day when we do activities like walking and running and there is now an encouraging branch of research exploring whether doing therapy while walking increases the effects. The important thing is to let our minds wander freely as we engage in these activities. One of the very best practices you can cultivate in the pursuit of inspiration is to take a daily walk without company, and without distraction, for at least 30 minutes. This means leaving headphones at home and allowing the sounds and sights to wash over you, while your body moves and your brain processes. I believe it is no coincidence that EMDR was conceived during a walk through a park.

Novelty and originality

One of the greatest ways to promote inspiration is to expose ourselves to new and novel situations that provoke us to think outside of our usual frames of reference. Simonton (2021) writes, 'creativity is enhanced when people are jarred out of normal, everyday thinking' and are given the opportunity to view things from more than one perspective. He refers to these as 'diversifying experiences', which are 'experiences that help weaken the constraints imposed by conventional socialisation' (Simonton, 2000). By deliberately putting ourselves into the world in a way that creates new experiences, we are increasing the material that we can refer to in our creative work but are also loosening and challenging the way we view things. Without even meaning to, we can become fixed in our perspective and find ourselves entrenched in a way of seeing the world around us that becomes second nature, to the extent we don't even notice it. I am so comfortable and accustomed to the idea of a 'chair' as something with legs, a seat and a back, that I do not have to consciously decode what is in front of me before sitting down. Of course, this sort of mental shortcut is essential in allowing us to function in a vaguely efficient way, but it can also limit possibilities and stop us from truly 'seeing'. If I come across a chair that challenges my assumptions, perhaps by playing with material, or proportion, then I am forced to stop and suddenly think consciously about what is before me. This is the sort of opportunity we want to engineer – the chance to be forced to see in a mindful, clear way that steps outside of the usual mental gymnastics that we routinely do.

To really get the most from being in an unusual or unfamiliar situation, we also need to purposefully set out to be open to the experience and engage with uncertainty and unfamiliarity. Openness to experience is consistently identified as one of the greatest personality variables associated with creative expression and performance, and this stands to reason. If we expose ourselves to a wider range of experiences, sights and sounds, we have more material to draw from and are increasingly able to make connections that move past the obvious. If you allow yourself to adopt a curious, open attitude to what you encounter, then you are more likely to apply that thinking when you stumble across new ideas and insights in your work, and are more likely to then follow up on these leads. This pushes you further towards a creative life that sustains itself and is rich and full.

Both openness to experience and divergent thinking are really concepts that point to a general way of being and perspective on living. They point to a thinking style that expands rather than pins down, and which allows possibilities to remain open. Within this are related concepts like being able to take risks and tolerate failure, being able to sit with uncertainty and being able to take joy and value from the process of making art, not just from the product. With regard to inspiration, it means suspending your internal critic and sceptic and allowing yourself to act on the impulse of inspiration as it arises. Sure, not every idea will lead you to create a career-defining work of art, but it might, and you won't know if you don't try. If you shoot inspiration down for being illogical, improbable or imperfect, then you shut down possibility and raise the bar of creativity so high that only a fully formed, credible idea can get past. But this is not how ideas work, they mostly come to us half-formed, imbued with a sense of something hinted at, and require a leap of faith to see where they might take you. If this is not your usual perspective, then there are ways of developing a more open, 'loose' outlook that allows insight and inspiration to flow past your 'quality control' default.

When I was researching for this book, I had the pleasure of spending time with practicing artists in a bid to understand what had got them to a place where they could create radical, original art. One of my favourite encounters was with Lucy Livingstone (http://lucylivingstone.com), who accepted my invitation to lunch completely out of the blue after I stumbled on her work and was amazed by its power and intensity. It turns out that this tendency to say 'yes' to seemingly random opportunities is at the centre of her journey as an artist. Over coffee, she shared countless times that she had thrown up her arms and answered 'yes' to whatever the universe presented to her, and how these invitations had inevitably led to opportunities to make unique, incredible work. The remarkable synchronicity in her experiences spoke to a spiritual dimension in her artist's journey, which many of the artists I encountered also referred to. They shared the sense that, if you allow yourself to be open to experience and do not judge what you encounter as either positive or negative, but just allow it to be what it is, then you are able to navigate life in a way that makes all experience grist for the creative mill. Lucy shared times that she experienced incidents that could have knocked her confidence or curbed her capacity to say 'yes', however she was able to integrate this into a coherent sense of the world as both 'good' and 'bad', and continue to remain open to whatever was presented to her. When I asked her how, she talked about the importance of allowing yourself to dwell in the possibility of uncertainty, not to expect that things will be neat and pinned down, but to expect the rough with the smooth, the synchronistic with the effortful. When I met her, Lucy was just relocating to the wilds of Scotland and remained curious and open to whatever experiences awaited her, certain that whatever she encountered could be used to inform her work. She talked about it in terms of allowing yourself to 'freefall', being open to the world and to experience.

If you are a person that is prone to anxiety, or that prefers certainty and a plan, then allowing yourself to surrender to the whim of circumstance may not be your natural comfort zone. I am not suggesting that you undertake a PhD in Arizona like Lucy, or relocate to the Highlands of Scotland, but I am suggesting that saying 'yes' more often to opportunities when they present themselves may open doors that you didn't know were there, and this may have a knock-on effect on your creativity. Studies of luck consistently show that what differentiates a person that considers themselves lucky from a person that believes themselves to be unlucky, is the tendency to say 'yes' and be open to possibility. We will explore this further in Chapter Seven.

When developing your ability to be open to experience, a good place to start is to mindfully place yourself in novel situations and be sensitised to what is going on around you and your reaction to it. Take yourself somewhere that is different to your usual haunts and spend some time just wandering around. Perhaps visit a neighbourhood that you have never been to, or a completely different city that was built in a different time period to your own. If you prefer to be in nature, take yourself to an unfamiliar landscape and allow yourself to get (safely) lost. What is it like to walk without a plan or an itinerary? Does it feel comfortable or threatening? What is your eye drawn to, and how does that differ to the usual sights and sounds that surround you?

One of the most interesting experiences I have had recently was allowing myself to get lost in my own neighbourhood, to channel my inner 'flaneur', and just wander wherever the whim took me. I took my camera and photographed what I found as if I was a tourist who had never seen the sights and sounds of the area before. What I 'saw' was completely different to anything I had consciously noticed before, despite living in the area for several years. Lucy also described allowing herself to become lost in familiar environments in order to cultivate the art of 'radical seeing', allowing yourself to look at the world with fresh eyes and to notice when you make assumptions about what it is you think you are seeing.

However you choose to experiment with the unfamiliar, the key is to remain mindful of your physical response to what you encounter; the emotions that arise and the thoughts that float into your mind. Being curious about these in a non-judgemental manner encourages associations to form and ideas and insights to present themselves.

Allowing yourself to play

When you watch children create, they do so in a playful manner where rules are suspended, and it is perfectly fine if the sun is green and a person has three arms. There is a lack of self-consciousness in the creative endeavours of very young children, as if it hasn't occurred to them that there is a right and wrong way to create; a concept that is most often introduced by the adults around them who accidentally fall into the role of novice art critic. How often do we praise young children or offer 'helpful' pointers such as, 'People only have two arms', rather than getting curious and asking the child to expand on what they have created. How often do we say, 'That's a *great* picture', rather than, 'Tell me about your picture!' This observation is not intended to shame, as offering praise is a natural response to being shown something, particularly by a child. The unintended consequence of this, however, is to introduce the idea that some ideas and forms of expression are worthy of praise, and by extension, some are not. The impact of this is to slowly reduce the child's willingness and capacity to suspend the rules and to create freely. As we explored in Chapter Three, children go through a series of brain developments meant to support their maturation into adults that can exist in social groups. This move toward social coherence, coupled with the initiation into the 'rules' of creating, means that by age nine or ten, most children have become significantly less playful and less willing to take risks in their creative endeavours.

One of the profound ways that we can increase our chances of being inspired while making work, is to regain and reclaim the sort of playfulness that came easily in early childhood. Allowing yourself time to experiment with new materials without an expectation about the outcome, or allocating a session in the studio to trying something new without the pressure to produce anything, creates an atmosphere of playfulness and experimentation. This atmosphere is light, frivolous and fun, and may even remind you of when you very first encountered whatever creative practice you have now. Maybe painting without any expectation to produce 'good' work will remind you of how it felt to put on an apron at primary school and use the large paint brushes and primary-coloured paint to make bold, uninhibited marks. Maybe 'playing' with clay will remind you of sitting at the kitchen table with playdough or plasticine and combining the colours over and over until you produced the inevitable brown. Being open to experience means being open to success and 'failure', and being open to valuing the process as much as the outcome.

One of the great gifts of allocating yourself 30 minutes of creative time every day, and of keeping whatever you produce private, is that is opens up a space for experimentation and play. We are less likely to be performative if there is no one to perform to, we are more likely to enjoy and value the process if the outcome will not be evaluated. If you have not yet allowed yourself to truly play during your daily creative time, then I urge you to purposefully cultivate an attitude of playfulness over the next few days. Put on upbeat music that makes you want to dance, choose mediums that are messy, imprecise, and even silly. Use bright colours, bold strokes, take nonsense photos, write nonsense words. Break out of what you believe creativity ought to be and allow it to be what it is. Make a mess, make a leap, make a 'mistake'. If you notice your inner critic surfacing to offer well-meaning opinions, then thank them warmly for their input but remind them that you are safe and you have no need for their protection right now. You are just playing. If you notice judgements coming up about the use of the time, or the space you are taking up, then again thank your mind for being so conscientious but warmly inform it that you don't need to account for this time. It is yours to do with whatever you choose. Move your body playfully, dance while you work, or sing loudly and badly. If you are still holding out on a medium that you have always wanted to use, then now is the time. Treat yourself to a roll of film, or a set of oil paints, or a slab of air-dry clay. Allow yourself the bright, glittery pens or the joyful, pastel paper that you would normally bypass. One of the most endearing things about the art that my four-year-old is currently producing is the addition of 'googly eyes' to absolutely everything. Trees, flowers, people, houses – all resplendently buzz-eyed. If you notice that you are taking your work too seriously, stick a pair of googly eyes on it and see where that takes you.

Exercise 25: The daily walk

In order to harness the power of bilateral stimulation, novelty and play, allocate yourself time to take a walk in an unfamiliar location every day for at least 30 minutes over the coming week. You can take routes around your home that you have not taken before or can travel to unexplored parts of your city, visit a new park or garden, or take a train or bus for a few stops and then just get off and walk. If the urge takes you to run, or to climb, then do so. If you feel led to change direction, then listen to the hunch and change direction. Practise sensitising yourself to the inner voice that pipes up with what you want and need. If time is tight, then taking a walk during your lunch break will do just fine. Take a meander around the hospital, office block or shopping centre that you work in. If you always turn left at a junction, then turn right and see what happens (I apologise in advance to anyone ending up in a stock cupboard).

Wherever you choose to walk, the important thing is that you walk with no distractions (preferably including headphones) and that you walk alone. This is time to just look and allow the rhythm of walking to throw up whatever thoughts and memories are there. Our senses are connected directly to our memories, therefore letting yourself listen, see, smell and feel the world around you will increase your exposure to insight and inspiration.

Make a note of what you saw and experienced and your reaction while walking. At the end of the week, review the process and what you have written. Was it easy to allocate the time, or did you find it a challenge? Did you find yourself looking forward to your walks, or did you find yourself having to overcome reluctance? Why? What supported your commitment to walking and what challenged it?

The importance of collaborations

One of the other ways that we can increase our cognitive flexibility and creativity is to spend time with other creative individuals and their work. Research shows that being exposed to the ideas of other people has a significant impact on the originality and creativity of our own ideas (Fink *et al*, 2012). It appears that being around other creative people stimulates the parts of our brain that are involved in creating and has a demonstrable impact on our work. It is not only our output that benefits, consciously creating a community of artists creates an environment for encouragement, helpful critique and support, and can help buffer you against both success and failure.

Collaborating on a piece of work with someone who uses a different discipline to you also opens up the possibility for work that steps outside both of your usual frames of reference. For example, I went for a cycle with my photographer friend and we stopped on a bridge overlooking an amazing river that swirled and danced in every direction as it flowed over the uneven riverbed. The light through the trees cast shadows that joined the dance, and an overflow pipe added the percussion. Of course, my friend took photographs while I listened to the musical sounds that the whole ensemble created; we were viewing the same phenomena but from very different perspectives. I wondered to him what would happen if he filmed rather than photographed the scene so as to catch something of the movement and music, which he obligingly did. The resulting film is like a piece of curated performance art, with each part adding to the mesmerising quality of the work. Had either of us encountered this alone, we would have brought only our own insights and perspectives to bear, but somewhere in the dialogue something new and interesting was born. This is a small example, but it highlights what can happen when we meet and communicate about art. If there is little opportunity for this in your life, then I would urge you to go looking for your tribe. Start a writing group, an art critique or ideas-sharing group, or even just spend time in the cafes that are connected to studios, visit galleries and exhibitions, and get talking to the people you find there.

Expose yourself to art

The act of collaborating is fantastic for taking and developing an idea and adding in different perspectives, however there is also something to be said for just plain exposing yourself to the work of others. You do not have to limit yourself to the discipline that you use, creative work of any variety will spark inspiration as you relate to the art and to the artists. One of my favourite things to do is to take myself to an art gallery for an hour and just listen to the dialogue that it sparks in my head. I enjoy noticing what I find myself nodding appreciatively at, and what sets me arguing silently inside my mind. Some work is inspirational simply because of the power with which you disagree with it, the key is to ensure that you don't simply stop with disagreeing, but you make the counter-work in response. If you hate a piece of writing because the perspective of the writer irks you, then write from your perspective in reply. If you don't like the glaze application on a pot because it feels like it ruins the form, then make the pot that you see in your mind's eye, glaze and all. If you dislike a painting because you find the scale of it stingy and just wish the artist had made it much, much bigger, then get out your paints and create something the size that you want to see. They always say that impersonation is the greatest form of flattery, and it's true that inspiration can come in the form of things you like, but it can also arise in response to what you *don't* like.

There is also something here about the role of purposefully exposing yourself to new and unfamiliar things to broaden what resources you have to draw from and to increase your capacity for 'divergent thinking'. If there is a gallery or exhibit that normally would not attract your attention, then make a point of visiting. If you generally avoid film or live music or the ballet as it is 'not your thing', then get tickets and go as an experiment in being open to experience. If you hate it, then you have confirmed what you at first believed, but be curious as to why and wonder what that tells you about your own work. If you find that you come away with an inspiration for work, then follow up on the moment by making a rough draft of whatever you felt moved to make as soon as you are able.

You do not have to visit a gallery or a formal art space to expose yourself to creative works; one of my favourite things to do is visit the 'antiques quarter' in my city and to just walk around, exploring and examining what I find. Sometimes it is ceramics that takes me, but other times it is exquisite bits of furniture or curiosities that could easily be repurposed. I have a love for objects that exist only because the maker was inspired to make it; I have recently fallen in love with a ceramic wall lamp in the shape of a moose wearing a smoking jacket/dressing gown and slippers. I found myself going back time and time again to examine another detail on this lamp, the brocade cord around his waist, the quilting on his trousers and the folds of the collar around his neck. For me, the care and thought that went into that creation, just because the artist was moved to make it just so, summarises what I find magical and inspirational about human creativity.

Acting on inspiration

Many people tell me about times that they have felt inspired by a piece of music that came floating out of nowhere in the shower, or an unexpected idea for a novel or a painting that came out of the blue when on the train to work. When I ask how they plan to act on it they look at me as if I am mad. It is so very rare that I hear accounts of inspiration taken seriously and ideas explored for all they might be worth. Instead, the next sentence is usually something self-deprecating that rubbishes the artist and the art. Over time, I have come to understand this as a sort of reaction to the perceived risk of investing in something that may appear whimsical, playful, or not 'dead certain' in terms of success.

When we talk about allowing inspiration and insight to guide our work, and taking risks in the creative process, what risks are we talking about? We know on some level that taking ourselves and our art seriously involves a level of risk, but does that risk have a tangible shape and form? Do you even know what you are afraid of when it comes to creativity? One way of digging deep into our fears is to ask yourself the 'and then' question over and over until you reach the nugget of anxiety that is wreaking havoc. Start with the moment that an idea occurred to you, and just keep asking 'and then' until you instinctively feel you have arrived at something. It will likely go a little like this.

> I had a great idea for a play that I think my drama group would perform brilliantly. I would love to offer the idea, but I'm worried they would think it was silly.
>
> *And then?*
>
> Well then, I would feel embarrassed and a bit like a fool.
>
> *And then?*
>
> Well, then I wouldn't feel able to show my face at rehearsals anymore.
>
> *And then?*
>
> Most of my friends go to the same drama group, so if I stopped going, I would lose a lot of important friendships and would be lonely.

And then?

I hate feeling lonely, I think it would drive me mad!

And then?

I worry that I wouldn't function, that I'd slowly get more depressed and if I had lost all my friends and no one would know I wasn't coping.

And then?

I guess life would be really miserable and there would be no one to help me. I'd be pretty hopeless.

And then?

If I was alone, not functioning, and hopeless… well, I think I'd want to die!

And then?

Wanting to die scares me. I don't think I'd ever be brave enough to kill myself, but I worry that I'd get sick or something, that I'd give up hope and just die.

When you make the jump straight from sharing an idea for a play to losing the will to live and ultimately dying from hopelessness, it feels very extreme. However, if you break any fear down into the steps by asking 'and then', you often find a series of assumptions that start fairly innocuously and end with a dreadful situation involving a lonely death, social ostracisation or something equally awful. Of course, you could challenge any point in that series of steps, but how often do we really step back and ask ourselves honestly what we are afraid of? Fear of failure, loss, destitution, death and annihilation can quietly derail our creativity without any sense-checking unless we are able to identify what lies at the heart of our hesitation and inaction.

Exercise 26: And then…?

Take a pen and paper. Begin by asking yourself what you would love to do if there were no consequences or barriers. If time, money, reputation or skill level were not considerations. Nothing to stop or limit you. Then ask yourself, if you allowed yourself to do this right now, what would happen? And keep asking 'and then' until you reach a point where you hit on an absolute; the sort of fear that seems total or irretrievable.

Now take a look at what you have written. How does it feel to look at your fear written down. Does it seem threatening, benign, plausible, ridiculous or terrifying? (This is a genuine question, sometimes what we unearth is very frightening, and makes great sense of why we are avoiding something.) How big is the leap between what you desire and what you are afraid of? Are there steps in the way that could be altered to prevent the outcome that you are trying to avoid, for example in the scenario above, the person could find ways to support themselves through feeling 'embarrassed and a bit like a fool' in a way that did not consist of not attending the group anymore.

Intuition and 'gut instinct'

If I could teach people one thing with the aim of improving mental health and decreasing suffering, it would be how to listen to their intuition and act on it without second-guessing themselves, talking themselves down or introducing the benefit of the doubt. So many of the stories I hear in the therapy room begin with a scenario where a person has a sense that something isn't right but ignores themselves because we have been conditioned to place being 'nice' and 'polite' and doing what is socially expected over being happy and safe and well. So often, people have a very clear sense of what is the right choice for them, but do not act for fear that it will cause a fuss, offend or rock the boat. The number of relationships that last far beyond the point that they become unhealthy because neither party is willing to act on the niggling feeling 'this isn't okay'. The number of times people tell me about staying in a situation when every fibre of their being is screaming at them to get out. Our gut instinct, or intuition if you prefer, is often relegated to the same pile as superstition, a sort of second rate, illogical voice that is best ignored. It is completely the opposite. Our intuition is a by-product of our brains constantly scanning the environment for threats and for anomalies – anything that does not match our typical schema for how things should be. If you get a sense that a person or a situation is off somehow, this is likely based on your mind picking up tiny cues in the environment that do not compute, thus triggering a feeling of unease. Likewise, if you come across a studio that you've never visited before and just get the sense 'this is somewhere I could work!', then it is the same system at work.

When I was younger, I vividly remember watching an interview with a firefighter on television. He had been leading a routine response to a fire at an industrial building when he had the powerful, intuitive feeling that something was wrong and he should evacuate his colleagues. He acted on this instinct and made the somewhat unusual call to pull back despite everything seemingly going to plan. Moments after the last person withdrew from the building, it unexpectedly collapsed. Researchers analysed the footage from the fire and noted an unusual pattern in how the smoke was curling, which indicated the presence of unusual combustibles. This gave a cue to the seasoned firefighter that something was amiss, something was deviating from the normal pattern that he recognised from many years of fighting fires. That knowledge was not transmitted consciously, it was only after the footage was analysed that this information came to light, but his subconscious mind was able to notice and respond by generating unease. I was unable to find the original source for this story, but in looking for it I stumbled across scores of similar stories of times when firefighters did, or did not, act on instinct. In a study of these phenomena completed in 2021, researchers found that expert firefighters do indeed complete a subconscious scan of the environment, a kind of pattern recognition exercise to look for anomalies (Okoli *et al*, 2020). The more experienced a firefighter, the more sensitised they became to the patterns and any deviation from the usual sequence of events.

These phenomena are not specific to firefighters but occur in all walks of life. A driver in the Monaco grand prix in the 1960s instinctively knew that there was a crash around the corner and slowed down, unaware of any conscious cues but compelled to act by an overwhelming sense that something was amiss. There was in fact a crash, and what had alerted him was that the spectators were all looking the wrong way as he headed down the straight; a fact that was not perceived by his conscious mind but was all-too-evident to the part of him alert to patterns. As creative people, we too become sensitised to patterns and develop an intuition or gut instinct about what might work, what might be possible, what might happen if we try this or that. If we are able to listen carefully and respond, we can take advantage of the brain's incredible ability to attune to the world around us and to provide us with cues, even if we are not consciously aware of what we are responding to. Developing the 'artist's eye' for the perfect moment to take a photograph, or an ear for the exact right note to follow a sequence, or an instinct that a story would make an excellent screenplay, are all examples of artistic intuition, a process of subconscious recognition that provides a world of information if only we are able to listen and act.

So why don't we all walk around listening to the voice of intuition and the 'gut instinct' that it gives rise to, particularly as this is a system that is designed to keep us safe? Like many things, we are socialised out of this from infancy, and it takes time and deliberate attention to rediscover the skill of listening to what we already know. It is very unusual to hear a parent attend to and support a child's gut instinct in a way that communicates its validity, in fact you often hear the complete opposite as a parent makes it very clear the child is being 'ridiculous' or 'unnecessary'. We are taught to value social cohesion over our own sense of reality and risk, and have to go back to retrieve and recalibrate our relationship with intuition. Unfortunately, this is a lesson that I have had to repeatedly learn as my tendency toward compassion can mean I opt for 'the benefit of the doubt' over snap judgements or can talk myself out of what I know to be the right decision in an attempt not to hurt others. However, every time I have ignored a gut instinct or felt sense, I have regretted not acting more than I would have regretted a moment of viewing myself as judgemental or uncompassionate. Our intuition is made up of more than mere speculation or superstition, it is the culmination of our experiences and the huge amounts of data that we have collated about the world around us. If you have the hunch that something might benefit your work, or an idea might have legs, then act on that hunch.

Creativity and spirituality

I have hesitated to explore the role of spirituality until this point, as it can so quickly alienate people that do not identify themselves as religious and find the idea of a 'higher power' difficult to work with. It would be impossible, however, to complete a book on creativity without giving some space to the question of spirituality, as what has been apparent from my meeting and talking with scores of artists in various guises, is that artists often talk about their work and the inspiration for it in spiritual terms. The specific form that takes varies from person to person – some describe feeling connected to nature in a way that speaks to their soul and channels directly into their work. Others talk about a creative force that manifests to them as either God, or the Universe, or a spirit who directs their work and lays inspiration in their path. Others refer to the 'collective unconscious' as a kind of shared mental space that we can all tap into and that connects us all regardless of time and physical location.

I hear account after account of moments of synchronicity where a person has decided, 'I'm going to take up painting', and has been invited to a class by a friend the very same day, or has declared, 'I used to love taking photos, I'm going to take up photography again', and has then been offered a used camera by a family member who is clearing out their house. I have had moments such as this on many occasions, both related to creativity and to the more domestic concerns of living. What is interesting is how each of us reacts to these moments, and how we integrate them into a sense of who we are and how the world is.

I was fortunate enough to walk the Camino de Santiago (a 500-mile pilgrimage across Spain) a few years ago and managed to somehow lose the plastic end from my walking pole about 200 miles in. I was making an irritating 'thud, clink, thud, clink' sound as I walked that was driving me and everyone within earshot to distraction. After several hours, I commented out loud to my friend Carina that I *really* needed an end to my pole, but the fact that we were currently up a mountain and at least 50 miles from the nearest town made it unlikely that I would be able to get one any time soon. As if I had issued a challenge to the universe, less than 200 yards further down the road, was the exact end for my pole on a rock, right on the path in front of me. I didn't even break stride as I slotted it into the opening and kept walking, enjoying the consistent 'thud, thud' as I went.

Different people would interpret this incident differently depending on their beliefs about spirituality, the world, themselves, and other people. There are of course well-evidenced psychological models that give a plausible explanation of how our interpretation shapes the meaning that is ascribed to such an event, and there is an invitation for me to lay them out for you here. However, perhaps surprisingly, when it comes to creativity, I do think that there is room for suspending logic and allowing such experience to form part of how we relate to the world around us. It appears to me like any encouragement in the course of living a creative life should be savoured and enjoyed as sustenance for the road. For me, I smiled warmly and deeply at the synchronicity and the little joke I now shared with the world, and continued on my way. However you view such experiences, the important element appears to be that you are open and willing to engage with them in a reciprocal 'yes', with whatever spiritual force you connect with.

The connection between God and creativity is a complex question of philosophy as well as psychology and has existed as long as both concepts have been in existence, which, depending on your theology, is always. In many religions, the initial act of creativity was performed by a deity, therefore any attempts by mortals to bring something into being must be understood as a spiritual exercise. The 'flow' state is often compared with a spiritual encounter in that it separates us from the often-pedestrian experience of being human and absorbs us for a time in something that feels bigger than the individual. The act of creating places us outside of time and can allow us to communicate things that are bigger than the sum of our parts and our capacity for language. Art can convey something in a moment that words might struggle to ever convey. The act of gazing upon a remarkable piece of art can be transformative to the extent that the work of one human can change the path of another centuries later. It is no wonder, then, that creativity takes on spiritual dimensions.

If you have a spiritual belief, then experiment with ways of integrating your spiritual and creative practices, for example ask for inspiration directly and see what comes to you, or make art, music, film or poetry to express your spirituality. If you do not conceive of yourself as spiritual, then identify what situations cultivate a sense of connectedness and being part of a larger whole. Perhaps this is perched in the middle of a busy shopping centre and peacefully observing the flow and chatter of the people as they move in a shoal around you. Or, in contrast, perhaps you feel most connected to the world when sitting alone in the middle of a forest and just listening to the noises of growth and life around you. It is not the 'truth' of spirituality that matters, it is the subjective experience of your place within the cosmos and the impact that has on your art. Existential topics such as the nature of life and death have always been the haunt of artists who seek to covey concepts that connect us all in our common humanity but defy being neatly pinned down by language. It is this ability that makes art in all its forms so powerful.

Conclusion

This chapter has focused on developing a relationship with inspiration that recognises its importance in the creative process and gives permission to place it high up your list of priorities as you move forward. Consciously creating time to expose yourself to art, to nature, to beauty, to each other, and all the ideas this generates, ensures that the 'well' of creativity is replenished and does not run dry.

If you find yourself struggling to make work, then one place to start is to deliberately put yourself in the path of inspiration. Down tools, walk out of wherever it is you are making and take an unknown direction down an unknown street and just drink in whatever you encounter. Let your mind wander freely, and be open to experiencing whatever comes to you, both in the world around you and from within. Protect and fight for the time to do nothing, the unstructured space into which ideas and insights can drop. Listen carefully for the voice of inspiration, whatever you call it and however you make sense of it, and respect it enough to act upon it without second-guessing, censoring, or getting caught up in the likelihood of its success. If you are able to cultivate this attitude of openness and willingness to experience, then you set yourself up for a creative life that is as long and stimulating as Glynis's. If you are really lucky, you may also be eating pizza well into your 90s.

References

Abel NJ & O'Brien JM (2010) EMDR treatment of comorbid PTSD and alcohol dependence: a case example. *Journal of EMDR Practice Research* **4** 50–59.

Beaty RE, Nausbaum EC & Silvia PJ (2014) Does insight problem solving predict real world creativity? *Psychology of Aesthetics, Creativity and the Arts* **8** 287-292.

Centonze D, Siracusane A, Calabresi P & Bernardi G (2005) *Removing pathogenic memories. Molecular Neurobiology* **32** 123–132.

Fink A, Koschutnig K, Benedek M, Reishofer G, Ischebeck A, Weiss EM & Ebner F (2012) Stimulating creativity via the exposure to other people's ideas. *Human Brain Mapping* **33** (11).

Gilbert P (2009) The Compassionate Mind. Hachette, UK.

Gilbert P (2014) The origins and nature of compassion focused therapy. *British Journal of Clinical Psychology* **53** (1) 6-41.

Hase M, Balmaceda UM, Hase A, Lehnung M, Tumani V, Huchzermeier C et al (2015) Eye movement desensitization and reprocessing (EMDR) therapy in the treatment of depression - a matched pairs study in an in-patient setting. *Brain and Behaviour* **5** (6).

Hase M, Balmaceda UM, Ostacoli L, Liebermann P & Hofmann A (2017) The AIP Model of EMDR Therapy and Pathogenic Memories. *Frontiers in Psychology* **8**.

Hoffmann J & Russ S (2012). Pretend play, creativity, and emotion regulation in children. *Psychology of Aesthetics, Creativity, and the Arts*, **6** (2), 175–184.

Kaufman SB (2016) Opening up openness to experience: a four factor model and relations to creative achievement in arts and sciences. *Journal of Creative Behaviours* **47** 233-255.

Nasseri P, Nitsche MA & Ekhtiari H (2015) A framework for categorising electrode montages in transcranial direct current stimulation. *Frontiers in Human Neuroscience* **9**.

Okoli J, Watt J & Weller G (2020) A naturalistic decision-making approach to managing non-routine fire incidents: evidence from expert firefighters. *Journal of Risk Research* **25** (2) 198-217.

Oleynick VC, Thrash TM, LeFew MC, Moldovan EG & Kieffaber PD (2014) The scientific study of inspiration in the creative process: challenges and opportunities. *Frontiers of Human Neuroscience* **25** (8).

Plucker JA, Beghetto RA & Dow G (2010) Why isn't creativity more important to educational psychologists? potential, pitfalls, and future directions in creativity research. *Educational Psychologist* **39** 83-96.

Shapiro F (2001) *Eye Movement Desensitization and Reprocessing - Basic Principles, Protocols, and Procedures*. New York, NY: Guilford.

Simonton DK (2000a) Creativity: cognitive, developmental, personal and social aspects. *American Psychologist* **55** 151-158.

Simonton DK (2021) Creativity In Society. In: Kaufman JC & Sternberg RJ (2021) *Creativity: An Introduction*. Cambridge University Press, Cambridge.

Zmigrod S, Colzato L & Hommel B (2015) Stimulating Creativity: Modulation of convergent and divergent thinking by Transcranial Direct Current Stimulation (tDCS). *Creativity Research Journal* **27** (4) 353-360.

Chapter Six: Action

Creative 'blocks' can happen at any point in the creative process; it may be difficult to generate an initial idea, a struggle to get going and actually put pen to paper or brush to canvas, or you may feel immobilised when the time comes to share your work and therefore keep it stashed in a garage, under a bed, or saved on a computer. This chapter is about the things that can impede the taking of *action*, that is, the practical act of making, writing, painting or sculpting. So many of the people that I work with tell me about ideas, plans and dreams for pieces of creative work, but experience some sort of block between these imagined works and the practical act of bringing them into existence. I hear all manner of highly plausible reasons for this, 'I don't have time', 'I don't have the money', 'work is just so demanding', but these reasons often point to an underlying issue that has not been explored, named and resolved.

I am currently sitting in a restaurant about five minutes down the road from my clinic. The space is large and has been intentionally made to look rustic in a way that inadvertently robs it of any genuine soul. Some perfectly ignorable music is playing at low level and people are sitting in groups talking, many of them on their lunch break. I have 45 minutes until I am due back for an afternoon of assessments, but have escaped to seize this brief window to write, typing with one hand while I eat pizza with the other.

Up until fairly recently, I had the fixed and immovable belief that I would finally write this book when I was in a position to take six months off from work to devote my time and attention to the task. I had fantasies of long days spent penning my thoughts, interspersed with introspective walks and bouts of reading related texts. It was during a long and animated conversation with an art teacher friend about the utility of psychology in the teaching and learning of creative arts, that it dawned on me that these magical six months were never going to present themselves. At no point on the horizon could I see the arrival of the sort of sun-drenched, peaceful and productive days I thought I needed to collect my thoughts. If this book was going to happen, it was going to happen now, in amongst parenting two children under four and juggling three jobs. In between trying to prevent us drowning under piles of washing or dog hair and remembering to feed the animals. This book comprises snatched moments before the children wake, tiny pockets of time freed up by a no-show at clinic or a last-minute cancellation, and nights when the children finally fell asleep, and I could type and drink wine by the light of my laptop. The reason I tell you this is not to induce pity, but to share the biggest and most profound insight that I have stumbled across when it comes to creativity; it can happen regardless of what else you are juggling, but only if you can suspend the belief about what needs to be in place before you start.

When we are really honest with ourselves, investing fully in our creativity by prioritising and putting our work forward, is a risky business. This book is a risky business. What if my editor hates it and tells the publisher that it should immediately be dropped? What if it sneaks past the publishers but is lambasted by artists, or other psychologists, or both? What if I am found to be a terrible writer, or, even worse, a terrible psychologist? One way of never really having to face these fears is to never actually write the book. I can avoid any sadness or regret that might be attached to that by convincing myself that the moment to write it is just around the corner.

Creating an idealised fantasy of the sort of circumstances in which we would be able to make work offers us a kind of 'get out of jail free' card if the work we produce outside of this magical situation is not as good as we would like or is not well received. If this book does not invite a positive reception, I can tell myself that it is because I am typing in a busy café and am not sitting at a dedicated desk on a writer's retreat. I can tell myself that I could have done *much* better had the context allowed. This is another nifty, cognitive defence to inoculate us from failure. However, like all psychological mechanisms, it can result in us failing to prioritise our work and never quite doing our best in case it is found wanting. In actual fact, it turns out I write much better with a constant supply of complex carbohydrates and coffee, so I have no excuse.

What is the difference between taking six months off to write unimpeded and the kind of cobbled-together process that has birthed this book? Well, the first and most obvious is that the latter allowed me to actually write something. If I had held out for the fantasied sabbatical, the book would have remained a collection of thoughts that I occasionally, and passionately, ranted about when presented with an interested audience. If I am truthful, the 'sabbatical' served two purposes: it provided me a perfectly valid reason not to write while also allowing me to hang on to the idea of the book as a real entity that I would undoubtedly get round to when the time was right. It allowed me to believe that the responsibility to make this book happen lay outside of myself, and to live in the fantasy that I would have several books completed if it wasn't for the (unavoidable) unfairness of life. By avoiding actually putting pen to paper, this project was essentially 'Schrodinger's book'; like the cat in the box, it was both alive and dead at the same time. When kept in the realm of the hypothetical, this book could be simultaneously an excellent read and a terrible failure, and I could consider myself a writer without ever having to fact-check that claim.

I see this phenomenon around me all of the time, which leads me to conclude that this is a facet of human nature that is not just related to creativity. When I worked in a community mental health team, I witnessed many patients sit on a waiting list to see me, sometimes for *years*, who would then fail to attend the appointment they were offered. Without exception, when I wrote to inform them that they had been discharged from psychology, they would telephone the service and implore to be placed back on the waiting list. By never actually meeting me, the possibility that I held the answer they were looking for was kept alive. If they had attended the appointment and engaged in the messy and uncertain dance of therapy, then they would have had to face the possibility I would disappoint, or fail, head on. Better to remain on the waiting list with the belief that help was just around the corner, than to risk failure and disappointment. Better to believe that whatever creative work that is incubating in your mind will happen *any day now*, than to risk starting and failing.

In actual fact, if I am found out to be both a terrible writer and a terrible psychologist, I hope that I have cultivated the ability through therapy and through experience to be kind to myself and to withstand the blast. I will be disappointed and sad that what I thought was an exciting topic is only exciting to me, and I will tell myself that it is fine to feel both of those things. I will spend time with my friends who like me and will cycle out into the countryside and reconnect with a world that is much bigger than me. I will allow myself time to grieve and then will get on with living and creating. I will *survive*. Most of the time, when we truly face down failure and disappointment, we realise that both are survivable if we are able to use self-compassion and take support. For me, therapy was a huge part in reaching this place, so I would urge you that, if the threat of exposure or failure is what stops you from creating, consider whether therapy might be the place to work through these fears.

We have all manner of inbuilt psychological mechanisms to protect us from social exposure and the shame of failure. If we do not allow ourselves to consciously explore these defences, then they can interrupt our creativity and block our ability to make art. There will always be competing demands vying for time and attention, the question is, why does creativity rank where it does and what is stopping you from changing your hierarchy of priorities?

One of the other tendencies that we need to be aware of is our propensity for 'black and white' thinking, operating only in 'all or nothing' terms. Either I am a full-time writer with no other commitments, or I write nothing at all. Either I am a full-time artist making a living from my work, or I am a failed artist and might as well give up. It can be hard to cultivate the sort of middle-ground thinking that is likely to lead to an increase in your creative productivity, but noticing times when you think in polarities is the first step. Watch out for absolutes in the way you think about a project, 'I need to dedicate at least six months to this', 'I can't create today, I only have an hour and won't get anything useful done', 'I haven't got any clear days over the next few weeks so there's no point beginning anything'. This sort of thinking will inevitably stall creativity and just isn't true. Great works of creativity can happen incrementally, bit by bit. An hour is more than enough to get started on a project, and the time in between bursts of productivity can be used to mull over what you have made and what your next step might be. The key is to just make, whenever you can, for as long as you can. If you find yourself hesitating, ask yourself what might be going on under the surface; are you worried that the work will not be good enough? That there might be a backlash to what you create? That other people will judge you, or that you might judge yourself? Focusing on these underlying concerns, rather than whatever clever reason your mind has presented as the reason for inaction, is likely to be far more effective in helping you push past blocks.

Exercise 27: Identifying fantasies

Is there a project that you hold in your mind with the belief that you will begin when the circumstances are right, or a development in your creativity that you tell yourself you will make when your environment allows? For example, have you told yourself that you will make the move from acrylic to oils when finances permit, or will make larger work when you have a studio, or will begin to use clay once a wheel is available? Will you make the film that you have been incubating in your mind only when you have a full year to dedicate to it?

Now ask yourself, if a miracle happened and the circumstances became just so, what would be different? Would you have more space, more time, more resources? Would you have a clearer mind to bring to the project, or would you be less tired? How would that impact your ability to make work?

Take a look at what you have written, are there ways that you can begin to build in what you need in smaller increments? For example, if a studio space is not available, could you clear a corner of your garage? If you need a clearer head, could you start a mindfulness practice, so you are more able to block out competing noise? If you need more time, are there ways that you can rearrange your daily commitments to create chunks of time for creativity? What would it be like to break down the project into smaller increments, for example writing just 300 words a day, or painting one layer of a painting at a time? If you need more resources, could you find creative ways to acquire what you need? Could you swap for something you do have, or offer a service or skill in return for supplies?

Understanding procrastination

In her book *The Right to Write*, Julia Cameron advises that you begin writing where you are and about what you know. Well, I know about procrastination. I naturally struggle with attention and often have to drag my mind back to a task several thousand times before it is completed. One of the ways I have learned to deal with my attention issues is to leave things so close to a deadline that the fear and anxiety regarding getting whatever it is finished overcomes my inattention and forces me to apply myself. For me, procrastination is a tool that I use to induce terror that then allows me to get stuff done. But there are unintended consequences to that; I make careless mistakes because I never have a chance to read things over properly, I rush most of my work so never feel like I have quite done my best, the anxiety of not completing is real and unpleasant, and I stress out the people around me with my panic and late nights. There are also times when this strategy just won't work, mainly when the sort of project I am working on cannot be completed in a short space of time, for example this book! As such, I have had to find ways to negotiate my relationship with procrastination, so I can move through it when I need to.

It is likely that you will have your own relationship with procrastination, too: perhaps it is a benign concept that doesn't feature heavily; or perhaps it is troublesome and serves a particular function; maybe it poses a significant barrier and therefore requires some thought. If you notice that every time you go to make work, you are distracted by something, or find something more pressing that needs your attention, then you might be procrastinating and putting off making work. There are often plausible reasons for procrastination, but what underlies it is a difficulty with moving into action and getting stuff done. This section will explore what experts say about procrastination and will then consider the implications for creative artists.

Exercise 28: Mapping your relationship with procrastination

Before we get into the topic of procrastination, take a moment to think about what this word means to you. Take a pen and write it in the middle of the page and then allow yourself to 'free associate', that is, let your mind generate anything that it deems related to the subject. Note down whatever comes up until you have encircled 'procrastination' with all the related words and concepts.

Take a look at what you have written. Is there anything that jumps out at you as particularly interesting? What are the 'hot' words on the page in front of you? What emotions are present as you hold the concept of procrastination in your mind? If you are unsure, bring the word to mind and check in with your body. Do you notice any changes? Does anything come into your awareness that wasn't there before?

When I did this exercise, I noted the word 'boring', which really surprised me. It turns out I find the delaying of work tedious, and time spent procrastinating boring; it is time that I kill while I wait for the panic to set in and spur me into action. Sometimes when we really drill down into an experience, our relationship with it is not as we might have imagined. The technique of just allowing whatever comes into our minds to arise without censorship can support us to uncover what might have previously been out of our awareness. You can use this technique to expand your awareness of any of the concepts we have explored in this book, you can even use it to make sense of a situation where you feel blocked or unable to create. Take a pen and paper and just allow yourself to write any words that feel relevant, without censoring or screening. When you are done, you can stand back and review what you have told yourself.

The concept of 'procrastination' has become increasingly recognised over recent years and has been absorbed into the mainstream vernacular, with 25% of adults identifying procrastination as a problem that impacts their functioning (Abassi & Alghamdi, 2015). But what are we talking about when we use this term? Jane Burka and Lenora Yuen are psychotherapists who have specialised in procrastination for the past 30 years and are the authors of *Procrastination: Why you do it, what to do about it now* (2008). Burka and Yuen conclude that their myriad experiences in the area 'have reinforced our idea that procrastination is not primarily a time management problem or a moral failing but a complex psychological issue' that is more related to the relationship with oneself, a 'shaky sense of self-esteem' and a 'problem of self-worth'. This is actually great news, as even complex psychological issues are amenable to change.

Possibly my favourite part of this book is where Burka and Yuen describe setting up a group for procrastinators, which they almost have to cancel due to initially low numbers, then have to book a larger room when the deadline for applications hit and they are flooded with participants. This is a wonderful example of the nature of procrastination and its relationship with boundaries and deadlines. The problem with creativity, however, is that there often are no deadlines. Sure, there may sometimes be a submission date or an exhibit that requires work to be produced in time, but for the most part creative artists are a self-governed bunch. This means that, in order to move into action, we need ways to understand and work with the tendency to procrastinate that does not rely on external limits and boundaries.

Factors that contribute to procrastination

Burka and Yuen put forward a host of factors that can result in procrastination, some of which may resonate powerfully with you, and some may not. These factors interconnect and become 'an interweaving' system comprising 'not only individual psychological, behavioural and emotional issues, but also social cultural and technological dynamics'. I invite you to be curious about how each of these apply to you, and what impact they have on your creativity, making notes about what areas may need some attention. If you hit on something that feels like a reoccurring pattern or common theme in your life, then interpret this as valuable information about what may be underpinning challenges to moving into the 'action' stage of creativity.

One potential mechanism underlying procrastination is the tendency to avoid confronting one's own limitations. By this I mean finding it hard to brush up against where our abilities end, or where the possibilities afforded to us by our environment end. If you have always secretly hoped that you had a talent for photography but have put off buying a camera by endlessly researching the technical specifications of equipment, then you may be using procrastination as a way of avoiding testing out whether you do indeed have a talent or just wish that you did. If you have always been told that you have a way with words but have delayed starting a writing project until right at the last minute, then you may be using procrastination to avoid ever getting an accurate gauge of your ability. If we never test the boundaries, then we can never be truly sure where they lie. If we never push ourselves to the edge of our own limits, then we never have to confront the reality that there is an end to what we are capable of. Procrastination therefore becomes a sort of artificial limit: it introduces an alternative hypothesis for why a piece of work might not live up to expectations and removes the need to ever test what we are capable of. The downside is that we can feel frustrated, uncertain, unfulfilled, thwarted, or anxious. If this is you, then ask yourself what does it mean for you to be unable to do something, or to meet a limit? What is your relationship with limits? What does the word mean to you?

The second potential root of procrastination involves the fear of failure. If you fear that you might fail at something or might not be able to meet your own or others' expectations, then procrastination becomes a way to avoid or delay the 'uncomfortable feelings' this elicits, such as disappointment, anxiety and shame. Imagine a child is given a task that they find challenging and expects to be publicly judged on the results; they may pre-empt humiliation and a knock to their social standing and might procrastinate and put off starting to delay the inevitable unpleasantness for as long as possible. This strategy also provides a plausible reason for poor performance; the feedback 'could do better' is far less crushing than 'tried their best and failed'. After a time, this can become a habitual way of responding to anything that is perceived as hard or that risks failure. If this is you, then ask yourself what does failure mean to you? How does it feel when you are unable to achieve something, or worry that you are unable? Bring the word 'failure' into your mind and float back to the earliest experiences that come into your awareness. How did other people react? What feelings do you remember? What did this or these experiences teach you?

This third factor that can contribute to procrastination, is the tendency to connect your self-worth with your ability and performance. Dr Richard Beery (1975), a colleague of Burka and Yuen, outlined how two assumptions underpin procrastination: 'what I produce is a direct reflection of how much ability I have' and 'my level of ability determines how worthwhile I am as a person'. If this is you, then somewhere down the line your worth as a person may have become directly related to your abilities and your performance.

This means that, when you set out to create something, the 'value' of what you produce becomes indicative of your whole value as a human; no wonder you become immobilised in the face of the pressure to perform. If this resonates for you, then complete the following sentences without overthinking or censoring. What words immediately spring to mind?

'If I make something that isn't perfect, that means I am…'

'If I am not good at something, then I am…'

Once again, we cannot ignore the role of culture and context on our emerging sense of self and the connection we are encouraged to make between our worth and our achievements. If you live in an individualistic, competitive culture that values output and product over person and process, then it is easy to start confusing the worth of your work with your worth as a person. If your performance is inextricably connected to your self-worth, then setting high standards can be a way of attempting to maintain a positive self-image; it is easy to find yourself becoming a 'perfectionist' that finds it hard to tolerate anything other than excellence. You may say to yourself, 'I need to get an A on this test', because that A reflects a sense of who you are in a way that renders a C or D a blow that is difficult to tolerate.

Educational experiences in childhood can reinforce the perception that self-worth is directly related to ability and performance. If we accept that education grew out of industrialisation, then this stands to reason, as value in a capitalist system is also based on output. Children are regularly assessed at school and are openly judged on their attainment from a staggeringly young age, in a way that can inadvertently place emphasis on what they *do,* rather than who they *are.* Even the most talented, sensitive teachers must operate in systems designed to please regulating bodies and to satisfy political agendas. As a result, children are openly praised and given rewards in the form of stickers, stars and certificates for achieving a high score in a test or for completing a piece of work that is deemed 'good'. This sort of reward is often accompanied by 'softer', interpersonal payoffs such as receiving fondness, appreciation, admiration and recognition. The unintentional consequence of this is that it subtly introduces the idea that there are also 'bad' pieces of work and scores that are not worthy of praise. This realisation can be the enemy of enterprise, innovation and creativity.

This leads neatly on to the next contributor to our relationship with procrastination and difficulties getting started with making work: our relationship with expectations, high standards and the tendency towards perfectionism. Children are subtly encouraged to adopt perfectionist standards for their work, which can be paralysing when it comes to the arts. Prizes are given for the 'best', and a big fuss is made of the 'winner'. When creativity is so subjective, how do you win at making art? How do you judge perfection? If it sells? But then lots of great works don't receive commercial success in an artist's lifetime. If it is received well? But then, art that is radical or before its time can sometimes provoke heavy criticism. Creative expression requires the sort of leaps of faith that most people's early experiences do not set them up to make. No wonder so many artists procrastinate.

I can vividly remember the first writing competition I was encouraged to enter when I was somewhere around the age of seven. It was a national letter-writing contest and we were given the remit that the text must 'persuade' the reader about something that mattered to us. I wrote an earnest and heartfelt account of the plight of calves being transported internationally for the meat industry. I have no idea how I was even aware of this at that age, but I can still remember the opening line: 'Imagine, you are a calf. You have just been torn from your mother…' It went on like this.

I overheard the teacher saying to my mother that she thought I had a chance of winning, as I was considered 'good' at writing at that age. I envisioned how it would feel to win the prize, and naively considered it a done deal as my teacher was obviously the authority on everything. I did not win and was given the same conciliatory prize as the rest of the class. I felt such shame at this, as I suspected I had disappointed my teacher and worried I might disappoint my mum when I told her. The consolation prize was four pamphlets containing folk tales from around the world. I still have them. The story that stood out to me was an Inuit tale about a giant girl who lived underwater, and has her fingers cut off by some jaunty-looking people in a boat. Her fingers sink down into the depth and become the fishes and creatures of the sea. I felt that my fingers had been chopped off, and I stopped writing. I concluded that I was not as 'good' as I had been told, and so gave up.

The reason I refer to this is that this competition, and many others like it, are designed to inspire writing in children. In actual fact, by prematurely introducing external motivators and imposed standards, we can inadvertently rob children of their innate, internal motivations. I wrote because I liked making up stories; I stopped because I was prematurely judged and concluded that not getting a prize must mean I wasn't very good. And I was embarrassed. My friend Mel once exclaimed, 'You can DIE of shame', and she isn't wrong – the part of my young self that was a writer did indeed die of shame. Luckily, I found ways in adulthood to resurrect her, otherwise this would be a very short book.

These early experiences of being judged good enough, or found wanting, inform what we learn to expect of ourselves and how we set standards for our performance in adulthood, both of which can result in procrastination. If you hold the belief that the first album you write and record has to sell thousands of copies to be deemed of worth, or the first book you write has to win a Pulitzer, then you will quickly feel pressured and overwhelmed and will likely procrastinate and delay getting started. Even setting unreasonable expectations for the rate at which you work can give rise to anxiety and stress, and ultimately lead to procrastination. Who can start a writing session that has to produce at least 4,000 words to be considered good enough?

If we can negotiate our expectations and bring them into a manageable place, for example, 'I will write 400 words today' rather than 'I will write 4,000', then we are far less likely to rely on procrastination as an avoidance technique and stand a much greater chance of actually getting started. Once you are in action, you may find that you get into the flow and end up writing far more than you expect; the important thing is that you do not set the bar so high that you cannot start at all. This is partly the rationale for the 30-minute daily creative practice – it allows a habit to form that is about small chunks of work, not about producing instant perfection.

Setting high expectations for yourself can also make it much harder to ask for support and to take advice and input from others on elements of a project that might not be our forte. For example, I know that my organisation is very poor, to the extent that if I didn't have help with booking clinic rooms then there is a high likelihood that I would have to see patients in the car park. I know this, so when I set out to write this book, I was very honest with myself and the people around me that I would probably need some help with estimating time and in organising space to write. My friend Matt is the most organised person, with a talent for breaking things down into sequences and systems for most things. Where he struggles more is in generating ideas and spontaneously planning. He regularly asked me how and where I was making space to write and helped me think through whether I was creating enough time. In return, I booked us on an alcohol ink painting class and suggested we sign up for a cross-country cycle. Owning our limitations means that we can draw on each other for support and offer balance, however this can mean having to face down very powerful and challenging feelings such as shame, disappointment and exposure and vulnerability at having to rely on each other.

People often express a fear in therapy that, if perfectionist standards are renegotiated, then the pendulum will swing the other way and they will become lazy and 'slap-dash'. They believe that without the harsh push of perfectionism, they will allow standards to slide and will have to face whatever the imagined consequences are for mediocrity. In my experience, when making a change, the pendulum may initially swing a little further than you are comfortable with, but this experience gives you a feel for where the middle ground is and soon resolves into something that feels more sustainable. If you notice times when you are setting the bar very high, then pause and wonder to yourself if this particular task needs to be done perfectly, or whether such high standards are likely to shut down creativity? Experiment with allowing yourself to adopt a playful, more relaxed attitude to activities that you do not have to excel at and see how it feels. If it is awful, your standards can be immediately reimposed. If it is liberating, then continue the experiments and see where it takes you. Ultimately though, if you can be compassionate to both your strengths and your challenges, then you are less likely to become overwhelmed in a way that invites procrastination as a coping mechanism.

It is worth saying that finding it difficult to get started on a project can also be an indicator that the task you are avoiding might not be for you. It can be helpful to ask yourself, 'Do I *want* to be creative, or do I feel like I *should* be creative?' 'Do I want to paint, or do I feel like I should as I've already bought the canvas?' 'Do I want to write, or do I feel like I should because other people keep telling me I have a talent and should use it?' 'Shoulds' can very quickly become truths that are not up for negotiation, declarations that dictate how things are. Often, if we look closer, the 'should' is sitting at odds with our true will and desire and is therefore giving rise to procrastination. Of course, there are some things that cannot be avoided: we have to file tax returns for example (a task I leave to the last minute every single year), but there are other activities that are absolutely non-essential. If you have a talent for writing but don't enjoy the process, then don't write. If you have bought a canvas but find yourself unmoved to paint, then thank the canvas for clarifying what you really want and give it to someone who will use it. It might be that your talents do not match up with your passions; you may be a talented painter but your heart loves to sculpt, or you may have an ability with words but really want to experiment with film. A talent in an area is not an edict that you must pursue that path to the end; it is fine to explore other forms of self-expression that are more gratifying, and you will likely find yourself much less prone to procrastination.

The other great obstacle that might be standing between you and getting started with creativity is the ready availability of distractions that engage our 'drive' system, namely the ability to scroll the internet and social media endlessly on phones, tablets and computers, and to check emails and messages wherever you are. These dopamine-heavy activities are a constant source of temptation that can eat time in a staggering, 'mindless' (by that I mean the opposite of 'mindful') way that can be addictive and almost impossible to ignore. If this resonates for you, then it is important that you carve out a space for creativity that is free from temptation, meaning free from anything that can be scrolled, clicked or checked. I don't have internet in my studio, which means that when I am writing my laptop is essentially a glorified typewriter. I know that if I take my phone in with me, I will use it to search for something related to what I am writing and will then become embroiled in a digital wormhole that eats at least an hour, so I leave it in the house. Being honest about your own temptations and taking steps to protect yourself from intrusion is essential in cultivating the sort of 'flow' state that gives rise to creativity, and that is so easily disrupted.

Managing procrastination

There are two ways I have found to address the impact of early experiences on your ability to move into action. The first is to engage your 'adult' self in reconsidering what you were taught about self-worth and performance and to disentangle them as two separate constructs. Your wise, adult self can recognise that you are *not your output*, you are a living, thinking, feeling human being that is valuable and deserving of compassion, support and care, regardless of whatever you are producing or achieving. One way of doing this is to communicate directly with your child-self, using therapeutic letter writing.

Exercise 29: A letter to my creative child

Take a pen and paper and address yourself as a child. You can choose what age you imagine yourself to be. Tell them all the things that you like about them, for example their playfulness, bravery, fun, humour, creativity, open mindedness or willingness to experiment. What creative skills does your child-self have that you appreciate, for example imagination, use of colour, ability to make up stories, or love of music? If you notice a critical voice starting up, thank it, but inform it that it is not needed for this exercise. This is for the compassionate, adult part of yourself to address.

If you recall being given unhelpful messages about your creativity, then address these directly and add a counter narrative, for example, 'Mrs Wilson said that you would never be a dancer in front of the whole class. I'm sorry she said that to you, it stung and made you feel ashamed of the way you move your body. I want you to know that you are allowed to dance and to enjoy the way that it makes you feel. You are allowed to move in response to music and express yourself physically however you want to.' Acknowledge any hurts that child sustained and validate the emotions that resulted from those hurts, for example, 'You were so proud of the card that you made for Dad's birthday and was so crushed when he barely even looked at it. You felt rejected, dismissed and hurt. It was painful to have something that you worked so hard on feel unappreciated.' Try to avoid rationalising, explaining, justifying or excusing, just name and allow the feelings to be.

How does it feel to speak to yourself in this way? What emotions come up when you think about yourself as a child? Do any of these feelings impact your creativity in the here-and-now, and, if so, how? For example, if you feel angry with your creative child, does that anger manifest in whether you allow yourself to play or force yourself to work in ways ➔

you find dull or pressuring? If you feel embarrassed, does that shame lead you to push away anything that reminds you of your child-self? If you experience powerful, negative feelings when completing this exercise, then pause and write the letter from the perspective of the 'compassionate figure' you identified in Chapter Two. Notice what feels the same and what feels different when you purposefully occupy this compassionate space.

Now tell your creative child what you wish for them in the future and how you will support them with this. For example, 'I want you to love making art again, and I am going to make sure that there is time for you to play and make a mess without worrying about getting into trouble', or 'I want you to be able to express yourself freely again and I am going to make sure I don't censor or shut you down when you want to communicate something'.

It is up to you what you do with this letter. Some people find it very therapeutic to complete some sort of ritual, such as creating a fire and releasing the letter into it or burying the letter with 'gifts' for your child-self. If you prefer, you can keep the letter somewhere safe to refer to. The important thing is that you find a way to mark the end of the exercise and do something that feels fitting with what you have written.

The second thing is to then reclaim your right to play, to experiment, to be *medium* and to learn. This may mean emphatically reassuring yourself every time you run into doubt about your worth as an artist or as a person, and remembering that most people do not begin by being 'outstanding' in their chosen creative art. Instead, they develop slowly by increments over time. Actively provide yourself with opportunities to engage in activities that you are not naturally gifted at but are fun: surf, dance, paint, draw, cycle, trampoline, ice skate... whatever you find thoroughly enjoyable without having to be 'outstanding'. Above all, remember that if you rob yourself of the right to progress and learn, then you can only ever engage in things that you are naturally fantastic at first time. For me, that limits my creative potential to drawing a horse or baking a Victoria sponge. Everything else has been a process of trial and error, progress and setbacks, two steps forward and one step back.

Burka and Yuen also suggest some helpful ways to respond to procrastination, some of which we have already explored in previous chapters. Cultivating a state of self-compassion can support you to tolerate the difficult feelings that may arise from embarking on creative work. If you lift your paintbrush and are caught by a stab of self-doubt, then acknowledging that feeling and offering reassurance to yourself can help you move through the resistance. Reach for a favourite, soft jumper, put on some uplifting music, make a warm drink, and then turn your attention back to work.

Mindfulness, too, can be a powerful tool in supporting your thoughts to remain in the present and not rush back into what you should have already achieved, or forward to the future and the imagined dreadful consequences that await you. I am currently typing in my office; I can see all the familiar things around me which include pottery made by dear friends, a plant I have managed to not inadvertently kill, and a watercolour of flowers I painted just because I like the colours and it reminds me of my garden. I can hear my partner making coffee downstairs, and, further in the distance, the sound of the first lawnmower of the year. I can also hear my cat, playing frantically with a plastic cup left on the floor by my daughter. Being aware of what is happening now, I am free to write exactly as the words come to me, without fear of the future or regret for the past.

If you have a tendency to become paralysed by unrelenting or unreasonable standards for performance, then try setting what Burka and Yuen call the 'minimum acceptable goal'. That goal might just be to do your 30 minutes of creative time each day. Or to write one verse of one song. Starting with a reasonable, achievable aim is far less intimidating and aversive, and far less likely to result in avoidance.

Procrastination and the risk of success

A fear of failure can be a big driver of procrastination, but so can the imagined consequences of success. What might happen if you try and succeed at whatever creative medium you apply yourself to? What might be the interpersonal implications, both with the people around you and society as a whole? What are the imagined consequences for your current way of life, your emotional world, and your relationship with your art? It is as important to consider your relationship with success as it is your relationship with failure when exploring any block to taking artistic action.

One of the big things that concerns people about becoming successful is that their personal relationships may suffer or even come to an end. For example, there are many examples of women who died just at the point that their talent was about to mature and reach its full power, perhaps even threatening to overshadow that of their lovers. Frida Kahlo died only months after her first solo exhibition, at a time when her beloved Diago Rivera's career was in decline. What were the imagined consequences of success for her, and her relationship with Rivera? Sylvia Plath died just as her writing began to reflect the 'bitter force' (*New York Times*) of her lived experience, at a time when her marriage to fellow poet Ted Hughes had just ended, also within the context of infidelity. What did it mean for her to write, full force, and to arise out of the ashes of that marriage an acclaimed writer? It could be argued that it was the distress that drove the emotional intensity and success, a sort of emotional 'boiling over' that is reflected in the work, and ultimately contributed to their deaths, but I also wonder about the psychological and relational consequences of being as 'big' as it is possible to be. What did Sylvia Plath imagine would happen if she was as successful as she was capable of being? Of course, there is no way of knowing what passed through the minds and hearts of these women, but we can acknowledge that success, as well as failure, has interpersonal consequences, and be curious about this impact of this in our own lives.

If you imagine that you reached the full height of your power in your creative work, and achieve whatever constitutes 'success' for you, how do you expect people in your life would react? How do you imagine that unfamiliar people would relate to you? Do you experience any discomfort regarding this? Is there anyone in your life who might be hurt, angered or uncomfortable if you 'grew' to your full creative size? This is a very challenging question, but both the women in the examples above had lovers whom they regarded as a sort of life force, without which life was unimaginably painful. Do you have such a figure in your life? A kind of 'well' from which life energy originates, or whose care you rely upon and without which you fear existence? If so, how do you imagine they would respond to you if you fully inhabited your creativity? What is the impact of that on your work?

Some people hold very firmly to the belief that, if they begin to make money from their art, or experience a level of commercial success, then their relationship to it will be compromised. There can be a fear that something profoundly enjoyable and essential will morph into something riddled with pressure and obligation if it becomes 'work'. This can give rise to ambivalence, with one part of you wanting your work to be acknowledged and one part fearing the price of recognition. Other similar anxieties can exist around losing control of your work, or success creating a precedent that must be maintained. These sorts of internal dilemmas can give rise to procrastination, as the internal parts battle it out and create a kind of inertia. It is important to find a way to settle such disputes to move forward, as dilemmas, if left unchecked, can result in an impasse.

One way to resolve internal conflict is to borrow a technique from Motivational Interviewing (Rollnick & Miller, 1991) and take time to argue each position earnestly and thoroughly. By listening carefully to the perspective of both parts, you can begin to get a sense of the merit of each argument and may find resolution. You get a sense of when you might be operating from past experiences, or fear of the future, and can weigh up how helpful that is in your current circumstances. You can identify which anxieties are out of proportion and may therefore be amenable to challenge, and which are unlikely to budge. Some people find it useful to embody the different parts by moving between two chairs, allowing yourself to totally inhabit whatever part is represented by the chair you are in. If you cannot easily reach a conclusion, then pick a decisive course of action with the internal acknowledgement that you will change direction if necessary. An old supervisor of mine used to say that it is easier to change direction when moving, as anyone that learned to drive before power steering will attest. If you decide to exhibit your work but quickly realise that you intensely dislike the exposure, then you can take a step back and reconsider other ways to distribute your art. If you receive critical acclaim and then are seized with terror that your second body of work will not live up to the first, well, then you can decide not to make a second body of work!

Managing competing demands

Unless you are a hermit with sufficient funds to preclude the need for work, then the chances are you will have demands that compete with your creative practice for time and resources (both physical and mental). Children, partners, relatives, pets, friends, colleagues, employers, even neighbours, may jostle to occupy space in your life, and while this can create a rich relational world, it can also compromise and even derail your creativity. If you reach the end of the day without the mental energy or physical time for your 30 minutes of creative practice, then the chances are that, in the competition of demands, you are losing out.

The difficulty with relational demands is that they are unlikely to spontaneously reduce to the point that we can devote time to creativity; we must proactively make changes to make this happen, and this is easier for some than others. I have an artist friend whose unequivocal approach to art I find inspiring. He is a father and partner, family member and friend, but when he is making work, he is focused, honest and boundaried. He will state clearly when he is not available and will hold these limits in all but the most exceptional circumstances. My friend is the exception. What I hear every day in clinic are chronic struggles with setting limits, disappointing others, prioritising needs, and, heaven forbid, saying no. These themes occur across gender, age, social class and cultural background, though some of these variables also carry with them additional societal expectations regarding care-giving and appearing helpful.

It is very easy to place the responsibility for carving out space for your creative work in the hands of others, and to feel resentful and hurt when this is not forthcoming. We might hint at a deadline, or the need for time alone in the studio, but stop short of declaring this an absolute necessity for fear of appearing demanding or unreasonable. Or we may finally find ourselves picking up a longed-for paintbrush or pen, only to be derailed by a ringing phone which we left on so as not to appear selfish or unavailable. You may never even reach the point of picking up the paintbrush or pen, as all your creative time is swept away in the dramas and emotional needs of others, which you feel at a loss to handle as you fear seeming uncaring or rejecting. One of the premises that therapy is based on is that we have the power to change ourselves, and this may or may not result in changes in the people around us but will certainly result in changes to the relational 'dance' we do with them. If you change the dance, it is nigh-on impossible for the people around you to continue unmoved.

One of the greatest fears I hear expressed in therapy is that, if a person follows their desires and pursues what they really want, they will inevitably neglect their children, cause lasting damage, and be judged a 'bad parent'. This can result in people prioritising the needs of their children to the extent that their creativity essentially hibernates for decades. This is a totally understandable perspective, and one that I can certainly be pulled into at times. However, if our children do not see us respecting and prioritising our own creativity, how will they ever learn to respect and prioritise their own? This has been said so many times that it has become something of a cliché, but there is enough truth in it that it bears repeating. Children learn by what they *see*, not by what they *hear*. You can tell them as many times as you like that creativity matters, but if they see you constantly devalue your own artistic life, then what they will learn is that art is disposable or falls way down the list of priorities. If you tell them that women are just as creative as men, but what they see is the men in their lives fulfilling their passions while the women occupy caring roles, then they will learn that creativity is a male pursuit. I would also hasten to add that even if there was no knock-on benefit to the children, you are still allowed to occupy space as a human when you are a parent. However, in this case I would argue that there is a discernible benefit to your offspring that will set them up for fulfilling creative lives of their own. People who neglect their passions for too long end up angry, or depressed, or constantly irritable, or asking for a divorce, or snapping at their children, or at the very least unhappy. Habitually putting aside your own needs for the needs of your family does not work as a long-term strategy; it is far better to negotiate space for your creativity and self-expression in a healthy way that promotes self-respect and self-care, than to find yourself having to blast out of your own life as you can no longer breathe.

Of course, children are not the only people towards whom we might occupy caring roles. You may have formed a few, or many, relationships based on your ability to meet needs and offer care; friends, lovers, relatives, people in your community. Or you may have a job that constantly places unreasonable demands on you, leaving little time for self-care and creative expression. How you respond to the needs of others is likely to stem right back to your early relationships and the patterns developed in childhood – it is no coincidence that so many psychologists and therapists are the eldest child. The question is whether, in the quest to meet the needs of others, you find yourself habitually side-lining your creative time to the extent that it is blocking your work. If the answer is yes, but you feel that you make clear choices and enjoy what this role offers you, then that is fine. If you find yourself repeating a pattern in relationships that no longer serves you, or is a source of frustration, then it might be time to re-examine the 'dance' you are doing with others and consider how to renegotiate the boundaries.

This is another area of creativity where it helps to think in terms of reciprocal roles, i.e., the roles that we tend to occupy in relationships with each other. As a reminder, the way I imagine these is like each holding an end on the rope: when one pulls, the other is pulled. How I act impacts you, how you act impacts me; if you are caring, then I am cared for, if I am patiently listening then you are patiently listened to. If we are invited into a role that is uncomfortable or unpleasant, for example if someone is being abusive or critical, then we might respond in a way that shifts the dynamic into another reciprocal role, for example by rejecting the person, or even by becoming abusive or critical ourselves. The key is not to castigate any way of being in relationships, but to remain flexible enough that we have options depending on the situation and can resist being pulled into roles that are damaging to us.

It is perfectly possible that you have a very healthy relationship with boundaries and can hold the tension between your need to be creative and the other competing demands in your life. Or perhaps the above scenario didn't quite fit, but you sense the themes in your life in a different way or with different people. Sometimes, meeting the needs of others is another form of procrastination that comes about for all the reasons documented above. If we are busy tending to the caring role, then we don't have to take our art seriously or test out our talents and abilities. We can tell ourselves that we *had* to give up our creative time to answer a work email, or call a friend in need, or listen to the woes of a neighbour. This sort of procrastination comes with the added benefit of apparent virtue, but it is just as malignant as all the others when it comes to your creative work. It is important to be honest with yourself about the risks and payoffs of these patterns in relationships, as unless we are clear about both the benefits and the unintended consequences, then change is unlikely. Look at your 'map' and ask yourself what are the benefits to this way of relating? Does it make you feel useful, self-sufficient, or even omnipotent? Does it feel connected to your values as a person, or does it sit at odds? Do you hold a fear in your mind about what would happen if you renegotiated this 'dance', for example that you would become selfish, or might lose all your friends?

Exercise 30: Mapping the dance revisited

Take a piece of paper and a pen. Imagine that you have allocated an afternoon to your creative work, and then you receive a message from a friend informing you that they have argued with their partner and are distressed. This friend often calls or messages when they are experiencing conflict in their relationship, which can happen several times a week. You care about this friend and value their friendship. What is your immediate response? What thoughts go through your mind? Do you feel yourself pulled into action, and if so, what is it you feel pulled to do? What is your initial emotional response? Do you feel dread, guilt, resignation, indifference, anger, concern, or something else entirely?

Thinking in terms of your relationship with your imagined friend, write down the worst possible reciprocal roles that could be enacted in this situation at the bottom of the page, for example 'abandoning-abandoned', or 'rejecting-rejected'. Perhaps the most feared place would be something like 'exacting-crushed', or 'neglecting-neglected'. Would you be in the 'top' or 'bottom' role? What feelings would be associated with this? Remember that we can also enact reciprocal roles with ourselves, for example being self-critical-criticised, or self-neglecting-neglected.

At the top of the page, write the thing that you would ideally like to play out in this scenario, for example caring-cared for, or valuing-valued. Again, would you be in the top role or the bottom role? Or might you be enacting the reciprocal role with yourself, for example being self-caring or valuing yourself? If it is hard to think reciprocally, then just write down whatever words come to your mind when you think about how you might feel in this scenario.

Are there any adjectives that might preface the roles you have identified, such as boundaried, good enough, sufficient, totally, distantly, immediately or authentically? For example, is care enough, or does it feel like you have to provide 'perfect' care? If you fear that care will be exacted from you, does that leave you feeling powerlessly crushed or angrily crushed? →

How are you likely to act to resolve this? Might you neglect your own needs to make your friend feel valued but then feel angry or resentful? Or are you likely to keep the time that you have allocated to be creative, but feel guilty and like you are being depriving or withholding? If that were to happen, does that feel okay?

How do you envision you would respond? Might you send a message of comfort but then return to your creative time? Do you immediately move to offer support to your friend, but feel controlled as if you have little choice? Or do you neglect your own work but then feel critical and judgemental of your friend for having contacted you at such a bad time? Write down any words, thoughts or dilemmas in the space between the 'feared' and 'longed for' place. Perhaps you would feel no particular pull and would feel happy to continue your work, confident in the knowledge that your friend can handle the situation?

There are no rights and wrongs in how you imagine responding to this hypothetical scenario, and certainty no rules about how to negotiate the situation. What we are interested in is what the dilemma brings up for you, how you feel pulled to respond (if at all), what this tells you about the patterns you experience in relationships and, ultimately, about how you negotiate your creativity.

Take a look at what you have written and note any words that are familiar, both in your current relationships and in those as a child. For example, if you have written 'neglecting-neglected' at the bottom of the page, what is your relationship with that role? How would it feel if you were experienced as neglecting, and how does this connect with your own experiences? What about the roles at the top of the page? Do you recognise these roles as things that were required from you in early life and you habitually give now, or are they roles you struggle to occupy without feeling angry or compromised? How do you respond to strong feelings in others? Are they tolerable or do you feel immediately moved to 'fix' and 'rescue' them? How does that fit with the roles you have historically occupied in relationships? Is there a part of you that reacts to the needs of others by distancing yourself, a part that resists feeling controlled or powerless?　➔

How do these words and concepts on your 'map' impact your creativity (if at all), and how much of the time? Are these patterns flexible and situation-dependent, or are there some that feel fixed and automatic? If the person in the scenario had been your partner, or a child, would that have altered your response? Over the next week, notice times when you are invited into any of the roles that you have identified and observe how you respond. Be curious about the times when you have an emotional response to this, and times when you don't. Are there certain people or scenarios that elicit these roles more than others? Why?

If you decide that you do want to make some changes and carve out more protected time to create, then there are several strategies that might be useful. If you struggle to hold boundaries, then put yourself in positions where you can actively work on developing this ability. Join a martial arts or self-defence class, or an amateur dramatics group where you get to experience different reciprocal roles to your own when in character. Find activities that build your confidence and sense of certainty about your own perspective, for example join a debating or improvised comedy group. If all else fails, this is another excellent theme to consider taking to therapy and is often a strong motivator for the patients who come to see me.

If you find yourself habitually responding in a way that you don't find useful anymore, then the key is to observe yourself carefully at first. Notice what situations invite you to respond in unhelpful ways and become aware of the factors that contribute to this sort of 'dance'. Once you are clear about how and when these roles are enacted in your life, then begin to gift yourself a 'pause' before you act to give yourself time to consider your options. In the example above, you might pause before you reply to the message in order to 'feel' out what your needs are and gauge how much resource you have or want to spend supporting your friend. The pause offers a sort of circuit breaker which ensures that, even if you choose to react in the same way you normally would, the response feels like a choice that is conscious and considered. There are other, practical ways of introducing circuit breakers, such as not having your phone on you when you give yourself time to create; that way you are not tempted by the relational dance of others. This creates a legitimate break between the invitation and your reaction and often a situation has resolved by the time you respond.

One of the most important things when seeking to negotiate and hold boundaries around creativity is to be really clear with yourself about what those boundaries are and be sure to articulate them to others. We are not always taught how to do this in an overt way and can therefore rely on methods such as hinting or inferring what we need, which may or may not be picked up but the people around us. This strategy can give rise to frustration when the boundaries are broken or needs go unmet. When you are about to embark on any piece of work, tell the people in your life what you need and be prepared to reiterate or hold the boundary if necessary. This might look like informing people you are not available between the hours of 13-16:00 and making sure that you are offline, and your phone is on silent during this time. If someone tries to invade this space, then reiterate your limit and if necessary, take steps to hold it by resisting even the smallest invitation to capitulate. If a friend promises they will just 'swing by' to drop something off, but won't stay long, it can feel petty to say no. However, as a person who has made this mistake many hundreds of times, someone who is willing to break your boundaries a little bit, is usually quite willing to break them a lot, and will likely settle in for a conversation and expect you to make the coffee.

It is better to risk being petty than to lose an entire, precious afternoon that was dedicated to your creative work. I am not usually one for outsourcing or decision-making by committee, but if you struggle with holding boundaries then this is one scenario where it can be helpful to recruit the help of someone who is excellent at them. My friend is immovable in his boundaries and will hold his time for writing and recording music against only the most dramatic and urgent of invasions. If I am struggling to work out if a limit is reasonable or not, then I will sometimes ask him for his perspective. The certainty and unequivocal nature of his response will sometimes lend me the conviction necessary to hold a firm no.

Seasons in creativity

Before concluding this chapter on taking creative action, it is important to give some thought to the seasonal nature of creativity and the natural fluctuations in productivity. Some people fear becoming blocked because they believe that unproductive times are likely to last forever and will derail any hopes of success or development. In fact, creativity appears to come in waves, with times of productivity being followed by 'fallow' times of restoring and 'taking in' energy and inspiration. If you find yourself in a dry spell, then one way to respond it is to allow yourself to fully inhabit that space and enjoy what it has to offer. Rather than attempting anything terribly serious or aspirational, allow yourself time to play and enjoy creating for creating's sake. If you find that even that feels like a wrench or an effort, then it might be that you need to soak in, rather than put out work, and require time spent just observing the work of others, or the world around you, until inspiration returns.

As we explored in Chapter Five, putting ourselves in the path of inspiration stacks the odds that we will once again feel compelled to make work. Rather than wasting the 'downtime' feeling anxious, trust that if you continue to tend to your creativity by giving it ample opportunity to be expressed, and ample nourishment in the form of experiences, then it will once again return when the time is right. The important thing is not to become despondent and give up, as this can turn a fallow month into fallow years. Invest in your creativity regardless of your mood, even if it is a tiny creative action like cleaning your creative space or ordering new pencils or books. Little steps are still movement and can make fallow times feel less intractable and stuck.

Conclusion

Moving into the 'action' stage of creativity can be fraught with difficult thoughts and feelings that can render us immobilised. Diving under the surface of what can at first appear a simple tendency to procrastinate, can reveal deeper drivers that are impacting our ability to make work. Spending time becoming familiar with these, and the thoughts and feelings they elicit, can move them from unconscious anchors keeping our creative selves tethered, to conscious companions on the road to creativity that occasionally need some attention. It would be naïve to say that there will never be times when these issues raise themselves again, but removing the mystery and uncertainty means you are better placed to respond and free yourself up to move back into action.

References

Abbasi I & Alghamdi N (2015) The prevalence, predictors, causes, treatment, and implications of procrastination behaviours in general, academic, and work setting. *International Journal of Psychological Studies* **7** (1).

Beery R (1975) Special feature: fear of failure in the student experience. *The Personnel and Guidance Journal* **54** (4).

Burka JB & Yuen LM (2008) *Procrastination: Why you do it, what to do about it now*. Hachette Books Group, New York.

Cameron J (2017) *The Right to Write*. Hay House, UK.

Rollnick S & Miller WR (1991) *Motivational Interviewing: Helping people change*. Guilford Publications, UK.

Chapter Seven: If you build it, they will come

At some point in my early 30s, I was lucky enough to meet and work with a wonderful Italian guitarist called Lorena. She is the opposite to me in every way. I am a person that cannot hide my enthusiasm at all, and my energy frequently evokes that of a spaniel, just let out of a car, on a beach. I do not exaggerate one bit when I say that Lorena is the opposite; she speaks only when entirely necessary, smokes roll-ups, moves purposefully and gracefully, does not flap, and does not compromise at all when it comes to music. We were a two-woman act performing acoustic versions of heavy rock and metal songs, played on Lorena's guitar which was tuned an entire tone down so it resonated like a harp from hell. I loved working with her – she was so gifted, and the sounds of her guitar and my voice melded effortlessly and beautifully. I trusted her judgement and feedback and developed greatly as a performer in our time together.

We were both living in Newquay, a seaside town in the South West of England that is popular with stag and hen dos (or bachelorette parties depending on where you are from), particularly during the summer. One night, we were booked to play a bar that overlooked the ocean and had been asked to do a set of about an hour, starting around midnight. I was of an age where that was still possible without needing a nap, so we agreed. When we arrived, the place was full of people dancing to loud dance music, some of them dressed as brides, or nuns, or policeman, and sloshing brightly coloured alcohol over each other. I blanched, there was no way that we could get up and play acoustic metal covers to these people. For a start, they gave no impression of being the sort of crowd that might appreciate such music, and most of them were already in the 'drunk and dancing' stage of the evening. I began anxiously suggesting changes to the set list to make us more palatable to the assembled crowd and lambasting the promoter who had so foolishly booked us. Lorena finished her cigarette before she answered, a habit that imbued whatever she finally said with an air of such authority it was impossible to disagree, 'If we play our music, our audience will come. If they don't, we count it as a practice'. Then she went inside and proceeded to set up as planned.

I did not for one minute think that she was right and was dreading taking to the stage. I stood awkwardly while Lorena did a sound check of the guitar and did what I so hypocritically suggested you avoid doing in Chapter Four – downed a pint of beer and immediately asked for another one.

I'm the sort of singer that finds whatever nerves I have melt the moment I start to perform; I genuinely feel physically moved by music and enjoy nothing more than to let my voice soar along with whatever instrument accompanies me. I tend to close my eyes as it allows me to focus more on the music, but this time I kept them firmly open, in part so I could dodge any beer bottles that might be launched our way. What I observed has stayed with me in a way that fundamentally changed how I understand creativity and audience. Most of the very drunk people melted away, drifting like mist from the brightly lit dance floor towards the darkly lit edges of the room or back to the bar. From out of those same shadows came people that I hadn't noticed for the entire time we were setting up: *our people*. It was genuinely like a scene from a film where loose-bodied spirits free themselves from walls and pillars and float across the room. The space that until five minutes ago was full of writhing revellers, was now filled with a completely different audience. Our audience. Some of the dancers stayed, giving a well-deserved nudge to my preconceptions, and by the end of the night the space was full of people singing along and attempting to start a mosh pit.

That night was a staggering lesson in what Lorena already clearly and unequivocally knew. If you make what is authentic and real to you, your audience will find you. Others who love what you love will gravitate towards you and will connect with you because the part of you that is speaking, is speaking to that part in them. If Lorena hadn't forced me, I would have changed the set in an attempt to please the crowd. I would have played some sort of 'halfway house' set of less convincing, unpractised music that would have left both audiences unmoved and unsatisfied. I wouldn't have enjoyed it anywhere near as much as I did and that would have shown. If I had compromised my authenticity, I would have failed to find the part of my art in any of the people there. If you want to find your audience, your tribe, your people, then you need to make *your* art. Not art that is likely to sell, or likely to please, or less likely to offend. No, I am talking about the sort of art that speaks directly from your soul to the soul of another. This is the sort of art that provokes loyalty and the sort of following that allows you to try, to make mistakes, to fail, to apologise and to keep on making.

Amanda Palmer, the lead singer of the Dresden Dolls and solo artist with countless albums, collaborations, music videos and provocative moments of performance art to her name, is a fantastic example of exactly this point. She makes the sort of raw, uncompromising work that cannot easily be ignored, and has provoked the sort of harsh response from critics and the media bordering on slanderous that would leave most people reeling. She writes about death, life, parenthood, envy, abortion, rape and orgasms in a way that lays bare the raw experience of being human, and as a result, she has called to her the sort of consistent, longstanding fan base that most artists dream of. When she decided to make her first solo studio album, she turned to Kickstarter rather than a record label and raised over a million dollars to bring the album into existence. Since then, she has established a community on Patreon that generates enough income that she is free to make 'stuff' whenever and however she wants, free from the permission needed from a record label or promoters. You may think that you require an enormous fanbase to raise that sort of money, however this isn't the case. It is roughly the same 25,000 people that funded the album and then became patrons. What is interesting about Amanda Palmer's fanbase is that their connection with her has also set the stage for their connection to each other and many of them regularly share art and general life on two thriving, lively forums. Palmer describes that her artistic success is about 'a few people loving you, up close', rather than mainstream appeal from a distance. Developing strong bonds with your audience, whoever they are and whatever the number, is a prospect that can feel far less daunting than aiming for mass appeal.

If you find yourself second-guessing your art, or making changes to stack the odds that you will be successful, you may well end up achieving the opposite. Art is able to convey the mysteries of living unlike anything else, regardless of what discipline you choose. If you can tap into the mystery of your existence – and by this, I mean the things that cannot easily be conveyed in words, or that resist definition – then you might just speak to the existence of others. It is this connection that creates a lasting bond between an artist and their audience and will sustain your practice over the longer term. It is the difference between art that speaks to just a moment in time, and art that speaks to the enduring experience of being human.

Exercise 31: Exploring your artist's voice

Take a pen and paper. Look at the last thing you created in your 30-minute daily creative practice and ask yourself, if that piece could speak, what would it say? Keep the piece in your eye line, do not censor or overthink what you are writing, but write whatever comes to you. If this piece had a voice and there was no concern about consequences or the reactions of others, what would it say?

Take a look at what you have written. How close is the 'voice' of the piece and your own voice? Do you recognise yourself in what you have written, or does it feel unfamiliar and alien? Does the piece tell you something about your experience that maybe was out of your awareness, or does it represent a sort of 'otherness' that is hard to relate to? What state of mind were you in when you made this piece? What impact might that have had on what you created?

Healing creative injuries

There are lots of things that can stand between you and making authentic work, some of which we have considered in previous chapters. One such thing is unhealed, unresolved, or unacknowledged creative injuries that have left scars or marks which continue to impact you and your art. These injuries may not be evident in day-to-day life but become bitterly apparent when the moment comes to make creative work.

I was once told by a fellow writer that including myself and my experiences in my writing made me appear 'narcissistic'. Ouch. Is it? Am I? Oh Lordy… It was the equivalent of a shame bullet, and it lodged itself right in my chest. I spiralled into a place of self-doubt that left me editing out anything that pertained to myself for the next two years. Two whole years of adopting a writing style that wasn't mine in case other people shared this view and I was secretly being branded an egotistical maniac. This was a creative injury; a moment in time that changed the course of my creative expression and I had to find a way to heal it if I was ever going to write this book from anything like an authentic place.

Luckily, I was given *The Artist's Way* by Julia Cameron (1992), which has already featured several times in this book for good reason. Cameron talks about the power of acknowledging creative injuries and of finding ways to heal them head on. For me, following her advice and writing a letter about the author of this wound, allowed me to heal enough to move past it and finally put 'pen' to paper again. I chose to write directly to this person, though I did not send the letter, and in doing so I unfroze and remembered the context in which the incident had occurred. At the time, he was trying to finish his own writing project and had asked me to contribute to the introduction. Suddenly confronted with a writing style very different to his own and realising that he did not want a collaborator after all, he attacked it and me. I was able to contextualise myself, too, my own vulnerability as I began to explore what it meant to be a 'writer' (a term that can feel terribly formal for something we all do most days). We were both primed for this interaction by our own context and 'stuff', but I needed to undo it if I was ever going to reclaim how I write.

It might be that your own creative injury or injuries came to mind as you read that account and are now being relived in your mind. The exercise below is a common one used in therapy to resolve dreams or to work with traumatic memories, but it is one I like to use in my personal life too, if I need to shift my association with an event. If you struggle to hold mental images in your mind, then feel free to make a visual representation of the event to work with.

Exercise 32: Identifying creative injuries

Bring to mind the term 'creative injury' and then allow yourself to float back through your life. Where does your mind alight? What incident or incidents are called to mind and what was the impact of these moments? How did they change the course of your creative life? What do you feel as you remember these experiences? Whereabouts in your body do you notice sensations or emotions?

Now close your eyes and choose a memory to focus on. Call to mind a 'postcard' image that would capture the event in a snapshot. For example, the moment you opened the envelope that contained the rejection letter for a manuscript, or the time immediately after a friend had told you they didn't rate you as an artist. Include as much detail as you can; who was there, where were you, what was around you, what were you wearing, what could you hear, what were you feeling?

Hold in mind the memory and the feeling in your body, and ask yourself, 'If I had a magic wand, what would I add or remove from this picture?' Perhaps invite your art group to come and stand around you, each with a hand on your shoulder. Or place your family around the room, facing you, filled with compassion and love. You might choose to add your dog to sit on your feet, and your best friend to stand in front of you, wine glass at the ready. If no one safe comes to mind, then add colours, lights, objects, whatever your mind requires. You might imagine the letter turning to butterflies and flying away or becoming glitter and falling to the floor in a cloud of sparkles before settling between the floorboards. You might place a globe or 'forcefield' around yourself, imagining your friend's words bouncing off it and evaporating into the ether. Or you may add a wall of people who love you and support your art and place them between you and whatever caused the injury. A police person to arrest the offender, a duvet or exaggerated armour to protect your heart, whatever brings a lift to the feelings that you associate with the image and changes the moment from a negative experience to one full of warmth, humour and support.

What was that exercise like for you? What emotions arose? Did you expect to feel that way or was it a surprise? Are there other memories of creative injuries that would benefit from this technique? If you found it challenging, then it might be worth repeating but using images, either drawn or cut out, to represent the event and your alterations.

Putting your work out there

Some artists are freely able to create work but hit a block when it comes to letting go and sending work out into the world without them, where they no longer have control over how it is viewed, by whom, and how it is judged. Their homes and studios are crammed with work that gathers dust or props up furniture but never sees the light of day. This can be about many things, many of which are similar to the driving forces behind procrastination. If you never disseminate your work, you never have to hear what others think of it, you never have to deal with criticism and you never have to face disappointment or shame. For some artists, it is only by removing the audience that the freedom to truly create becomes available. Their work is for them, and they have no urge to show it. This calls to mind the photographer Vivien Myer whose collection of hundreds of rolls of undeveloped film was discovered after her death. The resulting photos have been shown all around the world and give an insight into a life completely governed by her art. Now, it might be that she never wanted to display her works, and she was quite happy with the process of taking the photographs in the knowledge they would never be seen. There are artists, though, who long to put their work out into the world but who are blocked by their relationship to the finished pieces.

If you have a tendency towards perfectionism, then it can be very difficult to tell when a work is finished and ready to be released into the world. There is always one more lyric to tweak, one area of shading to adjust, one final edit to complete. If perfect is your standard, but creative work is your medium, then how do you ever judge when something is finished? There are no objective measures of 'good' or 'bad' to refer to, no unanimously agreed 'bar' to reach, there is just subjective opinion and conjecture. Perfection is an oily, slippery concept that will squeeze and wriggle out of your hands as soon as you think you have a grip on it. A change in the light, in your mood, in your reference points, and the piece is back to its stubborn imperfection. If this is you, then I strongly suggest you recruit a small number of trusted people to inform you, firmly and decisively, when a piece is 'good enough' and you need to let it go. If you know that you tend towards perfectionism, then it can be helpful to create work without going back to edit, tweak or amend it until you have completed the entire first draft. After this, allow yourself a set number of edits, for example two, before you declare the work finished and move on. This sounds extremely calculated, but it is a way of introducing boundaries to what can become a time and resource-consuming quest for the impossible.

The other thing that can cause artists to keep hold of their work is the fear of being out of control once it is released. Out on its own in the public domain, your work is open to misinterpretation, criticism, being taken out of context, and being misunderstood. It may be viewed by people who do not understand it, may be bought by someone who does not appreciate it, but acquires it as a 'virtue signal' of their artistic leanings, or may even be destroyed. If you struggle with control and feel very uncomfortable when you are unable to directly exert influence, then you might find it challenging to know when to let go and allow your work to enter a dialogue with others on its own. There are many examples of works of art that, once in the public domain, have taken on lives of their own and have unintentionally ended up being figureheads for debates and political movements, or conduits for societal anxieties. However, there are innumerable works that have been received in exactly the way they were intended; the difficulty is that you cannot control what other people read into your work, it is both the beauty and the risk of art.

The sad and irrevocable lesson that I have learned from both sides of the therapy chair, is that a sense of control in any area of life is often an illusion. It's an illusion that I have personally found very hard to let go of, in fact I might even go as far as saying it's my favourite illusion, as it brings with it a sort of comfort from our existential precarity. However, if it is taken too far, we can end up being controlled by our need to control, an irony I have had to confront more than once in my own life. It can be a painful process to let go of control, but it can also be profoundly liberating. It is the psychic equivalent of kicking back in a swimming pool or lake and floating – it comes with the same release of tense muscles, unclenching of the stomach and breathing out. Yes, it might mean that you have to deal with some unintended or unexpected consequences, but if you have cultivated the sort of emotional coping skills and support that we have explored in this book, then you can feel confident of your ability to survive. Letting go of control allows more space for the unexpected and chaotic, which can be dazzling and beautiful at times and can provide inspiration for creativity in ways that a tightly controlled life may not. This does not come without anxiety though, so if the idea of letting go fills you with dread, then start small and build from there. As with many things, therapy can offer a safe and contained space for the dismantling and disarming of the control illusion if it is proving problematic.

Our attachment to objects can also impact how we disseminate our creative art; we might find it hard to let go of things that we have formed a connection with or maybe too flippant in how we dispose of work and then regret it. Up until recently, the implication of attachment theory was considered mostly within the context of our relationships with each other, however research now suggests that it may have implications for how we create art, respond to art materials (Snir *et al*, 2017) and how we relate to the things that we create (Mathes *et al*, 2020).

Attachment theory is one of those psychological concepts that has made its way into the public psyche, so you may be very familiar with the central ideas. In short, it is a way of understanding how we relate to each other and getting our needs for physical and emotional safety met. Originally developed by John Bowlby and then Mary Ainsworth, attachment theory can be problematic due to its political leanings and its historical focus on mothers as primary attachment figures. However, attachment theory has developed to include all caregivers and continues to form the basis of many contemporary psychological models. It can offer a sort of shorthand to explore how we manage and respond to relational closeness, distance and endings. A full overview of the theory is beyond the scope of this book but if it interests you there are references for further reading in the resources section. In a nutshell, attachment theory argues that the way we connect to each other falls into four broad categories or 'styles' that are informed by our early life experiences. They can be modified by relationships in adulthood and are usually activated at times of stress or adversity.

Imagine a pair of hands, held out in front of you, palms facing inwards. These hands represent two people who can move closer to and further away from each other. Some people are able to tolerate being close to others (intimacy) and being separate without becoming unduly distressed. If their relationships have been relatively stable and attuned, then separation does not represent a threat as they expect the other person to return and re-establish the connection. The hands are free to come close together and move apart, the line remains around each hand, and they continue to be separate, but the proximity changes. At times of adversity, they can draw closer to the people around them for support, and when they need to turn their attention to work or creativity, they are able to be separate for a time, before returning.

Some people's relational experiences mean that this sort of closeness is intolerable and threatening. They prefer to keep others at a distance where they feel safer – this is sometimes referred to as an 'avoidant' attachment style. The hands remain a great distance apart, regardless of the situation. At times of distress, the distance is likely to increase rather than decrease as the person attempts to feel safer.

Inversely, some people find this sort of distance intolerable and seek a level of proximity and intimacy that can threaten the separateness of the two individuals. The hands come together and squeeze tightly, fingers interlocked in a way that makes it challenging to differentiate one from the other. This is sometimes called an 'anxious/ambivalent' attachment style. When distress occurs, the person responds by seeking enmeshment to feel safe and may experience high levels of anxiety at the threat of separation.

If a person's experiences have been inconsistent or chaotic, they might move between the two, sometimes interlocking fingers in a bid for safety and sometimes wrenching away and separating to a great distance. At times of adversity, this person is likely to choose the strategy that is best likely to get their needs met, albeit not always consciously. This style of relating is called a 'disorganised attachment' as it does not follow a neat, predictable pattern.

Of course, we do not fall into neat little boxes, and these patterns may change over time and be more or less obvious depending on the circumstances. If you are unsure of where you fall, then consider how you tend to respond to relationship break-ups. Do you delete the person and digitally block them from everything, never referring to them again, or do you find yourself compelled to trawl their social media and ply their friends for information? How comfortable do you feel with separation and with closeness? There is no right and wrong, and neither style is pathological, in fact at least half of us relate to each other in ways that attachment theory would consider 'insecure'.

These tendencies not only impact our relationship with other people but can impact how we relate to our work. Creative works can become imbued with emotional significance and can therefore be very difficult to part with, or even to show to others. If you use creativity to express highly personal, or highly emotive topics or experiences, then the resulting work can take on a symbolic meaning that causes a wrench when you consider selling it. If you have a tendency towards avoidance, then the inverse might be true, and you may end up sharing or selling things without fully considering the implications and then regretting it. A wonderful artist friend of mine was bemoaning their decision to sell off all their early work very cheaply, and now felt that they lacked a reference point or a sense of their own artistic story, as any evidence of the process they had been through had either been sold or binned. The tendency to quickly retreat from or end relationships was present in all areas of his life and represented a kind of global pattern of relating to things and to people. Of course, this repeated in his relationship with his art. Around the same time, I was asked to dinner at another friend's house, who is also a painter. Behind and under the sofas were rolls and rolls of paintings, curled up and unframed, that had been there for years. They informed me that there were more under the bed, in cupboards, and in drawers. They observed that they found it very difficult to part with any art, or any possessions at all for that matter, as it made them feel anxious and worried that they would miss them and would be unable to replace them.

Neither of these tendencies is 'bad' in and of themselves; the question is how does your relationship to finished work impact you and your ability to share what you create, and is this still helpful? If you have piles and piles of manuscripts that never get sent to a publisher, or piles of canvases that are impeding your ability to get into bed, then it might be time to find a way to let some of them go out into the world. If you find that you rarely take time to digest and reflect on what you have made, created, or composed but allow them to be disseminated almost as soon as you finish, consider keeping hold of a few pieces for a few weeks and revisit them. Be curious about what you learn when you re-encounter a piece: what things are how you remembered and what things are different?

There can also be something about putting creative art out into the world that formalises an artistic identity, which can be validating, daunting, reassuring or deeply anxiety provoking. If you put forward a book for publication, and it is accepted, then it can feel like suddenly you are a 'writer' and must inherit all that the word carries with it. If you have an exhibition of your paintings and hold a preview that is well attended, then you and others might start to use the word 'artist', regardless of how you feel about that term. It may be that you have written or painted all your life but feel that the moment you put your work forward for scrutiny you gain a label. Labels carry with them ideas, concepts, even emotions, and often come with a set of rules and expectations. If you bring to mind the word 'artist', what do you picture? Or the word 'director', 'writer' or 'actor'? Humans tell stories about everything, which is fine if the story fits, but what if it doesn't?

Exercise 33: Wearing the word

Take a pen and paper and write whatever word describes your creative art. Writer, painter, ceramicist, artist, screenwriter… or maybe several of these words. Now write all the associated words, concepts and images that appear when you bring to mind the sort of person this word (or words) would usually describe. How do they dress, behave, eat, socialise, play, speak? How much money do they earn, where do they live?

Now ask yourself, what are the 'rules' of being a _____? Allow your mind to wander and alight without forcing or censoring. What do you become aware of? Perhaps you associate writing with drinking alcohol, in which case the 'rule' might be 'all writers drink', or perhaps you associate musicians with sex and drugs, so the rule might be 'all musicians sleep around' or 'all musicians do a lot of drugs'. Perhaps some of the 'rules' come with a level of expectation or pressure, such as 'all artists have attended art school', or 'all writers have an excellent grasp of grammar'.

Look at what you have written. How do you compare with the words you have identified? What things are the same, and where are there points of departure? Are there bits that fit and bits that don't, or do none of them resonate? What 'rules' do you break, or only partially adhere to?

Finally, write the sentence 'I am a _____' and then sit back and look at what you have written. What feelings come up? Does it feel comfortable or uncomfortable? Would you feel happy saying it out loud to an unfamiliar person, or would that bring up difficult feelings? What do you notice in your body when you imagine that? How easy or hard was it to write that sentence, and why?

Handling criticism

If you are going to be a creative artist that disseminates their work in any way, whether that is on social media, in galleries, through publication or through performance, then you are likely to encounter public review and critique. Critics come in many forms: some are insightful, thought-provoking and point the way to go, some are damning and unexplored in terms of their own unhealed artistic wounds and the wounds they inflict on others. Either way, to survive, you must find ways to manage criticism and learn how to integrate and use helpful feedback and withstand and resist indiscriminate blasts.

When you are surfing, it is wise to have two points of reference on the shore that mean you can keep your bearings amidst the powerful pull of rip tides and currents. Without these reference points it is entirely possible to look up and find that you have drifted far further than you realised and are now well out of the range of where you want to be. The same can be said for navigating the course of your creative life and deciding how and when to respond to criticism and input from others. Having two people whose opinion you trust and who can be guaranteed to give you clear feedback in a way you can use, but that won't completely destroy you, is essential if you are going to navigate the waters of life as a creative artist. The characteristics you are looking for in these people are the same characteristics you might look for in a great therapist. They need to have done their own journey with creativity, even if that journey is different to yours, and they need to know and have a handle on their own 'stuff', so it does not leak out and unconsciously become entangled with your stuff. You need someone who is not quick to envy, as you need to be as big and as small as you are in the relationships with them without fearing unconscious attack, and you need someone who understands the magnitude of what they are dealing with when it comes to your art. These people can be mentors, teachers, fellow artists, friends, colleagues, or even family members. But they must be able to 'get' you and your vision for your art if they are going to act as navigation aids.

These are the people that you trust to find the grain of truth that you need to listen to in a review, and to help you withstand and resist the 'noise' of critics that just don't get it. It is a fact of life that there will always be people who do not get what you are trying to do and are full of 'helpful' advice about how you could do it better. The key is to strike a balance between being so impervious to feedback that you halt your development, and being so porous that you find yourself changing direction in response to every opinion you are given. Having two people in your life who can help you through this process and with whom you can share creative 'wobbles' will ensure that you are resilient enough to hold your course even if you experience knocks along the way.

Critics are not independent of culture and context, and their opinion is as subjective as anyone else's, though perhaps better-informed with regard to the work that precedes yours and where a particular 'scene' might be heading. Critics have historically been afforded a great deal of power in many of the creative industries and have had a 'make or break' impact on the career of a great number of fledgling artists, musicians or writers. The formality of the critic's role is shifting as a result of social media, and the widening of dialogue about and access to art. It is still very easy to get into a 'black and white' relationship with people who review your work, however, shifting from a defensive 'they know nothing' to a deferential 'they know everything', or, at the very least, 'they know best'. This poses several problems. If you are in the 'they know nothing' place, then you are closed to feedback and may miss helpful observations about where you could develop your work. If you tend towards the 'they know everything' position, then you might be tempted to begin 'writing for the gallery' and 'dancing' to please them, a strategy that is almost guaranteed to end in disaster. The reality usually sits somewhere in the 'they know something' territory and means that any feedback you are given needs to be subject to a careful sorting process, with each bit being picked over to identify what is helpful 'grist' for the creative mill and what is chaff, which is more about the critic and cultural climate, and so can be disregarded.

Critics can be great; they can be funny, insightful, smart and thought provoking. But they are also human and are therefore immersed in the same cultural milieu as everyone else. Of course, this shapes their tastes, aesthetics and politics, and their subsequent opinions about what you are producing. Many incredible artists have failed to get anything like recognition from critics at the point they produce their defining work but are then lauded as a great example to the next generation by the same group of people that slammed them only years before. This is a natural part of cultural shift, the sort of societal tide that shapes and re-shapes how we see the world around us, what we consider valuable, intolerable, provocative and taboo. It is constantly moving, and you can either try and stay ahead of the tide by endlessly paddling, changing your work to reflect the current trends, or you can stand your ground and keep speaking from where you are, and hope that the tide eventually turns your way. There is no right or wrong, both are risky, but I believe that holding your ground stands the best chance of creating an artistic career that is rewarding, meaningful and enduring. Even if you do manage to catch a wave and become a 'trend', there is a risk that you will be washed up as soon as the tide changes again, which it will.

Making art that is honest and 'real' can make it even more difficult to withstand a public critique of your work that is unfavourable or harsh, as it is likely to feel far more personal and you may be more emotionally invested and attached to what you have created. Criticism of flippant work created for commercial appeal can be shrugged off in a way that criticism of exposing, personal works cannot. Powerful feelings of shame, anger, frustration and exposure can be triggered by reading something that lambasts work you love and are protective of, however the likelihood is that this will happen at some point in your career or may even happen frequently depending on the nature of your work. This is where it is important to have others to turn to that are invested in you and that can hold up an honest mirror, neither too harsh nor too sycophantic. They can help you in the sorting process and can support you while you tend your wounds and can then let you know when the time has come to get on with the work.

It is worth taking a minute here to talk about artistic 'demons' and vulnerabilities, as these can be triggered by a well-aimed criticism in a way that can leave you reeling. Artistic 'demons' can be unhealed creative wounds but can also be 'sore spots' derived from a lack or a failure. If you didn't have a formal art education and feel sensitive, or even inferior on some level, because of that, then a critic comparing you unfavourably to another artist who did have a formal education, may inadvertently trigger that demon. They then appear in a puff of malevolent, mental smoke and proceed to remind you of all the dark thoughts you have ever had about the issue. If you had a very public dressing down from an English teacher about copying from someone else, then receive a review that suggests you have 'drawn heavily' from another writer, you may find yourself reliving the experience in a way that is anxiety-producing. Likewise, if you have sustained a creative wound and someone hits on this by using similar language or sentiment, then you may find yourself tempted to withdraw into an artistic shell and stop creating.

One technique that can be really helpful here comes from narrative therapy and involves externalising the demon and giving it a form and even a name. When working with children with OCD, I would routinely get the child to draw their OCD in detail, and to name it so they and their family could begin to work out how best to relate to it. My favourite character to date is an OCD monster called 'Number Bob', who looked much like a Mr Man character with a wobbly outline and tiny arms. Once the demon is external to you, you can relate to it as if it is separate and can speak directly to it. It very hard to take something quite as seriously when it is fondly known as 'Nigel' and wears a pirate hat.

The most important thing to do in any event is to keep making work, even if it is effortful, uninspired, or forced. If you get back on the metaphorical horse quickly, then you don't allow the seeds of inertia to implant themselves and eventually grow into a thorny forest you can't escape from. The emotional coping skills we explored in Chapter Four can prove useful for responding to any powerful, negative emotions that arise when you receive criticism, particularly the ones pertaining to self-compassion. Compassion is the most valuable tool in responding to shame and will return you to your creativity faster than any self-criticism or rumination will. If you ever find yourself in the heat of a shame response to something you have just read about your work, that is a great time to call to mind the compassionate figure you developed in Chapter Two. What would they say about this? How would they respond? What would they suggest you do, and what things would they encourage you to avoid? What perspective would they bring to what you are reading? This can act as a wonderful buffer by offering support for you but also reminding you that there are always multiple perspectives on any given topic. The reviewer or critic has their perspective, but this does not denote a universal 'truth' that is non-negotiable.

There is a fine line between a compassionate response and a defensive 'they know nothing' position, but the key difference is the accompanying emotion. If you feel angry, defensive, attacking and outraged, then the chances are you are tipping into the latter. While understandable, this sort of defensive response does little to deal with the wound and may result in you swinging to the other end of the polarity and collapsing into self-doubt and recrimination. Actively choosing compassion allows you to engage in the sort of self-care that you need to survive such an emotional hand grenade and will stop you tipping into inaction and self-pity, a position that can be mistaken for self-compassion but is far from it. True compassion means remaining accountable and responsible and choosing the right thing, even if that is not the easiest thing. This usually means making work, even if you don't want to.

Understanding projection and envy

Sometimes criticism is deserved and, when delivered constructively, can be essential in developing you as an artist. At other times, criticism is in fact a thinly veiled attack that seeks to undermine and destroy. Envy and projection are two concepts that can clarify what might be happening so that critique and aggression are not confused.

The concept of 'projection' comes from psychoanalysis and refers to a person or a group taking something they find intolerable or anxiety provoking in themselves and 'projecting' it into another. Now that the uncomfortable part of themselves is located in someone else, it can be related to as if it is a separate entity and can therefore be attacked, or cared for, or destroyed. For example, Carl is murderously angry with his husband after years of feeling overlooked and neglected. He feels unconsciously anxious about the strength of his anger, and so 'projects' the anger into his partner, accusing him of being abusive and aggressive and threatening to call the police. The husband may feel bemused, unaware of any angry feelings and completely baffled as to why his husband is accusing him in this way. By projecting his anger into his husband, Carl is now able to relate to it as if it is outside of himself; he can both attack it and place limits on it by threatening the 'law' in the form of the police. Carl's anxiety is reduced as he does not have to own his anger, or fully consider the implications of experiencing such a powerful emotion.

Sometimes, the same process can occur between society and an artist or a piece of art; something intolerable or desirable is projected into the work, and people then relate to it *as if it is the projected thing*. This is sometimes the point of the work; it is part of the power and dynamism of art and its ability to represent far more than is literally conveyed. At other times this can occur when a work or an artist inadvertently taps into a feeling that is lying just under the surface of society. One person or one work can come to embody, and ultimately take the fall for, something that is located in society and cannot be tolerated.

Being the recipient of projection can be very confusing and can leave you fishing around for what is 'real': 'am I an angry feminist?', 'do I hate this particular person or people'? If something really doesn't fit, then it might be that you are unconsciously conveying something in your work that you were unaware of, or it might be that you are the recipient of projections that are less about you and more about things that cannot be tolerated in the people around you. Understanding projection does not necessarily make it feel less toxic, but it can make it feel less mystifying and confusing.

Another powerful psychological mechanism to be aware of as an artist is *envy*. As already discussed in Chapter One, envy is a powerful emotion that is discrete from jealousy in its compulsion to destroy whatever possesses the coveted quality or 'thing'. Imagine hearing a woman talking to a friend about being offered a new job, she is clearly excited and proud and is animatedly describing the details of what sounds like a great offer. Her friend then launches into a diatribe about the company and how unethical they are, moves on to her friend's skills and the likelihood she will be overwhelmed and hate the new role, and then settles on how she would never personally take such a role as it doesn't offer enough security. By the end of the conversation, the new job is in tatters and its owner is entirely crushed. This sort of exchange is not always conscious; if we could pause the conversation and enquire about the thoughts and feelings motivating the 'feedback', the friend may assert they are just looking out for their friend, are concerned about their wellbeing and just want to make sure they had thought it through. Whether conscious or not, the effect of envy can serve to destroy and crush, and make the sort of playful, experimental mindset needed to make creative work almost impossible.

There are lots of blocked artists in the world who carry around projects in the emotional equivalent of their breast pocket. Bruised and sad, these creative works are never brought into the light of day, but are disavowed, disallowed, or denied for a myriad of reasons. When that person encounters someone who has taken out, shaken off, and realised their art, it can provoke unconscious, uninterrogated envy which manifests as an unexpected and sometimes devastating attack. You excitedly share your plans for a new project with a friend and get a list of why 'that's not going to work' back. You play a new piece of music to a family member who coolly responds that it's not up to your usual standard, with no explanation or embellishment. These experiences can feel devastating enough to derail a project before it has even started or become a kind of mental 'ear worm' that plays over and over when you try and create. You ask yourself, 'What if the person is right, and this isn't going to work?' or 'What if this isn't as good as I think it is?' That is not to say that any criticism that is difficult to receive is an envy attack – the question is whether it is constructive and points to actionable, plausible changes that get you closer to your goal, or whether the entire project is crushed under the weight of damnation. If it's the latter, then the chances are you are on the receiving end of envy.

One way to protect yourself from envy is to keep any fledgling work safe and away from anyone who might, consciously or unconsciously, 'slap' it before it is formed enough to withstand the impact. Some creative works need nurturing into existence and can be sensitive to attack, requiring cosseting for a time before becoming fully formed. You may come under pressure to share elements of your new project and might even feel petty or withholding if you don't, however if you open yourself up too early, you may find it difficult to recover and may be unable to focus on your work without envious words floating in front of you. I am not always good at abiding by this and can quickly be invited into talking about work I am enthusiastic about, but I have found it is better to err on the side of caution, and anyone that is genuinely supportive of you and your art will respect that.

The capacity of envy to interrupt creativity is not unidirectional; our own envy can be just as incapacitating. If we are envious of the apparently superior circumstances or talents of others, then we can be rendered immobile by the unfairness of it all and stop creating entirely. The art critic and writer Jerry Saltz talks openly about the toxic and ultimately devasting impact of envy on his career as an artist in his book *Art is Life* (2022). He articulates the process of becoming consumed by envy and rage as he surveyed the privilege of others and compared it to the challenges he was facing, living in an unheated apartment with next to no money. Though there was justification for his anger about the lack of economic parity in society, he was ultimately so caught by the resulting envy that it derailed his work entirely and he stopped creating. Of course, Saltz found his way back to creativity and has written widely on the topic of art and how to be an artist as well as being an active art critic, however many creative people do not make it back from such experiences and take the sense of unfairness to the grave.

Time spent chewing over the unfairness of life is time not spent creating, and the resulting emotional knots of rage and sadness can eventually be crippling. One thing that being a psychologist has taught me is that life is unfair, and it's not personal. Bad things happen regardless of your virtue, and life can take cruel and unexpected turns that leave us reeling. That is the human condition: unpredictable and unfair. However, it is from this mess that we create, and if you can keep your eye on your own circumstances and be compassionate about them without moving into making comparisons with others, then these experiences can serve as powerful creative inspirations. That is not to say that art should not speak to the politics of the time, and highlight inequalities and disparity, but this needs to be channelled into the work and not used as an excuse for why you are not creating.

Defining success

Allowing the success or failure of a piece of work to be dictated by its market value is a serious trap to fall into; it will blind you to brilliant bits of work that might not yet be in 'vogue' enough to sell, or pieces that perhaps lack something of your creative 'voice' but hit on a popular aesthetic or trend. Where possible, keep the concepts of success and money separate by being very clear about what you define as success. It might be that 'success' looks like a small group of people who appreciate your work and are willing to pay you enough for it that your work can sustain itself. Or 'success' may be a certain number of followers on social media, an amount of work, publications or albums, a level of quality that you want to reach. It doesn't matter, as long as you are setting the parameters for your own success: not an agent, a label or a publisher. It is fine to dedicate time to commercially appealing art that will sell, as long as this is balanced with time that is protected to create work that speaks to you as an artist, regardless of whether it speaks to anyone else.

It can be very difficult to change direction when you have hit on a stream of work that is selling well and is getting your name known in your chosen industry, as there is always the anxiety that if you rock the boat, it will tip you out. If you have written a series of humorous scripts that have been received well but hit on an idea for a family drama, then it can take a lot of courage to bite the bullet and make the work. What if people don't like it and the work dries up? What if it isn't as well received? Creativity is something that requires constant replenishment and inspiration to keep fresh and vivid. If you pursue a road too far you will eventually reach the end and will need to find a way back, which can be even more challenging than changing direction. Yes, it is a risk when you have hit on something that is proving successful, however if you continue to listen to the 'voice' of inspiration and remain open to experience, then you leave the possibility open for a varied and long career. If you are confined too soon to a certain style or genre, then the road becomes narrower and narrower as you exhaust the material. Pay attention to your inspiration levels and take action if you feel that the work is becoming forced or effortful; this is a clear sign that you might need to renew your artistic vigour, which may include a change of direction.

Exercise 34: The miracle question revisited

In Chapter One we used the 'miracle question' to identify what you would like to be different by the end of this book. Now I would like you to revisit this question with regard to the success of your art. Take a pen and paper and jot down whatever comes to mind.

Ask yourself, if a miracle happened and you woke up tomorrow to find that you are a 'successful' creative artist, what would be different and what would be the same? What would your day look like? What would be the first thing you notice when you wake in the morning, or the last thing you become aware of when you go to sleep? Where would you be and with whom? What would people say about your art and you as an artist? What would you read when critics or reviewers critique your work? What do you feel as a successful creative artist? Who else in your life would notice changes and what would they be?

Now read back what you have written. What does this tell you about your concept of 'success'? What does creative success look like to you? Where and how does money factor, if at all? How does this align or sit at odds with the values you identified in Chapter Four?

Creating your own luck

I was walking down the street with my four-year-old daughter yesterday when she broke stride and did a kind of shuffle-leap-shuffle movement. Looking down, surprised, I asked her, 'What was that?' Her reply came with thinly veiled contempt: 'You can't step on the lines mummy, it's bad luck'. This incident immediately took me back to my youth, and the widely held conviction within my school that something dreadful would occur if we stood on an odd number of manhole covers – a sort of raised square on the pavement that typically come in twos and threes. This belief would result in me and my friends simultaneously leaping to avoid the third grate in a way that must have appeared completely bizarre to passing motorists.

We were not alone in this behaviour; it turns out human beings are a surprisingly superstitious bunch. A survey completed as part of the 2003 National Science Week revealed that 72% of British people consider themselves a little superstitious and carry out some form of behaviour based on these beliefs (Wiseman, 2003a). This is not just an example of British eccentricity; polls undertaken in America suggest at least half of the general population hold some sort of superstitious beliefs.

A belief in luck, fortune and superstition appeals to the human need for order and certainty and reflects the reality that lives can be changed by small events. A chance encounter with an old friend leads to a successful business venture, a last-minute decision to attend a party results in meeting a future partner, a seemingly random choice to drive a different way home sees you avoid a particularly nasty accident. A belief in luck is not detrimental when limited to avoiding marks on the pavement or walking around ladders: however, it can become problematic if a series of unfortunate events are taken as evidence of *bad* luck, or if a reliance on fortune prevents you from creating your own luck.

When it comes to getting your work out there, whether that is through exhibitions, publication or airtime, there are several things you can do to stack the odds that you will get the opportunities and openings you need, none of which rely on fortune or luck. Richard Wiseman is a professor of psychology in Hertfordshire who specialises in luck and has identified four basic principles that separate those who consider themselves lucky and those who do not. The first is the ability to *notice and respond* to chance opportunities. In a witty study, Wiseman asked 'lucky' and 'unlucky' people to count the number of photographs in a newspaper. The people who considered themselves unlucky set about the task by diligently counting the pictures, however they missed the two-inch message that read 'stop counting, there are 43 photographs in this newspaper' that was emblazoned across the second page, and which the people who considered themselves 'lucky' spotted immediately. On the surface, a difference in fortunes can appear to result from a difference in the number of opportunities that present themselves; in fact, it appears that the difference stems from whether these opportunities are spotted.

Once again, this phenomenon appears to be related to the 'openness to experience' concept that so powerfully underpins creative expression. Wiseman (2003b) observed that those who consider themselves to be 'unlucky' are more anxious and tense than their 'lucky' counterparts, and this seems to result in them becoming far more focused on a specific course of action, only seeing what they deem relevant to a task or goal. Wiseman is describing how becoming too set on one course of action can shut down your receptiveness to opportunities and circumstances that you were not expecting. He states, 'lucky people are more relaxed and open, and therefore see what is there, rather than just what they are looking for'.

Cultivating the ability to spot opportunities relies on cultivating the ability to really see what is going on around you. When you take your undistracted walk, deliberately vary your route and look out for what is *actually* there. The old building being converted into a café that might be looking for work to hang on their walls, a covered courtyard that might be a perfect arena for a spoken word night, a gallery that you hadn't noticed tucked between two buildings. Say yes to social events, especially if they're not your usual 'thing' and allow your mind to take in all that is around you and try and find ways to speak to people that you might not usually engage with. Consciously introduce flexibility and curiosity into how you engage with the world; this will not only provide inspiration but is likely to present you with opportunities. Go on holiday somewhere you would never normally choose, attend venues that have never been on your radar and engage with the people you find there. Try saying yes to the next five invitations that come your way (unless you have a strong gut instinct to say no, in which case listen to that), even the ones that you would normally consign straight to the bin. Keep a note of what happens.

Saying 'no' to invites and opportunities that don't 'feel' right is also an essential skill to build. The ability to listen to 'gut' instinct and to make decisions accordingly is another guiding principle in making your own luck, according to Wiseman. Being able to 'listen' to your sensory system and instincts means you can tap into the wealth of subconscious but essential information that sits just outside your awareness. If you get a bad feeling from a person offering you a record deal, walk away. This instinct is unlikely to come from nowhere, but will be a culmination of non-verbal cues, previous experience, incongruities, and verbal hints. We all have examples of times when we have looked back at a situation and wished we could rewind and listen to what we already knew. There can be a level of anxiety associated with this as we risk losing an opportunity that may not present itself again, and it can be tempting to take an offer that we know isn't right and hope that we will 'make do'. This sort of thinking overlooks the risk of introducing the wrong people, at the wrong time into our creative world. Accepting something that isn't right for you is not a benign act: an insensitive editor, a harsh record executive, or an agent that doesn't get your work can derail and even end a career. Following your 'gut' is easier said than done, but if you are able to use your values and instinct as a guide, then you are far more likely to draw the sort of opportunities and people that you actually need.

Bad things happen to everybody, but your interpretation of events and the perspective you form about yourself is pivotal in determining whether you are 'lucky' or 'unlucky'. Imagine that you have had an offer from a local gallery to display your work in your first solo exhibition. You jump at the chance and immediately set to work making a large body of work to display. The night before you are due to install your work, there is a fire and the gallery burns to the ground. No one is hurt, and the gallery is insured so it can be rebuilt, but your exhibit is put on an indefinite hiatus. Is this lucky, or unlucky? The answer is, it depends on how you interpret the event and your perspective on whether things could have been better or worse. If you instinctively think, 'Oh thank goodness the fire happened *before* I installed my work, as I could have lost the lot', then you would consider the event a lucky escape. If you immediately think, 'Of course the gallery would burn to the ground right before my first solo exhibition, that's just my luck', then the incident will be chalked up as further evidence that you are unlucky and just cannot catch a break. It is this difference in perspective that Wiseman believes is essential in how we view our experiences, how we feel about our lives, and, perhaps most importantly, the hope we then hold about the future. If you view the fire as an inevitable result of your terrible luck then you might not proactively look for an alternative venue, convinced that any future endeavours will also be doomed to failure. If you see the incident as a fortuitous escape, then you might be quicker to conclude the exhibit was 'meant to be' and seek out a different venue. Over a lifetime, these subtle differences amount to a completely different trajectory that ironically serves to reinforce whatever belief underpins it. If you believe you are lucky, and act lucky, then you are likely to be lucky, creating what Wiseman terms a 'self-fulfilling prophesy'.

The art of asking

A powerful tool in creating the sort of artistic life that can sustain you is the art of *asking*, a term coined by the aforementioned Amanda Palmer in her 2013 TED talk and subsequent book of the same title. There is a powerful myth that people don't want to pay for art and will rip you off by copying your work, downloading your music, or pirating your film if they find a loophole, but that is not the case when you are in a meaningful, connected relationship with your audience. There is also a myth that asking is synonymous with begging and is somehow a shameful, one-sided act. These myths deny the profound exchange that can exist between artists and their audience, a two-way relationship that ultimately sustains both parties. Art is a currency that has the power to enrich lives, bring connection, articulate the mysteries of life, and bring comfort. Money is a currency that allows artists to keep making and creating without worrying about what they are going to eat. Platforms such as Patreon allow this transaction to happen without the intercession of labels, publishers, galleries or agents. It allows a direct flow of money and art to move between artists and audience and it makes the art of asking a reciprocal exchange, 'please make art', 'please pay for my art'.

This sort of connection is based on mutual vulnerability and involves the capacity to both see and be seen and speaks again to the importance of making work that conveys something of your internal world. What matters to you is likely to matter to someone else, what is beautiful to you is likely to strike the chord of beauty in others. Engaging in a dialogue that lets the people around you know what you need allows people to support you. Maybe you need a venue, somewhere to work, materials or a practice space. What would it be like to ask? What have your experiences of asking been in the past? The vulnerability comes from the possibility that you will be told 'no'; that's the deal when it comes to genuinely asking. Try it and see.

Conclusion

It can be a daunting prospect to put your work out into the world, particularly if the work is personal and speaks to your experiences. If you are able to find your artistic 'voice' and can support yourself enough to risk publicly using it, then you are more likely to draw people toward you that get what you are doing and want to support your work. Cultivating the ability to ask for what you need, taking chances when they present themselves, and listening to your instincts, will stack the odds that you will create the opportunities you need to be your version of successful. Bolstering your resilience to criticism and finding ways to navigate through the 'noise' of feedback will mean that you can sustain this success without compromising your art.

References

Cameron J (1992) *The Artist's Way*. Atlantic Books.

Mathes BM, Timpano KR, Raines AM & Schmidt NB (2020) Attachment Theory and hoarding disorder: A review and theoretical integration. *Behaviour Research and Therapy* **125.**

Palmer A (2014) *The Art of Asking: How I learned to stop worrying and let people help*. Grand Central Publishing.

Saltz J (2022) *Art is Life: Icons, iconoclasts, visionaries & vigilantes, & flashes of hope in the night*. Ilex Press.

Snir S, Regev D & Shaashua YH (2017) Relationships between attachment avoidance and anxiety and responses to art materials *Art Therapy* **34** (1) 20-28.

Wiseman R (2003a) *UK Superstition Survey* [online]. Hertfordshire: Psychology Department, University of Hertfordshire. Available at: www.richardwiseman.com/resources/superstition_report (accessed May 2023).

Wiseman R (2003b) The Luck Factor. *Sceptical Inquirer* Volume **27** (3).

Chapter Eight: Moving forwards

Endings

I am in my studio at the bottom of the garden. It is the first day of May and most of the tulips are open and dancing in the snowdrift of petals falling from the apple and cherry blossom. When I started this book, I had just tucked up the bulbs ready for the winter, the trees were losing their leaves and the garden was quickly fading into its winter brown. I have trampled down to the studio in rain, heavy snow, grey drizzle, and, more recently, blazing spring sun. I have relied on the heater to keep my fingers from freezing on the cold days, and just yesterday I had to open the door and the windows to keep from boiling. This book has been a companion through autumn and into Christmas, slowly forming in the moments between puddle jumps with the kids and Christmas shopping. It was my new year's resolution and saw me through the bleakness of January and February. I am submitting the manuscript tomorrow, just as the risk of frost passes and I can get to planting out the seedlings that are currently languishing in the cold frames that surround my studio. It is an ending of a process and a way of life that has been meditative and consuming, a psychic retreat and a silent friend that has accompanied me everywhere, much like when I was pregnant.

Ending a piece of work is not without its share of complex feelings. In some ways, I am amazed to have done something that I really doubted was possible before I started this project. Could I really write that many words? Commit to a project for that long? The answer is that, once I started to dance with this book, I found a rhythm I didn't know I had, the discipline of writing was easy to submit to when I was writing about something I care about so much. What happens now it is over? 'Real life' beckons again, and part of me doesn't want to answer; I want to tuck myself in a corner and start right away on volume two. Working on a project or work of creativity requires a kind of meditative concentration and focus that can be both demanding and protective from the usual 'life stuff', that is paused for a time. When it finishes, we can experience a sort of collapse, the likes of which I see regularly when someone has worked through a huge emotion in therapy. It is a kind of emptying, a release that leaves a sort of void for a small time. We can emerge disorientated and changed, and need to be compassionate and generous in our expectations while we recalibrate. If you find yourself struggling to finish a project, it can be helpful to ask yourself what finishing means for you? Does it deliver you back to the mundane but sometimes overwhelming demands of the gas bill and the hoovering? Does it leave you with a void until your next work becomes apparent? Identifying the meaning of an ending can help you figure out how to meet the need that will be left over by finishing and get to completion. For me, it raises fears about whether I will be able to sustain the momentum of writing, a process I have grown to love, without the structure of this book. In a glorious example of taking my own medicine, I suspect I will have to turn my attention to cultivating inspiration and moving back into action without the structure of a deadline. And I will have to encounter and manage any feelings that come up during that process; in truth, none of us is immune from the messy business of being human.

Keeping your own momentum

Coming to the end of this book is a bit like coming to the end of therapy – it marks a beginning point. A moment of launching and ultimately in evaluating what will stick and become part of your new normal, and what will fall away. There are a few things that I have found helps to cement and establish fledgling changes and stacks the odds that any gains you have made will be sustained.

The most important variable in any new endeavour is social support. Ensuring you have a 'tribe' to hold you accountable, and to remind you when your attention or commitment wane, will make lasting change more likely. Spending time with other creative people not only provides inspiration and increases originality, but also serves as a lasting reminder of the sort of life you want to live. Watching a fellow artist 'birth' a project can provide the energetic 'field' in which to embark on your creative work. In therapy, I encourage people to openly state their intentions moving forward to a couple of close family members or friends. Having a network of people who are rooting for you and who believe in the changes you are trying to make goes a long way to ensuring you can be resilient in the face of challenges and can remain robust, regardless of what life throws at you.

The other imperative is to expect hurdles, setbacks and difficulties, and do not interpret them as evidence that your progress is short-lived or cannot be sustained. Creative work is hard. It can flow easily or be wrenched forth effortlessly like the roots of an ancient tree. It can go smoothly or can involve meeting and subverting wall after wall of blocks, setbacks and unmet standards. None of this is indicative of the worth or quality of the work or of you as an artist; it is part of the unique process that each work demands. You will have times when you feel like you are floating on a tide of creativity, and times when you wonder if you will ever create again. This is normal. Experience changes moment by moment and neither the good nor the bad times endure, so do not fear, or get too attached to either. Both are true, both are valid, and both will end. The key is to cultivate the sort of habits that mean you can be productive in the fertile times and can survive, endure, and replenish in the fallow times. I suspect I will have a fallow time after this book, as I recover and recalibrate to my life. I will use the time to stock the cupboards of inspiration with visual images, sounds and experiences, so I am well-provisioned for the next project.

Exercise 35: Review

Take a moment to review the exercises that you did at the beginning of this book. Start with the 'miracle question' exercise from Chapter One. How does your answer, and the hopes you held for creative change, compare with where you find yourself now? Has the problem, aim or goal that you started with shifted in any way, or has your relationship with it shifted? How does it feel to be ending this book, and what emotions do you experience as you reflect on the process? Was it over or underwhelming? Encouraging, disappointing, affirming, or something else entirely?

Now look at the 'map' you created in Chapter Three. Have any of the patterns that you recognised in your relationship with creativity changed? Do you find yourself relating to your creative work in the same way, or has anything shifted?

How has it been to complete your daily creative time each day? Are you still managing to dedicate the 30 minutes uninterrupted or have other demands begun to encroach? What things have you discovered in your creative practice? What things have you experimented with and what was the outcome?

Are you still writing your morning pages, and if so, how are you finding them? If you have chosen to stop them, why? If you have continued, why? What have you learned about yourself by completing this exercise?

Think back over the course of this book and ask yourself what things you want to take forward with you into the next stage of your creative life? What things have stood out as helpful or challenging? What things do you need to keep hold of any of the changes you have made? What commitments do you need to make to yourself and whose support do you require to follow these through? It might be useful to write these down as a list of steps that you will take and resources that you will need to move forward. Did you encounter any difficulties while completing this book, and if so, how did you (or will you) overcome them?

Now take a pen and paper and write to your creative self in five years' time. What are your greatest hopes for them? How do you imagine them living, working, developing as a creative artist? →

What things do you hope to have changed since ending this book? What do you hope to have remained? What messages do you have for your future self, what words of advice or encouragement? Sign the letter with your most positive wishes, and then seal it. It is completely up to you what you choose to do with the letter; some people choose to save it, some to send it, some to burn it, or even plant it. It is important to find a ritual that works for you.

When to ask for help

There are lots of different reasons why people experience blocks in their creativity, and we have explored many of them in this book. I am never a fan of pathologising or labelling people's experiences, or their strengths and challenges, however sometimes the reason we are not creating is because our mental health has deteriorated without us recognising it. Sometimes difficulties with motivation, hope, procrastination and self-belief are indicative of an underlying depression, and it is only when you address that depression that your mood lifts enough to make work. Sometimes a fear of getting started, of failure, exposure or bad things happening is a symptom of anxiety that has become problematic, or a trauma that remains ready to trigger a 'flight, flight, freeze' response to perceived danger. If you suspect that your mental health might be playing a part in your creative blocks, or this book has raised things from your early life that feel unresolved and current, then I strongly recommend exploring these issues with a therapist. Having been both a patient and a therapist, I can reassure you that there is not a scale or threshold of difficulty that has to be reached before therapy is justified. A space to be curious with an interested, invested person is always a valid option. There are sources of support at the end of this book.

The same can be said for neurodivergence; sometimes difficulties with creativity are absolutely in the realm of common human experience and procrastination a result of the myriad reasons covered in Chapter Six. Sometimes they are not and are stopping you from working in a way that needs to be understood for you to move forward. If you find that your experiences seem to be enduring and are impacting your life in a way that is challenging to understand but appears to be different to the people around you, then I encourage you to find someone to take a careful look at your strengths and challenges and see whether there is a way of understanding what is happening. Knowing your neurotype is not about excusing or limiting yourself, it is about understanding yourself and being clear what you need in order to be the creative artist that you want to be.

I am in no way suggesting that everyone who continues to find it challenging to live their best creative life is experiencing poor mental health, or is neurodivergent, however if you have come to the end of this book and continue to feel that there is a 'something' that you cannot put your finger on, then it might be helpful to consider whether either of these might be playing a role. I strongly believe that diagnosis does not preclude you from doing anything, in fact there is research to suggest that certain neurodevelopmental and mental health conditions can increase creativity and originality: however, getting a clearer picture of your strengths and challenges and addressing any areas that might be impacting your work may help you move forward in a way that has eluded you to date.

The future belongs to the artists

We have visited and revisited the idea that human beings use stories to conceive of what is possible and to make sense of reality, both individually and as a collective. Most people struggle to imagine a future that looks markedly different from the present: however, we are now staring into a space where the way we have always done things is no longer available to us. The challenges posed by climate change and the inevitable need to move away from fossil fuels require solutions that are radically different in a way that is hard to imagine. The experience of a global pandemic has called into question many of our priorities and the way in which we live our lives. Economic and political instability raises questions about how we structure our societies and shine a light on whose voices are, and are not, being heard. This places us in a position where the very future of how we live and engage as a society now lies in the hands of the people who have the creativity and innovation to point the way for the rest of us to follow.

Within this context, prioritising your own creativity can and should be considered a radical and essential act and I hope that this book has introduced some concepts and tools to support you in this process. I urge you to continue the momentum that you have built during your time working through this book and believe that the best way to do that is to keep the daily creative practice as an indefinite commitment you make to yourself. If you write for 30 minutes every day, then soon 500 words will become 50,000 words and will eventually become a book. If you paint for 30 minutes a day, every day, then soon you will have a body of work that becomes an exhibition. Small, incremental changes amount to *work*, and ultimately to the sort of creative life that inspired you to pick up this book.

It is not enough for change to remain at the individual level however, we require conversations as a collective about how we move forward and renegotiate our priorities in the light of the difficult questions that confront us. Now more than ever before we need to foster the ability to think creatively in education and move away from a model that posits the idea that there is one 'right' answer. Young people need to be equipped to deal with the myriad of complex challenges that lay ahead, and that means being able to confidently rely on 'divergent thinking' that explores every possibility, rather than 'convergent thinking' that quickly shuts down potential answers and limits options. To achieve this, we need a radical change in the way we present information to children and how we assess their learning. By incentivising trying and failing, experimenting and adopting a playful, expansive attitude to problem solving, we cultivate minds that can adapt and respond flexibly to whatever confronts them.

We also need to rethink the value and importance of creativity on a much larger, cultural scale. If we continue to surreptitiously introduce the idea that the arts are an afterthought that can only be 'indulged' in when the real work is done, then we are undervaluing and disincentivising the very skills that are likely to sustain our ability to function as a society. It is imperative that we continue to fight, kick, scream and demand that we increase diversity and representation in the arts, otherwise the future, as well as the past, will belong to the privileged few. The dialogue has started, but any social change is vulnerable to relapse, and momentum can be lost without renewed pressure and commitment to challenging us all to do better.

Thinking on a macro scale is important, but so is holding onto the fact that change begets change on a micro level, too. In the time it has taken me to write this book, two of the people in my life have begun their own writing projects, spurred on by the observation that it is possible to write even in the middle of a busy life that competes for your attention. One close friend has signed up for a PhD, and together we have begun to put together the bones of a business plan for a centre dedicated to art education and creative development. The energy that resonates from creating is catching, and you will almost certainly find that, when you invest in your own creative work, you will subtly give others permission to do the same.

What is it all about anyway?

When I was training to be a clinical psychologist, I did a placement on a stroke ward in the city hospital. The ward was high up in the monolithic building that looked right out over the city – it was a constant reminder of the world that continued outside of those walls while the lives of those inside hung in the balance or were changed forever by the neurological fire that had burned through their brains.

I was 26 years old, newly in love, full of optimism and hope, and the sort of naïve belief in life that would be severely tested by my experiences that summer. Of all the memories of my time there, the one that stands out as vividly and starkly as if it were yesterday, is me standing at the door of Mary's room, trying to work out what my next move would be. She hadn't noticed I was there yet, and sat hunched on the edge of the bed, facing the window through which the summer sun was pouring. In a domestic setting, that sort of light would illuminate dust particles dancing and drifting and would be accompanied by the sound of bird song and lawnmowers. In the sterile emptiness of the hospital, the light fell only on the drab green of the walls and bed, absorbed by the greyness. Mary was silent, and still, and I stood there for a long while, paralysed for the first time by my own impotence and ineptness in the face of true human tragedy.

Mary had experienced a huge stroke several weeks earlier and was in the early stages of recovery, which is usually categorised by surveying the damage and working out what would likely improve, and what is the new way of life now. Simultaneously, Mary's husband of 42 years was in the hospital on the other side of the city following a catastrophic heart attack. The ward had been informed that he was unlikely to survive and so had arranged transport and staff to accompany Mary to say goodbye. They had spent tender moments together, holding each other for the last time, both in the wake of their own physical catastrophe, which would ultimately signal the end of their long union. When Mary had left, her husband was still alive, but he died soon after her departure. In a move of stunning tragedy that rendered me motionless at the door to her room, Mary had suffered another mini-stroke in the ambulance on the way back to her hospital bed, the impact of which was to fry the tenuous, fragile synaptic connections that were encoding the memory of her last moments with her husband. They were irretrievably erased and were now only held in the at-a-distance observations of the health care assistants that had accompanied her, who reminded her over and over of what had happened while she struggled to process the enormity of the implications.

When I finally entered that room, it was not as a psychologist in training, but as a human. None of the tools that I had learned could prepare me for this moment or could make me useful in the face of the wall of grief that Mary was facing. I sat down next to her, and she lifted her face, and wailed. Her body seemed to crumple towards me, and I paused for a moment, completely unsure what to do. In the end I did what any human would do, I wrapped my arms around her, and she wailed and wailed and wailed into my shoulder while I rocked her. The door was open, we were in plain view, and I knew that this was not common protocol, but in that moment, I had nothing else. We were bound by common humanity when confronted with the enormity of death and suffering and pain.

This formative moment was not the last of its kind, and in the past 15 years I have been confronted over and over with what it means to live and to die and to suffer and to face our ending. I have worked in hospitals and in the community, with physical pain and mental pain, and with adults and children. All of these experiences have left me with one conclusion: we are all in the process of facing down our own mortality and the only thing that really, really seems to matter in the end is love. The love of a dying husband, or of longed-for children, of friends and old colleagues. But also, the love of our own souls and of our art.

Our inhabiting of this Earth is fleeting and momentary, and can be besieged by all manner of unexpected events that derail and distract and demand from us. But, if you have a creative voice that whispers at you and urges you to make and make and make, then what will likely confront you when you eventually reach the end of your time here is the love of and attachment to that voice. Whether you have walked hand in hand with your creative world, or have dipped in intermittently, or have even skilfully avoided it by promising its time will come, this will govern how you reflect back on your life and the time you spent here. Just like all the other relationships in your life, your relationship with your creative self will be up for review when the superficial and meaningless parts of existence fall away. I don't say this to be dramatic or sensationalist, but to pop the bubble of fantasy that we have infinite time and can afford to not pay attention to the things that need to be expressed. One of the clever ways we cope with our fragile position on this planet is to keep death and the finiteness of our existence on the periphery of our consciousness, only becoming aware of it in the grip of a nightmare, or a momentary glimpse of someone else's mortality. The risk of that is we are lulled into a false sense of permeance, an illusion that tomorrow is a certainty, so we can put off writing, painting, sketching, dancing, creating until then. I have had a front-row seat on the implications of this and the devastating impact of regret on the process of aging and, ultimately, of dying.

You picked up this book for a reason. Some part of you reached out and opened the pages in search of something. You do not have time not to act on what you have encountered in yourself as you have read; you do not have the luxury of putting off until tomorrow the work that demands to be made today. Do not allow the illusion of life to prevent you from keeping in mind the limited time you have in front of you, and thinking carefully about how you allocate that time. It is a matter of life and death.

Resources

Neurodivergence

For further information and advice about ADHD, please contact ADDISS The National Attention Deficit Disorder Information and Support Service) here: www.addiss.co.uk

For more information, support and advice about Autism, please contact the National Autistic Society: www.autism.org.uk

For further information, support and advice about Dyspraxia, please contact the Dyspraxia Foundation: https://dyspraxiafoundation.org.uk

Mental Health

If you are worried about your mental health, please contact your GP who will be able to talk through what options are available to you in your area.

For advice and guidance, please contact MIND: www.mind.org.uk

To find a qualified therapist to support you to explore any issues this book has raised, please search here: www.psychotherapy.org.uk

Further reading in cognitive analytic therapy

Steve Potter (2020) *Therapy with a Map: A cognitive analytic approach to helping relationships*. Pavilion Publishing and Media, UK.

Steve Potter (2022) *Talking with a Map: A cognitive analytic approach to everyday conversational awareness*. Pavilion Publishing and Media, UK.

Elizabeth Wilde McCormick, (2017) *Change for the Better: Personal development through practical psychotherapy (5th ed.)*. SAGE Publishing, UK.

Further reading in compassion focused therapy

Mary Welford (2012) *Building your Self-Confidence using Compassion Focused Therapy*. Robinson, UK.

Deborah Lee (2012) *Recovering from Trauma using Compassion Focused Therapy*. Robinson, UK.

The Compassionate Mind Foundation: www.compassionatemind.co.uk

Further reading in acceptance and commitment therapy

Steven C Hayes, Kirk D Strosahl & Kelly G Wilson (2016) *Acceptance and Commitment Therapy: The process and practice of mindful change*. Guilford Press, USA.

Russ Harris (2019) *ACT Made Simple: An easy-to-read primer on acceptance and commitment therapy*. New Harbinger, USA.

Further reading in motivational interviewing

Angela Wood (2020) *The Motivational Interviewing Workbook: Exercises to decide what you want and how to get there*. Rockridge Press, USA.

Michelle Drapkin (2023) *The Motivational Interviewing Path to Personal Change: The essential workbook for creating the life you want*. New Harbinger, USA.

Further Reading in EMDR

Francine Shapiro (2012) *Getting Past Your Past: Take control of your life with self-help techniques from EMDR therapy*. Rodale, USA.

Francine Shapiro (2016) *EMDR: The breakthrough therapy for overcoming anxiety, stress, and trauma*. Basic Books, USA.

Index of exercises

References

Abbasi I & Alghamdi N (2015) The prevalence, predictors, causes, treatment, and implications of procrastination behaviours in general, academic, and work setting. *International Journal of Psychological Studies* **7** (1).

Abel NJ & O'Brien JM (2010) EMDR treatment of comorbid PTSD and alcohol dependence: a case example. *Journal of EMDR Practice Research* **4** 50–59.

Alrasheed M, Alrasheed S & Algahtani AS (2022) Impact of Social Media Exposure on Risk Perceptions, Mental Health Outcomes, and Preventative Behaviours during the COVID-19 Pandemic in Saudi Arabia. *Saudi Journal of Health Systems Research* **2** (3) 107-113.

Anglin DA, Lui F, Schneider M & Ellman LM (2020) Changes in perceived neighbourhood ethnic density among racial and ethnic minorities over time and psychotic-like experiences. *Schizophrenia Research* **216** 330-338.

Asakura K, Lundy J, Black D & Tierney C (2020) Art as a Transformative Practice: A participatory Action Research Project with Trans* Youth. School for Social Work: Faculty Publications, Smith College, Northampton, MA.

Averill JR, Chon KK & Hahn DW (2001) Emotions and Creativity, East and West. *Asian Journal of Social Psychology* **4** 165-183.

Beaty RE, Nausbaum EC & Silvia PJ (2014) Does insight problem solving predict real world creativity? *Psychology of Aesthetics, Creativity and the Arts* **8** 287-292.

Beck JS (2011) *Cognitive Behaviour Therapy, Second Edition.* Guildford Publications, UK.

Beery R (1975) Special feature: fear of failure in the student experience. *The Personnel and Guidance Journal* **54** (4).

Burka JB & Yuen LM (2008) *Procrastination: Why you do it, what to do about it now.* Hachette Books Group, New York.

Cameron J (1992) *The Artist's Way.* Atlantic Books.

Cameron J (2017) *The Right to Write.* Hay House, UK.

Centonze D, Siracusane A, Calabresi P & Bernardi G (2005) *Removing pathogenic memories. Molecular Neurobiology* **32** 123–132.

Chen H, Liu C, Zhou F, Chiang CH, Chen YL, Wu K, Huang DH, Liu CY & Chiou WK (2022) The Effect of Animation-Guided Mindfulness Meditation on the Promotion of Creativity, Flow and Affect. *Front Psychol.*

Damian R I & Simonton D K (2014). Diversifying Experiences in the Development of Genius and Their Impact on Creative Cognition. In D. K. Simonton (Ed.) *The Wiley Handbook of Genius.* Wiley-Blackwell, New York.

De Dreu CK, Baas M & Nijstad BA (2008) Hedonic tone and Activation Level in the Mood-Creativity Link: Toward a Dual Pathway to Creativity Model. *Journal of Personality and Social Psychology* **94** (5).

De Petrillo L & Winner E (2005) Does Art Improve Mood? A test of a Key Assumption Underlying Art Therapy. *Art Therapy* **22** (4).

Farroni T, Johnson MH, Menon E, Zulian L, Faraguna D & Csibra G (2005) Newborns' preference for face-relevant stimuli: Effects of contrast polarity. *Proceedings of the National Academy of Sciences* **102** (47).

Fink A, Koschutnig K, Benedek M, Reishofer G, Ischebeck A, Weiss EM & Ebner F (2012) Stimulating creativity via the exposure to other people's ideas. *Human Brain Mapping* **33** (11).

Foster-Wallace D (2009) *This is Water: Some Thoughts, Delivered on a Significant Occasion, about Living a Compassionate Life.* Little, Brown. USA

Gilbert P (2009) *The Compassionate Mind*. Hachette, UK.

Gilbert P (2014) The origins and nature of compassion focused therapy. *British Journal of Clinical Psychology* **53** (1) 6-41.

Guerrilla Girls (2020) *The Art of Behaving Badly*. Chronicle Books.

Harris R (2008) *The Happiness Trap: Stop struggling, start living*. Robinson Publishing.

Hase M, Balmaceda UM, Hase A, Lehnung M, Tumani V, Huchzermeier C et al (2015) Eye movement desensitization and reprocessing (EMDR) therapy in the treatment of depression - a matched pairs study in an in patient setting. *Brain and Behaviour* **5** (6).

Hase M, Balmaceda UM, Ostacoli L, Liebermann P & Hofmann A (2017) The AIP Model of EMDR Therapy and Pathogenic Memories. *Frontiers in Psychology* **8**.

Hébert M, Lavoie F & Blais M (2014) Post-Traumatic Stress Disorder/PTSD in adolescent victims of sexual abuse: resilience and social support as protection factors. *Ciênc. saúde coletiva* **19** (3).

Henriksen D, Richardson C, Shack K (2020) Mindfulness and creativity: implications for thinking and learning. *Thinking skills and creativity* **37**.

Higgie J (2019) *Plain Facts: The importance of Acknowledging Women Artists. In, 'Representation of Female Artists in Britain During 2019'*. Report, The Freelands Foundation.

Hoffmann J & Russ S (2012). Pretend play, creativity, and emotion regulation in children. *Psychology of Aesthetics, Creativity, and the Arts*, **6** (2), 175–184.

Jongsma HE, Karlsen S, Kirkbride JB et al (2021) Understanding the excess psychosis risk in ethnic minorities: the impact of structure and identity. *Soc Psychiatry Psychiatr Epidemiol* **56** 1913–1921.

Kabat-Zinn J (2003) Mindfulness-based interventions in context: past, present, and future. *Clinical Psychology Science and Practice* **10** (2) 144–156.

Kashdan TB & Rottenberg J (2010) Psychological flexibility as a fundamental aspect of health. *Clinical Psychology Review* **30** (7) 865-878.

Kaufman SB (2016) Opening up openness to experience: a four factor model and relations to creative achievement in arts and sciences. *Journal of Creative Behaviours* **47** 233-255.

Lin W & Shih Y (2016) The developmental trends of different creative potentials in relation to children's reasoning abilities: From a cognitive theoretical perspective. *Thinking Skills & Creativity* **22** 36-47.

Madjar N, Greenberg E & Chen Z (2011) Factors for Radical Creativity, Incremental Creativity, and Routine, Noncreative Performance. *Journal of Applied Psychology* **96** (4).

Mathes BM, Timpano KR, Raines AM & Schmidt NB (2020) Attachment Theory and hoarding disorder: A review and theoretical integration. *Behaviour Research and Therapy* **125**.

Nasseri P, Nitsche MA & Ekhtiari H (2015) A framework for categorising electrode montages in transcranial direct current stimulation. *Frontiers in Human Neuroscience* **9**.

Okoli J, Watt J & Weller G (2020) A naturalistic decision-making approach to managing non-routine fire incidents: evidence from expert firefighters. *Journal of Risk Research* **25** (2) 198-217.

Oleynick VC, Thrash TM, LeFew MC, Moldovan EG & Kieffaber PD (2014) The scientific study of inspiration in the creative process: challenges and opportunities. *Frontiers of Human Neuroscience* **25** (8).

Palmer A (2014) *The Art of Asking: How I learned to stop worrying and let people help*. Grand Central Publishing.

Plucker JA, Beghetto RA & Dow G (2010) Why isn't creativity more important to educational psychologists? potential, pitfalls, and future directions in creativity research. *Educational Psychologist* **39** 83-96.

Potter S (2020) *Therapy with a Map: A Cognitive Analytic Approach to Helping Relationships*. Pavilion Publishing

Richard V, Halliwell W, Tenenbaum GJTSP (2017) Effects of an improvisation intervention on elite figure skaters' performance. *Self Esteem Creativity Mindfulness Skills* **31**, 275–287.

Rollnick S & Miller WR (1991) *Motivational Interviewing: Helping people change.* Guilford Publications, UK.

Ryle T & Kerr I (2002) *Introducing Cognitive Analytic Therapy: Principles and Practice.* Wiley-Blackwell, London

Saltz J (2022) *Art is Life: Icons, iconoclasts, visionaries & vigilantes, & flashes of hope in the night.* Ilex Press.

Schutte NS & Malouff JM (2020) Connections between curiosity, flow and creativity. *Personal. Individ. Differ.* **152**: 109555.

Shapiro F (2001) *Eye Movement Desensitization and Reprocessing - Basic Principles, Protocols, and Procedures.* New York, NY: Guilford.

Simonton DK (2000a) Creativity: cognitive, developmental, personal and social aspects. *American Psychologist* **55** 151-158.

Simonton D K (2000). Creative Development as Acquired Expertise: Theoretical Issues and an Empirical Test. *Developmental Review.* **20** 283-318

Simonton DK (2021) Creativity In Society. In: Kaufman JC & Sternberg RJ (2021) *Creativity: An Introduction.* Cambridge University Press, Cambridge.

Smith S L, Choueiti M, Pieper K. (2018). Inclusion in the Director's Chair? Gender, Race & Age of Directors across 1,100 Films from 2007-2017 *Annenberg Inclusion Initiative.* https://assets.uscannenberg.org/docs/inclusion-in-the-directors-chair-2007-2017.pdf

Snir S, Regev D & Shaashua YH (2017) Relationships between attachment avoidance and anxiety and responses to art materials *Art Therapy* **34** (1) 20-28.

Social Mobility Commission (2021). *State of the nation 2021: Social mobility and the pandemic.* www.gov.uk

Tapper J (2022) Huge decline of working class people in the arts reflects fall in wider society. *The Observer, 10th December 2022.*

To ML, Fisher CD, Ashkanasy NM & Rowe PA (2012) Within-Person Relationships between Mood and Creativity. *Journal of Applied Psychology* **97** (3).

Tronick EZ (2010) Things Still To Be Done on the Still-Face Effect. *Infancy* **4** 475-482.

Wiseman R (2003a) *UK Superstition Survey* [online]. Hertfordshire: Psychology Department, University of Hertfordshire. Available at: www.richardwiseman.com/resources/superstition_report (accessed May 2023).

Wiseman R (2003b) The Luck Factor. *Sceptical Inquirer* Volume **27** (3).

Xi Y, Yu H, Yao Y, Peng K, Wang Y & Chen R (2020) Post-traumatic stress disorder and the role of resilience, social support, anxiety and depression after the Jiuzhaigou earthquake: A structural equation model. *Asian Journal of Psychiatry* **49**.

Zhu W, Shang S, Jiang, W, Pei M & Su, Y (2019) Convergent Thinking Moderates the Relationship between Divergent Thinking and Scientific Creativity, *Creativity Research Journal,* **31** (3)

Zmigrod S, Colzato L & Hommel B (2015) Stimulating Creativity: Modulation of convergent and divergent thinking by Transcranial Direct Current Stimulation (tDCS). *Creativity Research Journal* **27** (4) 353-360.